To: Brian and Bonnie

Jesse has given all of
us a message about
courage and looking to
the future.

I hope you will always
follow your dream!

John Davidson

THE
RIGHT
ROAD

HOW FAR WILL YOU GO

JOHN DAVIDSON

with

SHARON BRENNAN

Binea Press

Published in 2010 by
Binea Press, Inc
512-1673 Richmond Street
London, Ontario, Canada N6G 2N3

Tel: 519.660.6424
E-mail: bineapress@bellnet.ca
www.bineapress.com

Distributed by:
Binea Press Inc.
519.660.6424

Library and Archives Canada Cataloguing in Publication

Davidson, John, 1946-
The Right Road : How Far Will You Go / John Davidson with Sharon Brennan

ISBN 978-0-9812993-5-8

1. Davidson, John, 1946- – Travel – Canada. 2. Duchenne Muscular Dystrophy.
3. Walk-a-thon – Canada. 4. Canada – Description and travel – 1981-.
I. Brennan, Sharon, 1961- II. Title

RJ482.D78D39 2010   362.19' 7480092   2010-905959-X

Design by Pazzo Creative
London, Ontario, Canada
Tel: 519.878.8520

Printed in Canada by Friesens Corporation
Altona, Manitoba

· ACKNOWLEDGEMENTS ·

There are really two public groups of people – one a small group and the other a very large group – to be thanked in the creation of this book. The first group consists of those who worked on the mechanical bits and pieces, making sure the words, pages and pictures all fit together.

This first group of people would have had nothing to work with if it weren't for the second group – the thousands of Canadians, who lent a hand in whatever way they could, becoming part of a dream that continues to unfold.

Thanks go to the creative team consisting of co-writer Sharon Brennan whose love of the printed word guided her as she weaved the manuscript together. Editor and proof-reader Susan Greer combed diligently through every page (more than once) eliminating what could have been embarrassing errors. Amanda Jean Bolte worked her magic at the computer in creating the cover design and layout of the book.

To my long time friend Bill Brady, a Londoner and a community treasure who has championed so many causes over the years, thank you for the liner notes.

Special thanks go to Richard Bain at Binea Press, who believed in this book from the beginning and who was at the helm in getting all hands on the creative team to pull together. Secretly, I think they all just love the smell of a brand new book.

The second – and much larger group – is made up of people I know very well and people I've never met. They are the dozens of volunteers who were on the road with us (whose names I know.) They are the hundreds of police officers and firemen (whose names I don't know) who provided us escort. They are the broadcasters and newspaper reporters who told our story. They are the members of church groups and service clubs who fed us and at night time kept a roof over our heads as we made our way along the road.

Special thanks belong to the late Michael Woodward, who was there from the very beginning because he wanted to make a difference in the lives of others.

My friend Peter Garland, true to his word, did everything in his power to keep us going, including buying me a portable radio and a good Buddy Holly book (both of which I still have.)

Bevin Palmateer spent many lonely hours on the road, working up ahead of our little parade, as the advance man focusing on the media. Somehow he still managed to shoot both still pictures and video to capture our adventure on the road.

Bevin took the picture of me that is on the front cover of the book. He liked it because of its mystery – is it morning or is it evening? Is the figure in the picture going east or west, and is he walking toward you or away from you?

Thanks go to my friend Ed Coxworthy, from Bell Island, Newfoundland, who gave me a year of his life, free of charge. That's what Canadians do when they want to see a dream come true.

There are all kinds of unsung heroes whose names may seem to have slipped through the cracks. Not true. Time and space may limit us, but they know they were there and I know they were there.

Thanks to all those Canadians who waited along the roadside, the families at farm gates, the moms and dads and children who stood and waited (sometimes in the rain) in cities, towns and villages across the country.

And a heartfelt thank you to the all those disabled people, young and not so young, many in wheelchairs, who came to the roadside, sometimes with great difficulty so they could be a part of something special. You were the people who gave me the strength to carry on.

And oh yes, there was a third, not so public little group – my family who paid a price I can never repay. My wife Sherene is the quiet partner who always keeps me going, not just while we were on the road, but through all the broadcast years when working at night kept us apart. Thank you for your patience while I was writing this book and thank you for all the cups of tea served up with a smile.

To Tyler and Tim, who I often felt lived in the shadow of the events that surrounded them; I hope this book will help you understand where I was in those times when I wasn't home.

For Jesse
who taught me more about life than I ever taught him.

· PROLOGUE ·

It was Christmas 1994 when my wife Sherene and I broke the news to our extended family that I planned to push our middle son, Jesse, across Ontario in his wheelchair. The route – more than 3,300 kilometres from the Manitoba border to the Quebec border – would take us to Thunder Bay, across the top of Lake Superior to Sault Ste. Marie and Sudbury, south through the Muskokas and down the eastern shore of Lake Huron to Sarnia and Windsor. From there I would push Jesse to our home city of London and then on to Toronto and our final destination, Ottawa. There was stunned silence when I outlined the four-month journey. My sister broke the quiet when she asked, "How can we help?"

Our goal was to raise money for research into Duchenne muscular dystrophy (DMD), a fatal genetic disorder that gradually weakens the body's muscles. We hoped we would be able to help researchers find the answers prayed for by parents and grandparents of children with the disease. Blonde-haired Jesse had been diagnosed in 1986, when he was six years old. At the time it was an illness none of us had ever really heard of. Too soon it would become all too familiar. When we made the decision to tackle the cross-province trek, Jesse was 14 and I was 48.

So it was, the following summer, that my mother Sarah and father Jack followed our progress in the media as Jesse and I made our way across Ontario. They read newspaper stories and watched television accounts of us being welcomed in cities and towns throughout the province, often accompanied by the skirl of bagpipes.

The sound of the pipes always made them smile and in those moments they thought back to their younger years in Scotland. When my parents were planning their wedding, a grandmother I never knew told them, "If you two are smart, you'll get yourselves away to Canada as soon as the war is over."

It was a piece of advice they followed and never regretted. By the time they were able to act on the plan, they had two toddlers – my sister Dorothy, born in 1944, and me, born in January of 1946.

Dad went first, arriving in Toronto on the first all-Scottish emigration flight in 1947. Then in April of 1948, with a four-year-old daughter and two-year-old son in tow, my mother boarded the Cunard liner Ascania II to make the long crossing of the Atlantic, leaving Scotland behind and opening a new chapter in our lives.

Early into the trip my sister came down with measles, so we were isolated from the rest of the passengers and spent most of the journey in sick bay. My mother remembers how seasick she was – "so seasick that you would be happy to die!" But I never did become ill and mom describes me on that trip as a little boy with red curls, wearing my Davidson tartan kilt and spending eight days entertaining and being entertained by the crew. I spent most of my time playing in the doctor's office or in the ship's engine room with the engineer, who was from our hometown and seemed to have an unending supply of candy.

Following a train ride from Halifax, Nova Scotia, to Toronto, Ontario, our family was reunited at Union Station. In 1948 my mother and father didn't know a lot about the new land that would be our home, except how big it was, but like thousands of other families emigrating after the Second World War, it was the nation they had chosen in which to carve out a better future for their children. We settled in Brantford, Ontario, where mom and dad both went to work for Cockshutt Farm Equipment at a time when factory whistles told us the time of day. Our family was completed when my younger brother Alastair was born in 1957.

In school I enjoyed current events and history. I liked clipping newspaper stories and at night I would put on a bulky set of earphones to listen to short-wave radio signals from all over the world. The orange glow from the glass vacuum tubes of the radio was the telltale sign to my parents that I wasn't asleep. I would listen to everything I could, events in far-off corners of the world or maybe the voice of Foster Hewitt broadcasting hockey games from the gondola at Maple Leaf Gardens.

In 1960 we moved to Woodstock, Ontario, where dad was still working in the farm implement business, now with Massey-Ferguson. My mother was a reporter at the local newspaper, The Daily Sentinel Review, and following her lead, I entered the news business as a reporter at CKOX Radio in Woodstock.

By the time Jesse and I started our trip, Sherene and I had been living for 20 years in London, where our three sons, Tyler, then 18, Jesse, 15 and Tim, 12, were all born. I was given a leave of absence from my job at CFPL Television to undertake the project. But when our families pledged their complete support to keep Jesse's Journey moving forward – everything from fund-raising to cooking and laundry – they didn't realize our adventure would be the forerunner to an even bigger challenge.

Three years after pushing Jesse across Ontario, I started the second major phase of my fund-raising effort – a solo walk from one side of Canada to the other. One night when I was in Halifax in the early days of that second task, I found myself gazing from my hotel room window at Pier 21, a place where new lives began for so many people. I realized it had been exactly 50 years to the day from my passage through the gates of Pier 21 as a child to the moment when I dipped my running shoes in the saltwater of the Atlantic Ocean at Quidi Vidi, Newfoundland, the start of my journey across Canada to try to help build a brighter future for those with Duchenne muscular dystrophy.

· NEWFOUNDLAND ·

"God does not ask about our ability but rather our availability."
~ Unknown

On Labour Day weekend in 1997, as the wind took on a chill, everyone I knew was anticipating the changing colour of the leaves and the arrival of a new season. As others shifted gears to settle into the cozy routine associated with fall, I was thinking of little boxes, stacks of them, little boxes that needed to be moved. These imaginary boxes represented my dream, my mountain and possibly my undoing. Once again I laced up my running shoes, set my pedometer to zero and began training. But this time, I was not training to walk across Ontario; I was training to walk much farther, across the vastness of the true north strong and free. I was training to walk across Canada.

So why was I thinking about boxes? Whenever I have something large to accomplish, I like to break it down and visualize it as little manageable packages of work. At the beginning of a project the little boxes are all on one side of an imaginary line in my mind's eye and as I finish each unit of the task at hand, I move them one at a time to the "completed" pile on the other side of that imaginary line. When I have moved all the boxes, I have finished what I set out to do. A walk across Canada requires a lot of little boxes, 275 by my initial plan, one for each day I would spend on the road.

My intent as I was training that fall and winter was to work up to my goal of 33 kilometres a day, keeping in mind that reaching this mark too quickly could result in injury or burnout before I ever got to the starting point. I had to remember I was 52 years old and I was aware of the challenges this alone would bring. But I was determined and pushing Jesse across Ontario three years earlier had provided a solid and reasonable expectation of what was to come.

Training can be monotonous and I guess, given what I was planning to do, it is fortunate I prefer walking outdoors to working on a treadmill. So off I would go out to the country roads around London, taking in the fresh air and scenery along the way. Often I found myself at the farm of my friend Peter Garland. It was with Peter that I first shared the news Jesse had been diagnosed with Duchenne muscular dystrophy.

When Jesse and I decided to undertake the wheelchair marathon across Ontario to raise funds for research, Peter was there for us. So as I begin training again this time, I would walk to the farm, have lunch with Peter, chat for a while and then walk back home. Peter was supportive of what I was going to attempt in the months ahead and because he truly understood my desires in this regard, he was a wonderful companion as I planned for the walk. He can certainly be forgiven, however, for entertaining doubts. He would stare at me as I was leaving his house in the rain, heading down that gravel road all by myself, and told me later he would think, "Buddy, you have the world's courage in your heart to do this and to look to a cross-country walk ahead of you." It was then he vowed, "OK buddy, you've got me. I'll do whatever I can for you." From that point, Peter and his wife, Ann Hutchison, were true to this commitment and never wavered.

The dream of this journey started to turn into a reality when I began to visualize, which was just plain fun. The good thing about visualizing a dream is that it's free and there are no boundaries. When I could see what I wanted to accomplish, then there were questions I had to ask myself. Was my goal personally meaningful? Yes. Was it challenging? Oh yes. And the biggest question – was I committed to seeing it through? Yes, without a doubt.

THE RIGHT TEAM NEEDS THE RIGHT PEOPLE

As the weeks passed I was encouraged by the team forming around me. Some familiar faces were back, with invaluable experience acquired during the wheelchair push across Ontario. Mike Woodward was my master of logistics and Trish Federkow knew the ropes as road manager. Ron Calhoun, who had worked with Terry Fox, was my mentor and was with us again as national co-ordinator. There was only one new face on what would be our permanent road team.

On a wintry day before Christmas 1997, Bevin Palmateer, a London television

FIRST STEPS – Four-year-old Dorothy Davidson, left, and her kilt-wearing two-year-old brother John hold hands in Halifax, Nova Scotia on April 10, 1948, the day they arrived in Canada from Scotland with their mother.

VOYAGE TO A NEW LIFE – Sarah Davidson and her two young children travelled to Canada from Scotland on RMS Ascania II in 1948. Her husband Jack had arrived a few months earlier.

MR. SUNSHINE – Jesse had a smile for everyone. He was proud of his accomplishments and very proud of his brothers Tyler and Tim.

BRIGHT LIGHT – John and Sherene Davidson's oldest son, Tyler, 9 in this photo, now travels the world in his work in lighting and set design with Cirque du Soleil.

BIG SOUND – Tim Davidson (and friend), 4 in this photo, is the youngest of John and Sherene Davidson's sons. He is involved in the production of live performances, like his oldest brother, but his specialty is audio. He works in theatre in Toronto.

AT THE WHEEL – Sherene Davidson who grew up around construction sites as a kid, sits at the wheel of a tractor near the Davidson family home in London, Ontario in 2008

SWEET STUFF – Sherene Davidson has always been a busy mom. Here she gathers sap at a sugar bush near Mount Forest, Ontario.

reporter in his mid-30s, called on me at home to say he wanted to go across Canada with me. When I asked why he wanted to become part of the journey, he told me his mom had died of cancer in 1995 and that his stepmother, who three years before had been a vibrant woman, was no longer able even to feed herself due to the ravages of Lou Gehrig's disease. Bevin was choked with emotion as he spoke and it was then I knew he understood fully the need for research. Bevin was perfect for the job of managing the demands of the media.

We had found a fourth person for the permanent crew, but we still needed someone to co-ordinate the project at home. An old friend, the very capable Maureen Golovchenko, whom I first met when she was a journalism student at college, stepped up for what would be the most taxing job she had ever faced – getting the road team across Canada.

With the key players in place, it was now time to build the volunteer army, muster all the supplies we'd need and get underway.

As the leader of this adventure, I had to do a mental inventory of my own strengths and weaknesses before we could get things started. This required brutal honesty. What strengths did I have? What weaknesses could hold me back? I know I am persistent, but also patient and I like to think of myself as caring. On the flip side, I can be stubborn, a perfectionist and am probably too idealistic. That quick inventory gave me a pretty clear snapshot of the resources I had and what I still needed as I planned to take on this challenge.

My goal was clearly defined and was most definitely measurable, publicly measurable. I wondered if I was being realistic, but I knew what I had accomplished in crossing Ontario and I could use that information as a guide for this journey. I reminded myself no plan is perfect and stored that idea away to use as a balm on those inevitable, discouraging days when things did not go quite as I had conceptualized them.

It had been three short years since I pushed Jesse across Ontario in his wheelchair but this time, the task and the goals were much bigger. My intent was to create a lasting legacy, an endowment that would fund research forever. I was going to walk every step of the distance from the Atlantic Ocean to the Pacific Ocean and the starting date I had in mind was just a few months away. My dream was to make a difference and I wanted this to be a tribute to Jesse for all the courage he had shown in facing adversity in life. But this time I would face the road alone. The journey across Canada was going to take place in parts of two winters and I could not take Jesse with me. The risks were too high for him. But as for me, when someone you love faces a life-threatening struggle, you view life differently and personal risk can be reconciled. When I asked myself, "How far would you go for someone you love?" the answer changed my life in a very significant way.

SOMEWHERE THERE'S A STARTING LINE

The last days and weeks of winter were replaced by a hint of spring and then, seemingly without warning, it was time to say goodbye to the advance crew going ahead of me to the East Coast of Canada to put the pieces in place that would allow this adventure to unfold.

A five-person crew was moving a mini-convoy of two vans from London to St. John's, Newfoundland and it wasn't easy. In a.dash across Quebec in the aftermath of the ice storm of the century, the group was hard-pressed to outrun the floodwaters caused by melting ice. As they hurried through the Eastern Townships, roads were being closed behind them because of rising water levels. Memories of gushing deluges and damage caused by the ice storm stayed with the entire team as it pushed on toward the Maritimes. Their troubles didn't end when they left Quebec, as they encountered slippery winter conditions in both New Brunswick and Nova Scotia.

At the Gulf Ferry terminal in North Sydney, on Nova Scotia's Cape Breton Island, the convoy grew in size as the group picked up a motorhome left for them by Canadian Armed Forces volunteers who had moved it there from London. These folks also had battled tough weather to get to their destination.

In North Sydney our three vehicles were loaded onto the ferry for Port Aux Basques, Newfoundland, where the team bunked in for the night. But the windy and cold ferry crossing from the tip of Cape Breton was just a sample of what awaited in Newfoundland. The next day, high winds and snow pounded the motorhome and vans throughout the three-hour trip to Corner Brook, 200 kilometres from Port Aux Basques. It would have been a white-knuckle drive even for islanders who knew the roads. Finally, a week after leaving London, the five exhausted volunteers who made up the advance team, one motorhome and two escort vans rolled into St. John's, Newfoundland.

The winding roads and treacherous high winds, with snow blowing in all directions, had served notice that despite all our careful planning and discipline, the weather was one thing we could not organize, not here and not anywhere else across Canada. Newfoundland, with her rugged terrain and unpredictable elements, was a challenge to cross from west to east on wheels and it wouldn't be any easier going from east to west on foot.

SEEING WHERE YOU'RE GOING

On Monday, April 6, 1998, just four days before I was to start my walk across Canada, I left home knowing I wouldn't be back until I passed through London sometime in August. It was dark and our three boys were still asleep when it was time to go. I hugged my wife Sherene and as I kissed her goodbye, I told her I would try to do my best, something we both knew I would do no matter what. Jesse would turn 18 on the Friday of that week. It had been almost 12 years since he was diagnosed with Duchenne muscular dystrophy and our world had flipped upside down. In the pre-dawn darkness I held Sherene in my arms for a moment longer and hoped I was doing the right thing. Then quickly the luggage was loaded and we were on our way.

At the airport I connected with Bevin Palmateer, who was flying to Newfoundland with me. Several excited friends were waiting to see us off with good wishes, warm hugs and a few tears as we watched the sun rise over the hometown I wouldn't see again for almost a year.

My first image of Newfoundland from the air brought me to the reality that there was no turning back. My feelings were a mixture of anticipation and dread. Was I really up to the challenge? I was well aware that the days and nights of training and the hundreds of kilometres I logged in preparing for the challenge ahead hadn't reduced the 8,300-kilometre chore in front of me by even one metre. I reminded myself that probably every astronaut experiences a little nervousness just before launch. That is when you must trust in the effort you have already put in and the skills of those around you.

The water beaded on the window of the plane revealed only empty miles of dark green under a grey sky, with a thick blanket of white mist drifting in the wind. As the jet bounced onto the runway after the flight from Toronto, I thought about Jesse and the people who would benefit from the research dollars I hoped this journey would generate. Despite the sheets of rain hitting the tarmac outside, I felt a surge of adrenaline. I was now close to the starting point, both in geography and time. In a few days I would leave St. John's city hall and "Kilometre 0" in an attempt to walk the more than 8,000 kilometres of highway that link Canada's coasts; 275 days, I thought, and 275 little boxes.

I stepped out into the rain at the airport in St. John's carrying everything I would need for the next nine months in one big red duffel bag with the words Jesse's Journey stitched onto the side. I was thinking back to the time Jesse and I had spent together on the road and remembered how easy it became for us to pack our bags onto the motorhome, which would be waiting for us in another town at another motel. The hours I spent pushing Jesse along the highway in his wheelchair, as we caught up with the motorhome that had leapfrogged ahead, were so rewarding. If this solo journey came anywhere near to duplicating that experience, it would all be worth it.

The permanent road team and the first wave of volunteer drivers were being housed in bed-and-breakfast accommodations scattered throughout downtown St. John's. As we drove through the narrow, rain-slicked streets of the oldest part of the city, I caught a glimpse of the drizzly harbour and the city's most visible landmark, Signal Hill. At the top of the hill stands Cabot Tower. It was here that the Italian inventor, Guglielmo Marconi, received the first transatlantic wireless signal in 1901.

Visitors to St. John's can take a double-decker bus ride to the top of Signal Hill to look out over the rugged coast of Newfoundland. Southeast from the mouth of the harbour is Cape Spear, the easternmost point of Canada. Standing in the shadow of Cabot Tower at the top of Signal Hill, you can gaze out over the Atlantic toward Ireland.

The bus tours wind through the oldest parts of the city, past brightly painted "jelly bean" houses that stand side by side on the streets surrounding the harbour. These colourful homes, with their hanging baskets of flowers, often are used to represent St. John's in the pictures that fill art shops along Duckworth and Water Streets. On sunny days, visitors have other exciting options, such as whale-watching, boat excursions to see icebergs or puffins and visits to outdoor cafés and restaurants.

In the days just before flying to Newfoundland, I was busy with a lot of last-minute details and wasn't able to get out on the road to train. I made a mental note the first day in St. John's that the next morning, I would hike to the top of Signal Hill to give my legs a good workout. When I did just that, I was rewarded with a panoramic view of the old port city emerging through the fog. The harbour, the ocean and the coastline were all alive. As the sun cut through and with the wind blowing hard at my back, I looked out over the Atlantic Ocean and for just a moment, a little bit of nervousness came back as I wondered what I was doing on this windswept hill, thousands of miles from home, family and friends. As a reporter in my broadcasting career, I had often told the story of athletes and their pre-game nervousness and I knew exactly what they felt. It was the same thing I experienced the day Jesse and I began the wheelchair push across Ontario. I knew too that the butterflies would disappear as soon as I took my first step.

THE LAST-MINUTE CHECK

I gave myself a few minutes to feel the tension that had come over me and then thought again about why I was making this journey. I was not competing; I was simply committing to what I felt was the task I had been called to accomplish. And I knew I was going to do everything in my power to achieve what I set out to do. Suddenly, the anxiety and self-doubt about my ability to complete this job was gone. I mentally sharpened my focus and doubt was replaced by a sense of euphoria at having a chance to do something extraordinary, something that mattered more to me than anything else.

After the great experience of crossing Ontario with Jesse, this was a second "opportunity of a lifetime" and for that I was grateful. It felt like the wind had blown the cobwebs of doubt out to sea and the stage was set for a new cast of characters to step into the spotlight. Many of the players taking part in this adventure would be people I had never met and some would turn out to be people I will call friends for the rest of my life.

As we started to make final preparations for the launch of our journey, there was a noticeable excitement in the air. This was the rally point and the clock was ticking.

BE THE HARDEST-WORKING PLAYER ON THE TEAM

Everyone working on Jesse's Journey knew it would take a small army of people connecting with one another to make this project a success. No one knew this better than my friend Peter Garland, who had not forgotten that day back at the farm when he made a commitment to the cause. So, when it was time to take that first step, Peter was there.

Peter was born in the little Newfoundland outport of Lower Island Cove and his ties to his home province are as strong today as they were the day he set out as a young man to seek fame and fortune on the mainland. As he had watched me push my 52-year-old muscles to the limit in preparation for the walk, Peter had promised to do all he could to help get me safely across Canada, starting with the 960 kilometres of highway from St. John's to Port Aux Basques, a trek that would be beset by some of the worst weather conditions imaginable.

His first thought was to contact The Downhomer (now called simply Downhome), an island-printed monthly magazine mailed to Newfoundlanders all over the world. But he didn't anticipate how deeply his letter to the publication would move Newfoundlanders. Everywhere people showed up to help the father who planned to walk across Canada – not just to benefit his own son, but to enable research to aid all those youngsters just like his son. Peter's letter resulted in the knitting together of a formidable team of Newfoundlanders who tapped computer keys into the night, made calls and passed phone and fax messages across the province.

On the day before we set out to cross Canada's youngest province, an early 18th birthday party was held for Jesse in Mount Pearl, just outside St. John's. It marked the end of a whirlwind week of embracing the culture, sights and sounds of Newfoundland. I had been interviewed on radio and television endlessly and was feeling how Jesse must have felt on the morning we left London for the starting point of our journey at the Manitoba border, answering question after question about a journey that had yet officially to start.

The birthday party was a great success. Members of the Royal Newfoundland Constabulary (RNC) in their dress blues and the Royal Canadian Mounted Police in their red serge mingled with representatives of city service organizations and kids of all ages. Justice Combined, a band made up of RNC and RCMP members, filled the room with music and I was joined by a group of kids who helped me cut a huge cake as everyone sang Happy Birthday to Jesse.

Having kissed a cod, sipped a bit of Screech, the famous local rum, and wrestled with the tongue-twisting dialect, we were declared Honourary Newfoundlanders, a designation we all were delighted to accept. The party was our first full-blown experience of Newfoundland hospitality but it certainly wouldn't be our last. I just wished Jesse and the rest of my family could have been there to share in all these new experiences.

Then the day of truth arrived. For other tourists visiting historic St. John's and taking in the sites and sounds of Newfoundland, Friday, April 10, 1998 was probably just a routine morning. But this wasn't just another day for me. After seven months of training, today the distance would start to count for real. Today, I would take the first steps.

Through the third-floor window of my room at the Prescott Inn, our bed and breakfast on Military Road, I could see it was an overcast morning and St. John's looked cold and quiet. Although it was just before 7 a.m., people were starting to arrive at St. Thomas' Anglican Church across the street. Like most buildings in St. John's, the church, built in 1836, is made of wood.

It's the oldest wooden church in Newfoundland, painted dark brown with white trim. From where I was standing in the centre of my room, the wooden cross on top of the church was neatly framed by the window of my room. On the narrow street three floors below, a thick layer of frost covered the motorhome and escort vehicles.

People were bundled up in coats and scarves as they arrived at the church carrying dishes of food. I had almost forgotten it was Good Friday. With folks scurrying to get out of the early-morning cold, I decided to start this journey in a wind suit – navy blue pants and a bright red jacket with the Jesse's Journey logo stitched in white across the front. After lacing up my shoes and picking up my hat, I took a deep breath and headed downstairs, ready to begin the day I'd been waiting for.

Motorhome driver Mike Woodward of London and van driver Bob Seaton of Exeter, just north of London, were already in the kitchen, where the smell of coffee and toast filled the room. Mike was a veteran, having been on the road with Jesse and me in 1995. For Bob Seaton, a quiet guy with a brush cut, this was his first trip down East. He had been sitting at home reading the newspaper a few months earlier when the announcement of the walk across Canada and the need for volunteers caught his eye. Bob, who was scheduled to stay on with us as far as Goobies, Newfoundland, had been up since before dawn. He and I sat down to bowls of cereal and toast with a choice of two Newfoundland treats, bakeapple or partridgeberry jam. As we ate, the sun started to stream in through the windows, highlighting the potted geraniums on the sills. It was going to be a typical early-spring day in Newfoundland, with the weather constantly changing.

After breakfast, the motorhome and vans were warmed up as everyone gathered to travel together to the starting point at Quidi Vidi, the little harbour on the edge of St. John's where I would dip my running shoes in the Atlantic Ocean prior to the formal send-off at Kilometre 0 in downtown St. John's. On our way to Quidi Vidi, Jesse's Journey, part two, received its first donation – $10 from a 75-year-old woman who owned an antique shop at Quidi Vidi. Later, she told a reporter she had remembered seeing me on television and added how thankful she was to have four healthy grandsons.

FIRST PROVINCE – FIRST STEPS

It was April of 1998 and after months of planning and training, I was alone with my thoughts as I stood and surveyed the harbour and the jagged rocks that surrounded me. I locked in the picture. To the east through the habour's narrow opening was the Atlantic Ocean and, contemplating the task in front of me, I was very aware that I was closer to Ireland than to Vancouver.

The ocean rose as it pushed through the harbour entrance and the green and black waters climbed the face of the rock cliff before sliding back in white foam, pausing for just a moment before the cycle began again. As my eyes scanned the harbour, it was like looking at a postcard. Fishing boats in orange and blue were reflected in a saltwater mirror as they tugged at the ropes holding them to weathered wooden docks. Work sheds scattered around the inner harbour were draped in an assorted web of fishing nets hung to dry. Above the harbour, small houses clung to the cliff facing out to the sea. Some were red, some white and some yellow. Most looked pretty weather-worn. Smoke from the chimneys was quickly stolen away by the ever-present wind.

In the April cold, ice and snow covered the rocks and the roofs on the south side of the harbour, which is shaded by high cliffs. Snowdrifts were still tucked between the houses. On the sunny north side, the wooden docks looked warm and inviting. To the east the Atlantic rolled and to the west lay 275 days of walking between me and Vancouver.

BEGIN WITH THE END IN MIND

One thing I wanted to confirm was that my dream was squarely on the drawing board in front of me, where I could see it clearly from beginning to end. In the knowledge that this was where my journey would begin, I wandered out alone as far as I could on the tip of land that faced the entrance to the harbour. It seemed fitting to be by myself as I alone was responsible for the dream that brought us to this craggy shore and the start of another road adventure. With more than 8,000 kilometres of highway ahead, I took my time to make sure my focus was crystal clear.

There were little groups of volunteers and media people spread out across the rocks, snapping pictures to forever record the event. I dipped my running shoes in the frigid saltwater of the Atlantic and filled a glass jug with water as some of the locals looked out from behind curtained windows, snug indoors and probably questioning what we were up to on such a bitterly cold morning. I wondered how often they had seen others do exactly as I was doing before heading off down the road or out to sea. How many of those people had simply disappeared from sight as they set off on their journeys, never to be heard from again?

After months of mapping the route and paying attention to all the details, while at the same time trying not to lose sight of the big picture, this was where it would begin. Looking off toward Ireland for the last time, I said a little prayer and then turned to begin the most measurable undertaking of my life.

START THE CLOCK

Just as I crested the hill near city hall and Kilometre 0, the sun again broke through the clouds that had settled over the city. Because it was Good Friday and a holiday, most of the people of St. John's were probably just getting out of bed and plugging in their kettles when we were holding the official send-off. As I walked toward city hall, I could hear the familiar music of Justice Combined, who were back to show their support and were filling the downtown area with traditional Newfoundland music. I quickly learned to love this kind of willing spirit shown by Newfoundlanders.

For my friend and radio host Peter Garland, it was a memorable day. Back in London, his morning show was being broadcast live from his beloved Newfoundland. Peter, who had been conducting interviews since dawn, had a surprise for me as he emceed the formal portion of the kick-off from the steps of city hall. He had Jesse on the phone from London and while I was wishing him a happy 18th birthday and explaining how I kissed a cod the night before, something special happened. The crowd, which had gathered around the fire trucks, police cars and even a city bus that had stopped to join in the excitement, spontaneously broke into a chorus of Happy Birthday to a young man they had never met, the young man who was the inspiration for a journey that was to formally begin in a very few minutes.

There was one other piece of business to attend to before I set out on the road. On behalf of Jesse's Journey, I presented a cheque for $250,000 to Dr. Ron Worton of the Ottawa General Hospital Research Institute, discoverer of the gene that causes Duchenne muscular dystrophy. I made the presentation on behalf of Jesse's Journey, the charity we founded in the winter of 1993-1994, and it was, I hoped, a symbol of much more to come.

Kilometre 0 was very meaningful for me. To reach a dream you have to have a plan. There has to be a starting point and there has to be a way to measure progress as you move toward the dream. When the dream is to walk across Canada, there is a very distinct point at which you start to measure and to turn the dream on the drawing board into a reality. For me, Kilometre 0 was literally the point where the rubber met the road.

With a few more photo ops in front of the Kilometre 0 sign, a final wave to the crowd and after eight months of training, I took the first of the 10 million or so strides it would take to reach Victoria, British Columbia. In my mind I saw those little boxes again.

I barely noticed the gentle rain as I left St. John's and walked to nearby Mount Pearl, but by lunchtime the rain had settled into a steady downpour. As soaked as we were, our spirits were not going to be dampened on Day 1. Our faces may have been wet but they were also full of enthusiasm, an enthusiasm we didn't want to lose in the days and months ahead.

It got cooler in the afternoon and eventually the rain turned into flakes of snow. The highway was soon covered by a slick white blanket that made driving conditions greasy at best. The revolving amber caution light on the roof of the escort van was barely visible behind me. As I slipped and slid along the shoulder, I was passing cars that had veered off the road into the ditch. By the middle of the afternoon, the wind had come up and the snow was stinging my face. It was too dangerous to stay on the road. We knew it and the RCMP were telling us we had to stop, so this, our first day on the Trans-Canada Highway, ended after 22 kilometres.

As we drove back into St. John's, the snow turned to rain. To make up the shortfall in distance on the highway, I climbed off the motorhome, set my pedometer at zero and walked from downtown St. John's back out to Quidi Vidi, where I had started this first morning of my journey. By the time I returned to the bed and breakfast, it was dark and everything I had on was soaking wet, but our distance target for the day had been met. I knew April weather in Newfoundland could be very hostile and I considered the fact that it would be 28 days before we reached Port Aux Basques on the other side of the province. All I could hope was that those 28 days wouldn't all be as cold and wet as Day 1 had been.

I have never enjoyed a hot shower more than that night and as I sat down to write in my journal about my first day on the road, those little boxes slipped back into my mind. My method of measuring my progress was to think of one day as one box and my plan dictated that I had 275 little boxes of work to be dealt with, one at a time. As I had looked out over the Atlantic before we got underway in the morning, I had asked myself, "Can I really move all these boxes?" The answer – if I am being completely honest – was I don't know.

How could I know? But what I did know for sure was that I could complete that first day because I had trained and planned for seven months and I was ready to go. I was as prepared as I could be for what was to come and I saw no purpose in allowing serious doubt to enter my mind.

As I closed my eyes that night, I mentally moved one of those little boxes of work over to the "completed" side. And that became the first little box I wouldn't have to move again.

MOVING DAY FOR THE FIRST TIME

It was just past 6 a.m. on Easter Sunday when I climbed out of bed. St. John's had been my base for six days and the road team had been there even longer. It was a long drive out to our Day 3 starting point and the marker where we had finished the day before. The morning was quiet, with very little traffic and just a few donations, but things were about to change. After lunch, the four-lane highway narrowed to become a two-lane road and traffic quickly backed up for about a kilometre. For the first time, donations began to pour in as Easter holiday traffic from around the bay started to make its way back toward St. John's.

Yellow-vested men and women of the Whitbourne Lions Club were darting in and out of traffic and I had to slow down while they accepted donations from the windows of a steady stream of cars, trucks, vans and campers backed up in both directions. There was one minor fender-bender. I felt a little guilty about being responsible for people being delayed and apologized to a few drivers in the lineup heading home to St. John's. But in their typical East Coast manner and broad Newfoundland accents, they simply said, "Don'cha worry boy, you just take your time and good luck to ya."

We ended our day in Whitbourne with a Lion's Club supper of "fish and brewis," a mixture of hard bread, salt cod, onions and scrunchions, which are small pieces of pork fat fried to a golden brown. Fish and brewis is an age-old Newfoundland dish and after a busy day on the road, it proved very popular with our crew of mainlanders. By nightfall, we were blessed with full tummies, an army of new friends and had collected more than $2,300. It was a good day and I paused for a moment as I headed to bed. Alone in the long, dark hallway, I stopped to look at the door of the room, three down from mine, where Terry Fox stayed when he passed through Whitbourne on his Marathon of Hope almost 20 years before.

ALWAYS KNOW WHERE YOU ARE

In a way, Newfoundland is almost two islands. The Avalon Peninsula, bounded by Trinity Bay on the north side and Placentia Bay on the south, is the narrow land passage leading to St. John's and the easternmost pocket of Canada. Across this strip of land, the collision of the cold air from the waters of Trinity Bay with the warmer air from the Gulf Stream in Placentia Bay can create some dramatic weather, but on our crossing, we experienced mostly just rain, fog and a lot of very wet clothing.

My assigned distance for each day was 33 kilometres and I tried to complete as close to 20 kilometres as possible in the morning so the afternoon portion of the walk would seem a little shorter. I had developed a lunchtime routine that included closing the bedroom door at the back of the motorhome and sleeping for about 45 minutes before heading back to the road for the afternoon. It was never much fun waking up to the sound of rain and looking at more grey sky. While I napped, the rest of the crew continued to fine-tune their daily routines. With each passing day the rough edges were wearing off and the team was starting to function more smoothly. With an endless list of little things that had to be done in tight quarters, there was bound to be friction at times, but nobody told me about it. However, I was happy to hear when members of the group went off to look for whales or moose or just to see some of the colourful little Newfoundland villages nearby. It told me they were wise enough to know they needed to get away and find some breathing space.

Music and fun are the nighttime focus of Newfoundlanders and as they dish it up, they manage to find a way to turn it into giving. Early in our trip, a lodge owner brought in a band during our stay and on a particularly rainy night, in typical Newfoundland fashion, the casual merrymaking resulted in more than $1,000 raised for research.

Walking along the Trans-Canada Highway in Newfoundland is unlike walking anywhere else in the country. Waterfalls are everywhere and sometimes they were so close I could feel the spray. Wild rivers rushed under the bridges I crossed. At other times I could see waterfalls in the distance, but they were so far off, there was only silence. These were the moments, as I listened to my own breathing and the sound of my running shoes on the paved shoulder, when I would sharpen my focus in a calculated effort to store up the mental energy I knew I would eventually need. With each step and each breath, the distance kept slipping behind me at the rate of 33 kilometres (and one little box) each day.

There are hundreds of little fishing villages, called outports, dotting the rugged coastline of Newfoundland. At nighttime, the lights of these coastal villages stretch out like glittering diamond necklaces against the black of the ocean. It was the people of these little towns across the province who made us feel at home as they hosted the Journey road crew night after night. And as Newfoundlanders shared their life stories with me, I became aware of the hardships this province has borne. I realized that when I read future newspaper accounts of the plight of Newfoundland fishermen, I would see these people from a completely different perspective. I also realized this trip across Canada was going to include a big element of education for all of us. As we headed down the road to improve the lives of others, it was our lives that were being forever changed by the people of Canada and their stories.

Newfoundlanders have their own special sense of time and space and it didn't take me long to understand that everything in Newfoundland seems to be marked by its distance from the closest Irving service station. K. C. Irving probably never imagined these stations would become landmarks throughout the Maritimes. Whenever we asked directions, the answer always seemed to begin with someone stretching an arm out, pointing and saying, "Well, you go down to the Irving." From that reliable marker, we could get our bearings. Besides serving as route indicators, the Irving stations are drop-off and pickup points for people heading to the airport in St. John's, with mini-buses stopping regularly, at least according to Newfoundland time. When you ask when a bus will arrive you're told, "She gets here when she gets here!" Being as tactful as possible, if you ask when you should be at the station in order to catch this elusive bus, you're told in no uncertain terms, "You should be here when she gets here!"

THE FIRST BUMP IN THE ROAD

Continuing north toward Gander, the Trans-Canada Highway is four lanes of divided highway with a nice wide shoulder for walking. Along the way we reached Clarenville, which like so many settlements in Newfoundland, lies below where the highway sweeps across the province. Also like hundreds of Newfoundland towns and villages, Clarenville hugs the shoreline along the old road, where the water and the woods powered commerce in earlier days.

My first minor injury of the journey occurred when I twisted my ankle making my way up and down the hilly main street of Clarenville. I felt a lot better when I reached the town hall and saw a large number of young Sea Cadets, Brownies and kids with flags waiting to greet us. It hadn't taken me long to notice that the young people of Newfoundland are extremely polite and answer every question with "yes sir" or "no sir." These responses from kids who were so well-mannered somehow made me feel a little older.

Clarenville is where Ed Coxworthy, from Bell Island, Newfoundland, joined us as a volunteer. Ed was driving to the birthday party his wife Kay had organized for Jesse before we left St. John's when she casually mentioned we were still looking for a driver for a couple of weeks in Newfoundland. Ed said, "Don't look at me, I've done my part for the country." He had no intention of leaving home for any reason and certainly not to spend two weeks with a bunch of mainlanders. But after he heard me speak that night in St. John's, he told his wife on the way home, "Maybe I'll go for a week." He had more motivation than just my speech. His daughter Kari is a cancer survivor.

But whatever his motivation, we figured Ed would be a good addition to the team, even on the short-term. He knew his way around and there wasn't much he hadn't done. In his life, he had been a lobster fisherman, a seal hunter and a transport truck driver. He had been burned in a mining accident, had just one lung and had served Canada overseas as a peacekeeper in Cyprus.

When he joined us in Clarenville, we had no idea what lay ahead for the two of us. But what was immediately apparent was something else Ed brought to the team – a solid dose of Newfoundland humour. It occurred to me that if there was a Mr. Newfoundland who represented the fun, the dedication, the hard work and the love of his province, Ed was probably him. He was quick to inform us that he is a true Newfoundlander and his humour was evident when he told us he was born before Newfoundland decided to let the rest of Canada join it in 1949. While we laughed at Ed's dry wit, we soon learned his point of view is shared by many others across the province who were born before Newfoundland joined Confederation.

The Trans-Canada Highway is the lifeline of Newfoundland. The ferry from North Sydney, Nova Scotia to Argentia, in eastern Newfoundland, is only a seasonal run. So when winter holds the province in its icy grip, everything that's bound for St. John's arrives in Port Aux Basques and then has to be trucked almost 1,000 kilometres across the province. The fleet of transport trucks hauling everything from pencils and pantyhose to milk and motor oil is constantly on the move along the Trans-Canada and as word of Jesse's Journey continued to spread, truckers began responding with a friendly blast of the air horn as they passed by.

One trucker pulled his rig over and climbed down from the cab to shake hands and make a donation. He had heard on the radio about a father who was walking across Canada to help raise money for research. He too was a father and he understood why I was on this journey. It was just a brief meeting at the side of the road and after a couple of minutes, he began shifting through the gears as he drove away. Soon he was out of view and his truck became just another of the hundreds of rigs moving back and forth across the province. But it was an understated moment of understanding like many I would experience, as another parent reached out to me with quiet understanding.

MOVING IN THE RIGHT DIRECTION

Ten days into the journey, we had moved farther away from the Atlantic and the rain and snow had disappeared, replaced by a brilliant blue sky. As I headed north along the highway toward Terra Nova Provincial Park, in the distance I could see snow-capped mountains. Newfoundland was putting on a show.

Despite the stiff breeze, there were smiles on the faces of those in the escort van that followed along behind me like a shadow, matching my speed at five kilometres an hour. For the first time since arriving in Newfoundland, the road crew could roll down the windows and soak up the sunshine. I was hearing songbirds in the silence along the highway and the atmosphere in the motorhome seemed to have changed as nature teased us with a serious hint of spring.

But it was still early April and despite the smiles and upbeat feeling among the now well-organized crew, I had no doubt we would face more hostile weather before we moved to the mainland. I set my sights on Glovertown, next up on the map of Newfoundland. I didn't mind leaving Terra Nova National Park behind as some of its monster hills had taken more than an hour to climb. It was now just over a week since our departure from St. John's and my body was already giving me less-than-subtle reminders that I really was 52 years old. But despite having to nurse the aches and pains, my confidence had resolved itself into a steely determination hardened by the months of training. This was what I had chosen to do to have a lasting impact and help kids like Jesse. With that thought in mind, I kept moving the little boxes day after day, never losing sight of the big picture.

In Glovertown, for the first time since leaving Kilometre 0 in St. John's, I was reminded of suppertime back home. Instead of a restaurant, we were sharing conversation and the story of Jesse's Journey with the Churchill family, along with the town mayor and representatives of the Lions Club and Women's Institute. I would soon learn how important the Women's Institute is in Newfoundland. Its goal, "to strengthen the quality of life for themselves, their families and their communities," is one its members take very seriously as individuals and as a group and this is evident in everything they do.

This night their service to the community involved bowls of steaming-hot mashed potatoes, lima beans baked in molasses and all the goodies we could imagine being passed up and down the big dining room table. My thoughts strayed to another dinner table as I wondered what my family was having for supper at home.

Bits of news confirming that we were moving in the right direction, literally and figuratively, reached us each day. In Glovertown, we learned Irving Oil had agreed to provide us with free gas and propane across Newfoundland. We had no way of knowing it would be the only province where that kind of sponsorship happened.

When it was very quiet along the highway, there were times I wondered if anyone knew or cared that I was out here. But in the evenings, when I bowed my head and listened to someone saying grace in yet another church basement or community hall, I gave thanks that these generous people did know I was there and why and that they allowed me to share with them a potluck supper and the story of Jesse's Journey.

The journey's integrity rested on always picking up where we left off. So every day we had to budget time to accommodate the distance we had to drive, either forward or backward, from where we had stayed to where we had left our marker the day before.

Mornings became a routine of checking batteries on the portable radios, giving out the road assignments, getting a rundown on what radio interviews were scheduled and what time they were slated for, along with checking to make sure all the vehicles were fuelled up. Flashing lights had to be working and we had to have plenty of water on-board. It's surprising how dehydrated you can become even when the weather is cold and wet. We were very careful about our use of water, which was a precious commodity on the road. The risk of freezing temperatures had dashed any hope of having running water in the motorhome during the Newfoundland leg of the journey. This meant we had to make do with the two red plastic five-gallon containers we carried. Running water would have to wait until we reached the mainland. But we knew that when we hit cold weather in the West later in the year, we would have to shut the water down and get out the plastic containers again. After completing some stretching exercises and co-ordinating positions with our RCMP escort, it was time to get to work.

LISTEN TO THE OTHER STORIES

I made good time throughout the day, unlike the previous day, when my steps were short in response to strong headwinds. By day's end we were in Gander, "The Crossroads of the World." In the gathering dark of the late afternoon, I finished my distance and made a stop at the Silent Witness Memorial, a statue that marks the location where 256 members of the 101st U.S. Airborne Division on their way home for Christmas from overseas were killed December 12, 1985 when their aircraft crashed after a refuelling stop in Gander.

There was a light snow falling in the eerie silence that surrounded me. Directly in line with the north-south runway at Gander Airport, but on the other side of the Trans-Canada Highway, I could see a huge clearing stripped of trees. It ran for several hundred yards, exposing three levels of rock descending toward Lake Gander. The ill-fated plane, loaded with fuel, came down there in what was then a heavily wooded area, hitting the top of the first hill and then the two levels of rock below. The bald area of the crash site was dotted with stone cairns less than a foot tall, some with small makeshift wooden crosses tipped over by the wind. Draped from some were bits of ribbon or the remains of flowers, partially hidden by a light dusting of snow. Faded and weathered pictures of wives, girlfriends, parents and children were at the base of many of the crosses.

The U.S. Airborne Division's memorial to those who died in the crash is a larger-than-life bronze statue that depicts a member of the division in full battle uniform, holding the hands of a little girl and little boy standing beside him. The children are holding olive branches. It's a moving piece with an incredible amount of detail in the faces of the soldier and children. As I turned to leave, it started to snow a little harder as darkness closed in.

EXPECT THE EXPECTED

In the morning we woke up in the dark to the sound of a snowplough clearing the parking lot. When I opened the curtains and wiped moisture from the window, I was looking out at 10 centimetres of fresh snow. For the first time since leaving St. John's, I was not certain we would be able to get started. And even if we did, I was doubtful we would be able to put in a full day on the road.

But start we did, although the snow was heavy and wet and spray from passing vehicles made for a miserable and sloppy morning. When the plough went by, it scooped up a carpet of white and curled it into a wall of watery slush at the side of the road. The driver gave us a honk of the horn and the plough grew smaller and smaller as it moved off into the distance. With the shoulder scraped clean, the footing immediately became more solid and by midday, the sun had banished the cloud cover. The heat of the sun loosened huge clumps of snow on sagging tree branches and every now and then, the silence was broken by the sound of branches springing back into position and the dull thud of the snow as it fell to the ground.

A young woman and her husband stopped to make a donation on their way to St. John's from Cambridge, Ontario. I was touched by their gesture because they were going to St. John's for the funeral of the woman's father. I gave her a hug. I didn't know what else to do. But I thought about their long drive across the island and the circumstances, which made the fact that they took time to stop even more meaningful.

Late in the afternoon Newfoundland's weather turned nasty again, so quickly it seemed as if someone had pushed the switch from off to on. But every day, regardless of whether the wind and rain were stinging our faces or we were soaking in the warmth of the sun, the road brought new experiences. They caused a roller coaster of emotions as changeable as the weather and I never knew when the coaster would rise to a high point or plunge to a low. What I discovered is that I learned from both. There is no explaining why things unfold the way they do in life. We knew the ebb and flow of what happened each day on the road could not be controlled. The only thing I could try to control was my reaction to whatever happened. In a journey constantly packed with unpredictable twists and turns, controlling my reactions proved to be very important.

It was about 4 p.m. and starting to get dark when a man in a truck stopped to make a donation. I had no idea how he heard about us or why he stopped. Maybe someone told him or perhaps he heard me speak to a service club in a church basement or a community hall along the route. I was just grateful he took the time. Quite often people who heard me speak would bring their families out to support us on the road the next day. Some came just to see for themselves, curious about a 52-year-old father so determined to make a difference that he was willing to walk the entire distance across Canada. In turn, the 52-year-old father was thrilled to get the chance to meet youngsters like his own sons. These meetings helped fuel the fire of commitment needed to complete the thousands of kilometres ahead.

On our final night in Gander we were guests of a group of firefighters who gave us a tour of their firehall before presenting us with a cheque. Our conversation swung around to who had been where on the night of the Airborne crash. When I met the firefighter who was the first to reach the site, I could tell, as he looked down and shuffled his feet, that while it had been 13 years since the disaster, his memory of it hadn't dimmed. He didn't want to talk about it. Gazing out into the black night sky as we drove back to the motel, I thought about him again. Somehow at that moment, my load seemed a little lighter.

Heading west, I seldom saw the sunrise behind me as I walked along the Trans-Canada. But on the morning we left Gander on the way to our next stop at Lewisporte, I turned to look east and it was like watching the curtain go up on a spectacular stage set. It was still very cold as daylight pushed aside the night to reveal the highway that swept downhill and disappeared into snow-capped mountains sparkling in the early-morning sun.

It was midday when we met Michael Roberts from Bishop's Falls. He was everything an eight-year-old is supposed to be, with one exception. Like Jesse, Michael had DMD. Michael and his mom and dad were the first Duchenne family I met along the road. At lunch we were guests of the manager at the Irving Restaurant outside Bishop's Falls. I had to smile as I watched Michael's eyes light up when he found out he could have anything he wanted for lunch. A few minutes later I could barely see him behind a huge hamburger, a giant plate of french fries and a milkshake. As his mom helped him with the ketchup, I chatted with his father. Like so many Newfoundlanders, he was unemployed and the family faced a four-hour drive into St. John's every time Michael had a medical appointment. The hardships of life in rural Newfoundland were apparent almost every day and it was difficult to imagine the struggle of dealing with a life-threatening disease in such a remote place.

But people like the Roberts family don't dwell on the cards life has dealt them. Instead, they get busy and in this case, they organized donations for Jesse's Journey. As we walked through Bishop's Falls with a police escort, Michael was living every little boy's dream – sitting up high in the front of a bright red fire truck with the siren blaring at his command. As we made our way through town, people we thought had nothing to give gave everything they could because they felt it was the right thing to do. Sometimes when we think of philanthropy, we think of the photo op when a huge cardboard cheque is being presented by a large corporation. The people of Bishop's Falls taught us about real philanthropy, when you reach into your own almost-empty pocket to give without hesitation.

We completed the loop through town and back on the Trans-Canada, I leaned over to say goodbye to my new friend Michael. He shook my hand as he gave me an envelope with a cheque inside. Then he reached up and put his arms around my neck and gave me a big squeeze. He was only eight years old and yet it was as if he knew what the future held. This was his way of saying, "Keep going John. Help us find an answer. All we want is a chance to grow up like other kids." I held him for just a moment before his dad lifted him up to return home. I didn't know if I would ever see them again or whether Michael realized what a huge part he had played in Jesse's Journey and what he had given me that day. I turned back to the highway.

Late in the afternoon, just like clockwork, what started out as a beautiful day turned ugly. The wind rose and a stinging combination of rain and sleet attacked my face for the final hour on the road. Yet people were still stopping to make donations. It was almost dark when a car pulled over up ahead. The driver, who left his emergency lights flashing, got out and walked back to meet me through the rain and cold spray from passing vehicles. The stiff wind blew his trench coat against his body and sent the collar whipping against his face. He had heard me speak at a reception in Gander but here, in the middle of one of the most miserable hours I had spent on the road, he handed me a cheque for $500. He too had a son who suffered from Duchenne. If there were tears in his eyes, which I suspect there were, I couldn't really tell because of the wind and rain. In the headlights of the escort van, we shook hands. He was another father who understood exactly what I was doing and why. Without saying anything more, he turned, walked back to his car and drove away, vanishing from my life as quickly as he entered it. And so it went as the roller-coaster ride continued.

FOOD FOR THE SOUL

Another little box was moved at the end of another long day on the highway when we reached Lewisporte at the south end of the Bay of Exploits. Lewisporte is where the ferry leaves to make the 35-hour journey to Labrador. I must have been quite a sight, soaked to the skin and dripping water on the carpet as I shook hands with dignitaries at the town hall. It was cold, wet and miserable outside, but inside the hall was packed with people and we were treated to another big slice of Newfoundland hospitality. We were welcomed by the music of the Sea Cadet Marching Band and the smiling faces of more parents and kids. I spoke for 10 minutes about how kids everywhere would benefit from the research we would be funding. It was still early days in the walk across Canada but as several groups presented cheques, I thought that even as tired as I was, this was what I was prepared to do every day to reach my goal.

As guests of the Women's Institute in Lewisporte for supper, I again found myself in the company of a fascinating group. After spending hours on the road each day, sometimes with very little response, it was amazing to observe these remarkable women and to realize how well organized and powerful they were. I had the feeling that if the Women's Institute in Newfoundland ever fielded candidates, they would probably win enough seats to form the government, and perhaps they should.

Supper was served in a hall adjacent to the town's heritage museum. After locking the old wooden door to the museum behind me, I shed my wet clothing (everything I was wearing) in the silence and under the watchful eye of two mannequins in pioneer costumes. I laughed at the thought that there probably weren't too many Canadians standing naked in a museum in Newfoundland at that very moment. As I donned dry clothes, I thought this was not exactly what I had planned when I got up that morning. But it had rapidly become clear to me that no two days on the road were likely to be the same.

It was story-time for the 150 Newfoundlanders who had provided us with another marvellous potluck supper, topped off with a dessert made with bakeapples, a Newfoundland tradition. Bakeapple is often called cloudberry in other parts of the world and isn't an apple at all but a creeping raspberry with yellow or orange berries. I shared our story and hearts and wallets opened to help Jesse's Journey take another giant step forward. These were people I had never met before. These were the people of Lewisporte, Newfoundland.

The next morning in the pre-dawn darkness, the red duffel bags that made us look like a hockey team were loaded into the motorhome and vans, which were being warmed up for the day's work. We had a 55-kilometre drive to reach the marker at yesterday's finish point, which would be our starting point for the new day. The marker routine was pretty simple and very accurate. At the end of each day, we tied fluorescent tape to a guardrail or signpost at the edge of the road and then reset the motorhome's odometer to zero for the trip either backward or forward to wherever we were spending the night. Then in the morning we noted the distance and again set the odometer at zero before driving the same distance until we found our marker. This trip of 55 kilometres was our longest so far to reach our starting point. As we drove, the headlights of the motorhome revealed nothing but snow-covered trees and a long stretch of black highway. By nightfall, when I moved the next little box, we were in Grand Falls-Windsor and halfway across Newfoundland.

In our "normal" lives, we often spend much of our days looking at computer screens, reading reports and memos and answering telephone calls. Conversations frequently focus on work. Television often dominates our evenings at home and real conversation, the exchange of thoughts and ideas with others, seems well down on our list of priorities. But when you're on the road for seven or eight hours a day, you have a lot of time to listen to those who are taking turns walking with you. You get to know them in a way you probably wouldn't under different circumstances. The small talk dissipates in a hurry and it's then you get the chance to learn what really makes people tick. It's a rich experience.

At noon on Day 14, I spoke to a joint meeting of the Rotary and Kiwanis Clubs in Grand Falls-Windsor. The CBC taped my speech and I was surprised to receive a standing ovation. It gave me a good feeling as we made the trip by van back to where I left the road, although the lunch-hour appearance meant I had to skip my after-lunch nap, which had become an important part of my daily routine. The pay-off was that a lot more people had learned what Jesse's Journey was all about.

The road team was spread around several locations for the overnight stop in Grand Falls-Windsor and I was at a bed and breakfast with a real western feel about it. The lady who ran the business had 11 horses and also operated a riding school. As we pulled up to the gate there was a stop sign that said "Whoa Partner!" The sign on the paddock said "Please do not feed fingers to the horses!" The next morning, just up the road, I was about to see a real sign of the times.

LITTLE TOWN – BIG LESSON

When we reached the edge of Badger, Newfoundland, it was a cold spring morning, the kind of day where you can see your breath in the air. This was about as far as I could possibly be from a life of four-lane traffic, cellphones, fast food and too much noise.

Volunteers from the fire department were waiting with two fire trucks to provide us an escort. Fire engines are a major part of celebrations in small communities all across Canada. Thousands of hockey players can probably remember riding on the local fire engine after winning a championship. As we made our way through town, I could see smoke rising from the chimneys of the little wooden houses. From behind curtained front windows and warm inside their homes, people smiled and waved at the passing parade.

No one talks about the citizens of little towns like Badger and their day-to-day struggles. Badger certainly doesn't reflect the usual tourist's view of Newfoundland. It's about as close to the centre of the province and as far from the ocean as you can get by road. Before the railway tracks were torn up at the end of the 1980s, the town was a bustling logging community. By the time we arrived, it was struggling economically, with as many as 70 per cent of the 1,000 residents on social assistance of some kind. Most of the employed worked for Abitibi-Price, either in the forest or at the mill in Grand Falls-Windsor. Spruce trees in the area were earmarked for the mill, but the people of Badger were allowed to cut birch, aspen and tamarack for firewood. Some of the tired-looking buildings in town dated back to more prosperous times but inside the town's proud houses were some of the finest people you could ever hope to meet.

Even with the sirens of the Badger Fire Department splitting the morning silence, few people ventured outdoors and understandably, donations would be hard to come by here. While I was making my way to the public school, one elderly Badgerite paid us a visit. Ed Coxworthy told me later that a 93-year-old man stopped by the motorhome because he wanted to help. He had only $1 to give and that's what he donated. I was sorry I didn't get to meet him.

There were just over 80 students enrolled at Avoca Public School in Badger, which serves Grades 1 to 9. Avoca is an Indian word that means "the meeting of three rivers." The kids were just like school kids everywhere, full of life and wanting to help. When the teachers had heard Badger would be one of the stops on our itinerary, they wrote a song. The result was special as the junior grades sang Hello to welcome us to Badger. Some Newfoundlanders might not have a lot of money but it seems they all have the gift of song and I think that makes them richer than many other Canadians. A young girl presented me with a cheque on behalf of all of the students. It was 127 of the hardest-earned dollars we received.

I felt a bit like the Pied Piper as I left the school. All the students joined me in a walk through town as we made the loop back out to the Trans-Canada. One little girl never left my side. She was very quiet but as I waved goodbye to the kids when they turned to head back to school, my new little friend looked up at me and in a very shy voice said, "I'm going to be an astronomer when I grow up." Crouching down beside her in the snow and pointing to the sky I replied, "Every night, you look up at the stars because that's where your dreams are and I hope they all come true."

The honesty of children who have no agenda makes me wonder if we spend enough time listening to our own advice. How often do we actually step outside on a clear night and look up at the stars? One of life's pleasures for me still is to stop on a country road at night and get out of the car to stare up at a sky that looks like diamonds scattered on black velvet. It puts everything into perspective. Each of us is just a tiny fleck in the universe and we aren't here very long.

Back on the highway in the afternoon I had a lot of time to think about the people of this little town and the lives they were living. They kept their pleasures simple and avoided dwelling on their dreary economic outlook. The focus of the people of Badger was on taking care of each other.

When we returned to Badger that night, the Firettes, a group consisting mostly of firefighters' wives, had a roast beef dinner waiting for us at the firehall. Just after the fire department was formed in 1961, the Firettes hoisted the fund-raising banner and they've been hard at work ever since. The firehall was a beehive of activity when we arrived. It was nice to come in from the cold to the wonderful aromas coming from the kitchen. We spent the night on Second World War-vintage cots set up in the firehall. There were times when I rolled over in my sleep that I had the sensation my rear end was hitting the floor, but whatever shortcomings Badger might have had was more than made up for in its hospitality.

With my head on a pillow thousands of kilometres from home, I was feeling pretty lucky to have met so many wonderful people along the road. But I was missing Sherene and the boys. Our day in Badger had imprinted the word "family" on my mind and unable to sleep, I wrote in my journal that "Today we stared poverty in the face and it smiled back." In the morning we would move into the most remote part of the province and would face another test of stamina and commitment. In the meantime, another little box had been moved.

From Badger, the highway turns north toward Springdale, which is tucked into one of the many inlets that lead to Notre Dame Bay. There is no view of the ocean in this part of the province and in the rain it was a bit depressing. Along the narrow road was a large area destroyed by a forest fire about three years before. When you live in the city and the closest you come to seeing a forest fire is pictures on television, you can't conceive of the destruction. The scars from this fire were still visible and no new trees had been planted.

The day was a bit confusing as our police escort cars shuffled back and forth so officers could attend court. The officers told me most of the cases involved domestic disputes. By the end of the day, five different officers had handled the escort duty. But regardless of when I looked back, there was an RCMP vehicle right behind me with its roof lights flashing. That was great comfort as we kept moving along the Trans-Canada Highway.

There were few donations in this remote area of central Newfoundland, but a man loading a logging truck waved from the distance before he stopped what he was doing and drove up to the road to make a contribution. A group of little boys dressed in their Beaver uniforms waited to meet us at the turnoff to Springdale to present me with the toonies they had collected. They were smiling, excited and proud to be helping other kids. And there was a man in a pickup truck who drove by before turning around and coming back to make a donation. He shook my hand as he said he just wanted to help and there were tears in his eyes as he told me he had lost his precious daughter just a month earlier. As I gripped his hand, there was nothing I could say but "thank you."

I never got used to these moments, when strangers released and shared their most personal feelings. The pickup truck pulled back onto the highway and moved on down the road. I walked on to the next town, the next moment and the next lesson on life's highway.

Springdale is a town of just 2,500 people who, less than a month earlier, had never heard of John or Jesse Davidson. But with word spreading across Newfoundland, the Kinettes of Springdale had literally been stopping traffic to raise money. The women of the service club had organized a "boot toll" and raised almost $1,000 for Jesse's Journey.

Moose meat and scalloped potatoes were the highlight of dinner in Springdale, which was followed by a cheque presentation from the Kinettes. There was an unexpected gift from a woman who left her home on a rainy Sunday afternoon to make a donation on behalf of Springdale's Royal Canadian Legion membership. Newfoundlanders have a special place in their hearts for people who make sacrifices. Legion members from one side of the province to the other have never forgotten those young people from across Canada whose last steps on Canadian soil were in Newfoundland before crossing the Atlantic to fight for freedom. So many of them never returned.

JUST GIVE ME A CALL... OR NOT!

There are times when, if you don't laugh, you'll probably cry. Just beyond Springdale, Murphy's Law hit us with a vengeance and it seemed like everything that could go wrong, did. We had entered one of those geographic pockets we'd nicknamed "Never-Never Land" or "cellphone hell," depending on how many problems we were up against. Without cellphones, we couldn't contact the rest of the world and we would have to get to a land-line to conduct radio interviews or talk to the home team in London. The phone problem meant we had to do a lot of jockeying along the road to keep our time and distance accurate. To add to what had become a big day for minor problems, our computers weren't working and the walkie-talkie batteries wouldn't hold a charge in the cold weather. On the brighter side, we'd been assured the scenery ahead was spectacular and the road was mostly flat. At least it wasn't snowing as we made the turn toward Port Aux Basques and the ferry to mainland Canada.

On the last day of April, after what felt like many, many days in the wilderness, we finally reached Deer Lake, a funny name considering there are no deer in Newfoundland. The weather was a mixture of rain and snow, both swirling in every direction. For the next three days we were constantly soaking wet and we considered ourselves lucky if half a dozen drivers a day stopped along the highway to make a donation. I thought back to the words of my friend Darryl Sittler of the Toronto Maple Leafs, who was there when Jesse and I announced our intention to cross Ontario together. Darryl said, "It's real easy when the television cameras are here and everybody wants to talk to you. It's when you're all alone in the middle of nowhere and it's pouring rain that measures your courage."

There were no television cameras here and I was sure this was what Darryl would have called "the middle of nowhere." The cold wind and driving rain left our hands and faces red and raw. There was nothing to look at beyond low grey clouds, fir trees, rock and wet pavement. No one said much and the hours on the road were a real test. A stop for hot tea and fruit in the morning was an oasis from the misery. But soaking wet and with rain dripping from my chin, even the indoor picture wasn't very pretty. The motorhome was a maze of makeshift clothes lines hung with everything from wet socks to running shoes. All of us were learning a lesson in dedication and determination.

The rugged terrain of Newfoundland didn't always lend itself to finding a place to park the motorhome on the Trans-Canada Highway. A rest after lunch each day was part of my routine and I didn't want to be worrying that several tons of transport truck might be about to come through the bedroom of the motorhome when I was lying down. It became a game of cat-and-mouse and often Ed Coxworthy would have the motorhome hidden at the end of an abandoned laneway, partially obscured by the trees. With very little noise, these were great spots for getting a good nap.

As we headed southwest toward Port Aux Basques, our next stop was Pasadena. Things were looking up as the sun was shining and Newfoundland's gorgeous scenery was again on display. The weather was warmer and our rain-drenched clothing had finally dried out. The legs that had been struggling through snow were again starting to pump like well-oiled pistons as the kilometres fell behind us. We were on the home stretch in our traverse of Province No. 1.

The smoother routine on the road allowed my thoughts to drift home. I could see a younger Jesse walking home from grade school carrying artwork to show us at supper time. I saw him walking on the beach in summer, standing at attention in his Cub uniform, trying his best to kick a soccer ball and leaning on my shoulder for a family picture. Jesse had used a wheelchair since he was 12, so these mental pictures were cherished memories and I had them safely stored away. Every time I looked at the faces of schoolchildren, like the kids in Pasadena, I replayed those pictures over and over again in slow motion, because I wanted to be able to hang on to them forever. I saved every image I could in those early years, with as much detail as possible, because I knew the clock was running and I guess I knew a day would come when Jesse could no longer walk. It's something most parents never have to think about.

In Pasadena, the public school is high on a hill overlooking the road below. The kids had been let out of class and had formed a long line in front of the school. They were cheering as Jesse's Journey made its way through town. I got an extra workout as I climbed the hill and shook hands with each of the pupils. As I looked into the eyes of these children, smiling faces so full of life, the replay camera in my mind flashed pictures from another time and place.

There were days when our road team must have looked like a pretty ragged bunch when we arrived at luncheons we'd been asked to attend. Quite often our hosts would seat us at a special table and there we'd sit, sometimes dripping wet, sometimes sweaty or windblown, with our Jesse's Journey outfits making us stand out in a roomful of men in shirts and ties and women in business suits.

Each time I stood up to speak, I found myself looking at an audience of business leaders used to making tough decisions. But the story of Jesse's Journey always seemed to hit a nerve and I would see businessmen who'd been laughing over dessert and coffee suddenly become silent, sometimes even removing their glasses, exposing red-rimmed eyes. Women in the audiences often reached into their purses for a handkerchief. All I was doing was telling them about the courage of youngsters like Jesse, but it moved them deeply.

It was back to the highway after another midday luncheon appearance and having missed my noon-hour rest, I was very tired by early evening, when we finished our day on the road. The lights of the outports scattered along the coast sparkled in the dark, linking the villages together. Nighttime in the small towns and villages of Newfoundland isn't like nighttime in any other part of the country. In the cities, evenings for many people mean television time. In Newfoundland, nighttime is "each-other" time. This night's each-other time was at the firehall in Pasadena.

The sound of guitars, a stand-up bass and a mandolin mixed with the clear, powerful voices of The Sharecroppers, three singing schoolteachers from Pasadena who have performed all over the island and around the world. Neighbours chatted over coffee and sandwiches and there were young girls in kilts doing an impromptu Highland fling.

Everywhere I looked there were smiling faces, fingers drumming on table-tops and toes tapping on the floor as people sang "Fogo, Twillingate, Morton's Habour, All around the circle," lyrics from I'se the B'y, a traditional Newfoundland folk song. After I spoke to the people of Pasadena about the journey across Canada, the night at the firehall became another Newfoundland memory to be stored away when The Sharecroppers talked me into doing a solo. There was much laughter as this mainlander struggled through "I'se the b'y that builds the boat and I'se the b'y that sails her." This was nighttime in Newfoundland.

MAY IN MARBLE MOUNTAIN

On the first day of May we were just outside Corner Brook and looking up at Marble Mountain. Its pink marble, shipped all over the world, can be seen from the Trans-Canada, which makes a dramatic sweep upward as it rises above Newfoundland's second-largest city.

There were always frustrations along the road and just outside Corner Brook, I ran into one of them. I was using a cellphone to do an interview with CBC Radio in Corner Brook when I realized our media kit had obviously gone astray. I knew the interview wasn't going to go very well when the announcer called the project Jesse's Dream. From that point, it just got worse. Not only did he think I was running across Canada, but he thought I was going in the opposite direction and finishing in St. John's. I tried to be patient and to do my best to straighten him out, since there was nothing to be gained by getting upset. He already looked foolish. There was no point in both of us looking that way. When the conversation ended, I just shook my head. I reminded myself that it was just one interview, that it is wise always to expect the unexpected and that patience is indeed a virtue.

The Trans-Canada Highway at Corner Brook provides a panoramic view of Frenchman's Cove and the Bay of Islands. Besides its distinctive marble,

Corner Brook boasts one of the largest pulp and paper mills in the world. On that cool, still morning a plume of smoke from the distant mill rose straight up in the air. On the water, Canadian Forces HMCS Nipigon was making her way into the harbour. From this height, the frigate looked like a toy floating in a bathtub. I was told a group of grocery store employees from Corner Brook had stopped by the motorhome with a donation of $1,500. Focus and patience seemed to have brought their own reward.

With Corner Brook fading into the distance, life on the edge of the road once again settled into a quiet time of logging kilometres and moving little boxes as we headed southwest. Although we wouldn't be there for a couple of days, our next major stop was Stephenville. At the end of the day, the RCMP accompanied us back to Steady Brook, at the foot of Marble Mountain. A bagpiper led us in to a dinner hosted by the community Lions Club of Steady Brook and although I was starting to get anxious about finishing the Newfoundland leg of the journey, there was another audience who wanted to hear what Jesse's Journey was all about. Every time I was given a chance to speak, I had to remember the people I was speaking to were hearing it for the first time. As much as it hit a raw nerve every time to talk about Jesse and all those kids facing a shortened life expectancy, it had to be done. I couldn't slack off and had to give it everything I had at every opportunity. When I finished speaking that night about Jesse and the hope research holds, people were standing and there were more donations.

Finally the weatherman gave us a break! Back on the highway to Stephenville, the sun was shining and for the first time since the journey began, it was definitely warm enough to put on a T-shirt. It was great to feel the warmth of the sun on my face.

A truck driver who stopped to make a donation said he had passed us about 50 times. This was important because if he had passed me that often, I was pretty certain a lot of other truck drivers also knew exactly where we were on the road and that made life seem just a little safer. At our morning break, our RCMP escort officer, who had a CB radio, confirmed, "Oh yeah, you guys are a hot item out here." No sooner had he made the remark than the voice of a trucker crackled through the speaker in the cruiser asking, "Who the heck is that guy walking down the road?" Another trucker answered back, "That's

John Davidson from London. He's walking across Canada." When the first driver responded with surprise saying, "You're shit'n me," the RCMP officer grinned sheepishly. Then he picked up his microphone, pushed the button and said, "OK boys, let's keep it down at bit." It was all a part of life along the Trans-Canada.

On the day we reached Stephenville, the wind was blowing hard and it had been raining all day. But when I look west, the water I could see was the Gulf of St. Lawrence and beyond that was mainland Canada, just a few days away. That was good news. To reach Stephenville from the highway, we had to cross the Port au Port Peninsula past the hamlets of Lourdes, Grand Jardin and De Grau, originally settled by French seafarers.

The giant Abitibi-Price pulp and paper mill is the backbone of Stephenville, but the community was once home to the largest U.S. air base outside the United States. As we drove there on a rainy Sunday night at the end of our day on the road, it was like stepping back into history. You could almost hear the ghosts of yesterday. To reach the centre of town, we had to drive across miles of tarmac and past abandoned hangars ravaged by weather and neglect. In the headlights of the van, sheets of rain lashed the tarmac and the windshield wipers whipped back and forth as I squinted to look out at the empty buildings with their broken windows. I could imagine what it must have been like when thousands of young airmen were stationed there during the Second World War. There would be the sound of jeeps shuffling arriving and departing airmen back and forth across the tarmac amid the constant drone of the military flights taking off and landing on runways now fenced off and deserted. A fighter plane mounted on a pedestal in the centre of town is one of the last reminders of the time when Stephenville was of strategic military importance.

The town was dark, wet and dreary as we headed to our dormitory, which was a little spooky. Our floor was empty except for us. I decided to work on the blisters on my feet, which were in pretty bad shape after a day of pounding the pavement in the rain. It was time for a "blister popping party," which sounds pretty disgusting but was fairly simple and a good thing to do to keep my feet in good shape. Sitting on the counter in an empty washroom, I soaked my feet in very hot saltwater and then pricked the bubble portion of the blisters with a small disposable lance from the first-aid kit. The steam rising from the water made the tile walls even clammier than they already were. Rain ran down the outside of the washroom window, a black rectangle of glass with a wire grid that separated me from the night. I felt a pang of homesickness as I wrote in my journal at the end of Day 24 on the road and visualized moving another little box.

When I finally put my head to the pillow, I thought back to the highlight of the day, when a group of volunteer firefighters stopped by the motorhome to make a donation. They were from Burgeo, an outport on the south coast of Newfoundland, and had made a five-hour drive in the rain to meet us. It was another of those occasions when friendship was both instant and fleeting. On the motorhome, our guests had a chance to dry out and share hot chocolate. We laughed and joked and smiled for the cameras as the firefighters took still pictures and videotape to mark the day they took part in Jesse's Journey. They were a proud group of guys who typified the spirit of Newfoundlanders. As I learned about Burgeo, I realized this was a singular moment. A village I had never heard of, with just 2,500 residents, had just contributed $500 to help make life better for a lot of kids they'd never met.

The next morning we climbed Gallant's Hill, the largest hill in Newfoundland. The scenery was stunningly beautiful as the Trans-Canada began its plunge down into the Codroy Valley, which winds toward Port Aux Basques. As we moved south, the Gulf of St. Lawrence was off to the right, bright blue and sparkling in the afternoon sun. To the left were dark green mountains separated by what looked like giant inland fjords. Fog swept down in long wisps from the almost flat tops of the mountains, like steam from a witch's cauldron. Wildlife seemed to be everywhere, transforming this part of Newfoundland into the stuff of fantasy. Across a ridge were two moose, a cow and her calf, standing absolutely still, staring as we logged some of our final kilometres on the island. On the other side of the highway, there were caribou and a red fox. For the first time since leaving St. John's, I was wearing both a T-shirt and shorts as I prepared to shift gears into warmer weather.

After a final night of being anchored in Stephenville, the red Jesse's Journey duffel bags were loaded onto the vans and motorhome. This was our last moving day on the island. By nightfall we would be staying in Port Aux

Basques, our last stop in Newfoundland.

We reached our starting point for the day and set out toward Port Aux Basques. Ahead was a 16-kilometre stretch of the Trans-Canada Highway known as Wreck House. It's a high-wind zone and the landscape in this area is dominated by Table Mountain, which rises more than 500 metres above sea level. The winds here come rushing down the flanks of the mountain and blow across the highway. There are huge yellow signs along the road cautioning about the danger of 200-kilometre-an-hour winds. These winds are the stuff of legend, with stories of trains that had to be chained to the tracks and tractor-trailers tossed about like matchsticks. In bad conditions, drivers are usually cautioned to wait out the wind before venturing through the area.

It was another day that started out wet and cold, but by the time I was 10 kilometres down the road, the temperature was 10 degrees warmer. I shed three layers of clothing in less than 30 minutes, but then had to put them all back on again as the winds swept down from the mountainside late in the afternoon. Although I had changed shoes several times during the day, the wet weather was again causing problems for my feet. This was a serious concern as they were probably the most important part of my body at this point. The road team also was paying a lot of attention to my feet, underscoring the need to concentrate on the most important things to keep us moving day after day.

There were only a few donations along this road but I told myself not to be discouraged because there might be days when we wouldn't get any. If those of us with good health would stop for a moment to realize how vital research is, it would make all the difference. But I knew that if we persevered, a day would come when we would reach our goal and be able to give $1 million a year, every year, to research. That was the goal I never lost sight of. As if to prove the value of positive thinking, we were approached by a woman with a disabled son. She apologized that she could afford to donate only $3.50 because she was on social assistance. It's so impressive when people who have so little to give do what they can to help.

BLOWN AWAY – LITERALLY!

When I thought about Bob Dylan's lyrics, "The answer my friend is blowin' in the wind," I wasn't sure I could relate to the "answer" but I sure could relate to the wind. When I set out to cross Newfoundland almost a month earlier, I knew there was a strong likelihood the weather would be hostile at times. On my final day on the road in the province, Mother Nature decided to test my endurance one more time. A driving rain and very high winds ensured that the final 16 kilometres on the highway were completely miserable. Dressed in fluorescent orange rain gear in an attempt to be visible to the few vehicles on the road, I was in a real tug-of-war with the weather as I leaned into the wind, which sometimes blew me back a step.

Just after lunchtime, with the caution lights of the escort vehicle behind me blinking through the endless rain, we officially reached Port Aux Basques. It had been 29 days and almost 1,000 kilometres and we had completed Province No. 1.

There was a huge crowd waiting, indoors where it was dry, at the train station in Port Aux Basques. A legendary train, the "Newfie Bullet," now fully restored, is parked on the last 70 metres of track in the province. The engine, which once belched steam into the clear Newfoundland air, now stands silent at what was the head of the rail. CNR stands out in red letters on a background of dark green and black. Behind the engine are a baggage car, complete with a new, gleaming hardwood floor, and passenger cars, where thousands of travellers sat over the years. The leather seats have been redone and the car's pot-bellied stove looks brand new.

To say the Newfie Bullet is legendary is an understatement, but contrary to its name, speed was the last thing on the minds of those who boarded. There are tales of how the train would stop for those who wanted to pick berries or flowers before climbing back on-board to continue their trips. Newfoundlanders like to tell the story about a woman who gave birth on the train. When the conductor told her she shouldn't have been travelling in her condition, she looked him in the eye and said, "I wasn't pregnant when I got on this train!"

The day we arrived, the refurbished train station hadn't officially opened as a tourist attraction. But, with the RCMP organizing events for us in Port Aux Basques, town officials decided the arrival of Jesse's Journey was a good time to open the building to the public. I was really happy to see so many people out to welcome us. The building was jammed with school kids, Sea Cadets and people from service clubs, including a huge contingent of men and women from the Royal Canadian Legion.

Representatives of the Newfoundland arm of the RCMP were on hand to say goodbye as we prepared to leave for North Sydney, Nova Scotia. I had been told back in St. John's, "The Force will be with you," and for a month, through the wind, snow and rain, the RCMP had been right behind me. In my final speech in Newfoundland, I thanked the officers for their help. But I found myself struggling to realize I had made it all the way across the first province. All the little boxes that represented Newfoundland had been moved over to the "completed" side.

On Day 30 of Jesse's Journey, while most of Port Aux Basques was asleep, our motorhome and vans were being driven onto the ferry for the 96-nautical-mile journey to the mainland. The warm waters of the Gulf of St. Lawrence would soon separate us from the people of "The Rock," but the friends we had made in the last month would keep us tied to Newfoundland forever.

I looked back to shore as we began to make the crossing to mainland Canada and I felt good about one major aspect of striving for any significant goal – designing the plan so you can win. This is where people undertaking sizeable projects often stumble. It is important to have your dream where you can always see it and to know there is a plan in place. But the establishment of reasonable steps to achieve it is critical to success. Things can easily and quickly collapse when people overestimate their abilities. It's sometimes better to under-promise and over-deliver.

From the top deck of the Joseph and Clara Smallwood, I watched Newfoundland disappear into the fog as we slipped out of the harbour at Port Aux Basques. While I looked forward to reaching Cape Breton, I replayed the pictures I had collected and stored away in my memory bank over the last month.

There was the day in Corner Brook when the lobster season opened, giving rise to one of the most memorable conversations on the island. When we asked, "How much are the lobsters by the pound?" we were told, "We don't sells them by the pound, we only sells them by the each!" When we then asked, "How much are they by the each?" the answer was "$4.50 a pound!" And so it went day after day, all across the island.

My memory reviewed pictures of history, pictures of poverty and pictures of hope set in the magical charm of Canada's newest province, which boasts such places as Blow-me-Down, Bumble Bee Bight, Hearts Content, Ireland's Eye and Little Cat Arm, along with Butter Cove, Bread Island and Empty Basket. There was the wit and wisdom of the good people of Newfoundland. There were the smiles and handshakes of encouragement from moms and dads and grandparents all across the province. These were salt-of-the earth people who listened and gave thanks that their children had the ability to row a dory, climb the rugged mountain terrain and walk the province's saltwater shores. They were parents who wanted all children to be able to share in that experience.

Threaded through my pictures of day-to-day life in Newfoundland were memories of the ever-present humour that helps its residents vanquish hardship and the harsh climate. But most of all, the islanders had shown me their love of life, music and laughter. These create a buffer from the fast-paced world Newfoundland seems so far removed from. As the bow of the Smallwood cut its way through the waters of the gulf, leaving a churning wake of turquoise foam, I allowed myself the pleasure of leisurely flipping through the never-to-be forgotten mental snapshots in my island scrapbook.

· NOVA SCOTIA ·

"A good plan today is better than a perfect plan tomorrow."
~ General George Patton

The Smallwood and its sister ship, the Caribou, make the six-hour crossing of the Gulf of St. Lawrence twice a day. The motorhome and escort vans were major clues to the other passengers that the Jesse's Journey team was on-board. Some of them had seen Jesse's picture on the sides of the vehicles, smiling as he waves a Canadian flag.

The fog finally lifted just as we arrived in North Sydney and the captain invited us up to the bridge to see the ship approaching port. Docking requires precision work, with a lot of tinkering at the controls to guide the ship gently into its slip. Once the lines have been secured, the bow of the Smallwood opens like the mouth of a giant sea monster to disembark its cargo of vehicles and people.

Under a blue sky and to the strains of bagpipes, I stepped onto the Nova Scotia soil of Cape Breton Island. Old friends were there to greet me, along with a Mountie in his bright-red dress uniform. But most important, there was a 10-year-old boy named Trevor who suffers from Duchenne. He was with his dad and grandfather. It was for kids like Trevor that I had come to Nova Scotia. Jesse's Journey was for him and all those incredible youngsters, most of them boys, who show us every day what real courage is all about.

MAY ON THE MARITIME MAINLAND

The day after we arrived on Cape Breton Island was Mother's Day. It was Sunday and by early morning we were back on the highway, walking the road from North Sydney to Sydney, the capital of Cape Breton from 1784 until 1820, when the island became a part of Nova Scotia. It's a rugged part of the country, where coal and iron ore deposits led to industrial development in the mid-19th century and made Sydney "The Steel City." In an area that conjured up pictures of smokestacks and slagheaps, tulips just about ready to bloom swayed along the highway. The grass was a rich green as it soaked up the morning dew. The sun was beginning to feel warm on my back and the road ahead held a promise of spring.

The first donation of the day came from a young woman driving a pickup truck. She had her three young children with her and she had driven out to the highway specifically to shake my hand. Like every person I had met along the road, she had a story and visibly struggled with her emotions as she told me about the children. The conversation lasted less than a minute and was like a camera shutter clicking and bringing the big picture into focus.

I couldn't believe how fast the traffic was moving in comparison to the slower pace in Newfoundland. One driver, rubber-necking to see what we were doing, almost ran into the car in front of him, hit the brakes and sent his car fishtailing back and forth across the highway. He was lucky there was nothing coming the other way on the narrow section of two-lane road. Soon after, there was another close call when a transport truck screeched to a halt just short of the car in front of it. Blue smoke and the smell of burning rubber filled the air as the truck left two long back skid marks on the pavement. We hadn't been in any accidents and I was hoping today wouldn't be the first. With 33 kilometres completed, we drove back to North Sydney for one more night. I packed the duffel bag in preparation for morning and then phoned my mom in Brantford, Ontario. Tomorrow was moving day, but tonight was still Mother's Day.

Highway 4, which runs along the south shore of Bras d'Or Lake, is a difficult stretch. The road is narrow, with no shoulder to walk on, and there are lots of twists and turns. There also are a lot of hills and while short, they are very steep, not like the long gradual grades of the Trans-Canada in Newfoundland. With no police escort available in the afternoon, I was much more aware of how vulnerable I was on the edge of the road, even with one of the mini-vans behind me. It was the first but it wouldn't be the only time I felt a sense of danger. While there were few donations along the road, I wasn't discouraged. There really wasn't anyplace to stop a vehicle without creating a real hazard.

Cape Breton was putting on a floral show of blue, pink, purple and white lupines in full bloom everywhere you looked. As I reached the top of one of the short steep hills, I saw that Bevin Palmateer was busy shooting videotape of me as I walked toward him. I didn't know why he was aiming my direction because if he had just turned around, there was a fabulous view across Bras d'Or Lake that could have been in a travel brochure for Scotland.

Bevin asked if I noticed anything special about this spot, but other than fields of lupines and little yellow buttercups blooming at the side of road, there didn't seem to be anything outstanding about this piece of the highway. With the camera still rolling, Bevin broke into a smile and said, "Congratulations my friend, you just finished the first thousand kilometres!"

Sometimes in the pursuit of a dream we can become too driven; life becomes a win-at-all-costs situation. Things get distorted and the beauty of the dream we want the most morphs into an "all or nothing at all" proposition. With a rainbow of lupines swaying in the sunshine and buttercups beaming, I realized this was a real stop-and-smell-the-roses kind of moment, so to speak. With 1,000 kilometres completed, we paused briefly to acknowledge our success. I wanted to clear my head and give my dream room to breathe. It seems a contradiction but the more often you stop, the farther you'll go. With some back-slapping, hugs and handshakes, we posed for a couple of pictures and a little roadside celebration. When we got going again, the hills seemed easier and my pace that much quicker.

The air was warm and with a huge, blue sky overhead, the scenery again reached the level of spectacular. Bras d'Or Lake is a bit deceptive. It's actually a part of the Atlantic Ocean and was formed when the sea flooded a glacier-depressed valley. St. Peter's Canal to the south and the Great Bras d'Or Channel to the north link the lake and the ocean. Bras d'Or Lake is known as "The Great Inland Sea" and has 70 kilometres of coastline, barely perceptible tides and a saline level half that of the ocean.

The few days on Highway 4 along the shore of Bras d'Or Lake were very quiet. After the rain and cold weather in Newfoundland, it was a pleasure to take advantage of the sun's warmth. I settled into a routine of soaking my feet in sea salt and cold water three times a day. Ed Coxworthy, our Newfoundland driver, said to me, "By the Jesus, Johnny, you got feet like the leather of a baseball glove." (Every sentence he spoke seemed to start with "By the Jesus,

Johnny.") I took that as a rather weird compliment that my feet were getting tougher. The blister problems seemed to have disappeared now that we were enjoying drier weather.

The few communities in this area were spread out along the highway. White clapboard churches surrounded by green lawns marked the villages of Ben Eion, Big Pond (hometown of singer-songwriter Rita MacNeil), Irish Cove and Johnstown on the shore of Bras d'Or Lake. The stones in the graveyards told the history of the area.

As I walked the narrow roads of rural Cape Breton, I saw old wooden houses that had been abandoned. These were the kind of deserted buildings you see in the pages of black and white photography books. People who came from Scotland once occupied these farmhouses. Many of them arrived in Cape Breton late in life and didn't have children, so when they died, the farms fell into ruin. The way the law is structured in Nova Scotia makes squatters who might want to occupy a house hesitant about doing so in case long-lost relatives suddenly surface after money has been spent to restore the property. And so these houses sit empty, a reminder of earlier times.

WHEN THE STUDENTS BECOME THE TEACHERS

The moments that stay with us in life often come without warning and one of those unscheduled moments began with a knock at the door of the motorhome one day in Cape Breton. It was lunchtime and we were just north of the Mikilometresaq Reserve at Chapel Island. An energetic young woman who was teaching on the reserve said the school was right alongside the road and she asked if I would please stop and say hello to the children. I told her I'd be happy to. She told us that when she began teaching on the reserve there were just 13 children taking classes. Now enrolment was up to 75.

When we reached the school I was immediately surrounded by dozens of happy, smiling children. One of the pupils was a little girl in a wheelchair, a six-year-old with cerebral palsy. She looked up at me with the biggest brown eyes I have ever seen and handed me an envelope that contained a cheque for $100 from the schoolchildren. These kids wanted to help other kids.

Chapel Island Reserve is home to many caring people. They are proud of who they are and what they have achieved. Their homes have window boxes filled with flowers and there's an orderliness about the place. The reserve was the complete opposite of the stereotypical images I had been carrying in my mind. Before we said goodbye and moved south with our band police escort, the chief of the reserve presented me with a book of native poetry. As I headed down the highway, three ladies from the Chapel Island Women's Club came to the roadside with a donation. The good people of Chapel Island had opened my eyes.

The final day on Cape Breton Island was warm and sunny and I felt content to be here, rather than in Ontario, where we'd heard it was a sweltering and sticky 31 C. As we headed toward Port Hastings and the causeway that crosses the Straits of Canso, it was a gorgeous day, 28 C. with a light breeze. We crossed out of Cape Breton on the Canso Causeway, which was built between 1952 and 1955. It is more than a kilometre long and its rocky base fills the Canso Strait to a depth of 65 metres, making it the deepest causeway in the world.

In one motel after another, I kept moving the little boxes as we pushed deeper into Nova Scotia. Kilometre after kilometre and hour after hour I pressed on, sometimes struggling to stay focused as I tended to tire mentally. On the days when it was very quiet along the road, my thoughts drifted home to the family I was missing. I thought about the dreams we all have and how we frequently take the path to those dreams for granted. It isn't until life takes a dramatic turn that we suddenly realize the road is full of hurdles and we begin to see things differently. We may discover we have to create a different kind of dream.

I snapped out of my daze as I became aware of the soft crunching sound of the tires of the escort van behind me rolling over the gravel at a rate of five kilometres an hour. I had lost complete track of time and wondered how long I had been thinking about dreams. But such thoughts helped me strengthen my priorities. My dream was to help researchers find a cure to Duchenne muscular dystroyphy and my goal was to someday be able to provide them with $1 million annually in funding.

I didn't know if this introspection was an asset or a liability but one thing I did know was that I was stubborn. I suspected there were a lot of people who didn't think I could make it and with more than 7,000 kilometres still ahead, stubbornness would be an advantage and would fuel my conviction that quitting was not an option. I also knew I would have to be patient. There was no short-term fix when it came to building an endowment to fund research in perpetuity. I had to be in it for the long haul.

Since the inception of our undertaking in the winter of 1993-94, we had managed to build a brand new charity and to give parents hope, something they had longed for. Thousands of people had given their time and energy to Jesse's Journey. Through our investment in research, we had already ignited a fire in the scientific community to find a treatment and, eventually, a cure for an insidious disease that robs parents of their children.

The families of disabled children who face life-threatening illnesses for which there is no cure find it difficult to be patient. It's too hard when they live each day in a race with time, and the clock keeps ticking. Alone on the road, I also could hear that ticking clock and yet I had no choice but to be both stubborn and patient. It wasn't easy to accept that maybe young people like Jesse had only a slim chance. But I also knew that what I was doing could make a real difference. The sound of the van tires still rolling over the gravel was reality. Regardless of how much money we did or didn't raise on the road each day, the big picture was clear. We had to keep moving.

YESTERDAY, WHEN I WAS YOUNG

I was on the road with Dave Meadows, who had decided his Halifax law office could survive without him for a week. David and I are two fathers who met in the summer of 1969 when we were in our early 20s, still single and living at the same fraternity house in London. We were both working in radio during what the music world would label "the summer of love." In upstate New York, Woodstock was about to go from a small rural community to a generational landmark. The musical Hair was riding the crest of a pop wave and Aquarius was one of the most popular songs of summer. Zegar and Evans were on the charts with In the Year 2525, along with Sly and the Family Stone and Hot Fun in the Summertime. Beauty, horror and triumph were all performing on a psychedelic stage. It was the year Ted Kennedy's hopes for the White House were dashed at Chappaquiddick and the horrific Manson murders took place in California. It was also the summer the world stood still as Neil Armstrong stepped onto the moon. Dave and I didn't know what our futures would bring.

Scottish roots run deep in the university town of Antigonish, where a civic reception marked our arrival. On the way into town, I walked through a portion of the campus of St. Francis Xavier University, established in 1861. An architectural highlight of Antigonish is St. Ninian's Cathedral. Built from locally quarried blue limestone between 1867 and 1874, it honours the fifth-century saint who brought Christianity to Scotland.

On the highway from Antigonish to New Glasgow, I was joined on the road by two politicians. At the time, Peter McKay was a 32-year old rookie Conservative Member of Parliament for the Nova Scotia riding of Pictou-Antigonish-Guysborough. He was young, enthusiastic and did not know his political career would see him become Canada's minister of National Defence. John Hamm was the leader of the provincial Conservative Party in Nova Scotia and would go on to become premier of the province. A tall man with a long easy stride, the 62-year-old Hamm had no trouble walking the highway and collecting donations.

But as for my walking, a lot of little physical problems were starting to pile up. In addition to persistent nagging blisters, I now had to ice both knees, as well as the ankle I twisted back in Newfoundland. It was a nuisance fussing with these things, but I knew I had a long way to go and a lot of people were counting on me. I had to be careful and I couldn't afford to ignore these issues.

The days along the road leading into Halifax became what I called "paying your dues" days. There were very few donations, but every now and then there was a nice surprise, like the Sunday afternoon our volunteers collected more than $750 at a stock car racing track outside New Glasgow. But on Victoria Day, along the road to Truro, we raised only $40. In my mind I had already dealt with the issue of "good days-bad days." Not everything was about money. I kept on walking and kept moving those little boxes, one at a time.

The first 18 kilometres of our route from Truro to Halifax had me walking southwest along a multi-lane divided highway, before I had to shift over to a secondary highway. It was pouring rain as traffic sped by, rushing back into Halifax at the end of the Victoria Day weekend. The last couple of days in the rain had been a series of blurred pictures and conversations. There was the mayor of Truro presenting town pins, a car dealer dropping by the motorhome with a cheque for $100 and a memory of steam rising from the

Irish stew and hot chocolate we were served at lunch. There were members of a vintage car club donating $200. There was me soaking my feet while doing a radio interview and the remembered sound of cars and trucks honking and spraying us with water as they whipped by in the rain. Then there was a mother and father from New Glasgow and their son, who suffered from the same disease as Jesse. They came out to the highway to make a donation and offer support. I held on to that picture longer than the others.

The sun had finally broken through to shine on the farming communities in this part of Nova Scotia when I was approached by Steve Casey of London, a volunteer who was with us on the road when I pushed Jesse across Ontario in 1995. He was one of those guys who liked working in the background and who would do whatever had to be done to keep the whole project moving. He knew the last few days had been tough in terms of donations and after we'd ascended one of the longest and steepest hills in Nova Scotia, he asked me if I ever thought of giving up. I told him exactly what I had resolved when thinking about those who didn't believe I'd make it: "Whenever that question comes up, and I'm sure it will from time to time, there's a five word answer – 'Quitting is not an option.' "

Six kilometres into the day, we marked the highway and headed into Halifax for a news conference and an unexpected moment. The room was packed with supporters, including business groups, school kids and a young boy in a wheelchair with Duchenne. Having covered this sort of event myself in the past, I knew the television and radio reporters were looking for the right "sound bite" for the six o'clock news or the right audio clip for the day's radio newscasts. The program began with a short video of Jesse and me on the road together in 1995, after which the mayor of Halifax, Walter Fitzgerald, was scheduled to welcome us to his city. I was to speak to the crowd after the mayor's remarks.

The lights were dimmed and the video ran before the hushed crowd. When the lights came up and the mayor stepped to the microphone, there was a long pause. Fitzgerald was suddenly so choked with emotion he couldn't continue. With tears running down his cheeks, he took a handkerchief from his pocket and wiped his eyes as he struggled to gain control. After what seemed like a long time, he faced the microphone and began his remarks. It wasn't necessary, but he apologized to the gathering as he continued to dab his eyes. Then, with a little smile between the sniffles, he said, "You know, I've been in politics a long time and people who know me will tell you I'm never short of something to say, but today you got me!" That comment broke the tension and elicited a warm round of laughter. Then the mayor gave us a heartfelt welcome to Halifax.

Before I returned to the road, it was my turn to get a little choked up as I said goodbye to Ed Coxworthy, who was heading home to Newfoundland. We were very lucky to have a volunteer like Ed, who kept us laughing in tough times and tough weather. His comments had become legend. There was the day he stepped out of the motorhome and spotted two rabbits doing what rabbits do quite a lot. We were reduced to tears when he described the scene: "By the Jesus, Johnny, he was just a stitchin' her coat something fierce! A sewing machine didn't have anything on that boy!"

Ed, who hadn't planned to take part in the project at all, had been on the road with us for 37 days. After saying farewell to the crew, he thanked me for showing him parts of his own province he had never seen. We knew we would miss this congenial man who dropped what he was doing and gave us a chunk of his life, who not only entertained us, but helped look after us along the road.

If we could find a way to place a value on laughter, it would rank very high on a list of the world's greatest commodities. People come and go in our lives all the time but seldom do we give them enough time to show us how they shine. I had known Ed for just over a month and yet I knew I could trust him with my life. He is one of those gold nuggets that shines from the moment it comes into your line of sight. Does someone or something bigger than all of us send such nuggets our way at just the right time? No matter how it had happened, Ed was a gift.

The events in Halifax put me behind my distance goal for the day so back on the road, I walked until almost 6 p.m. As I edged closer to the city, I knew there was no margin for error when it came to charting our course through Halifax, both in terms of road distance and appearances at promotional events. We would have to stick to a very tight schedule. We collected only $20 in donations that afternoon – another case of a low following an earlier high.

THIS OLD HOUSE

Province House, built in 1819, is the oldest and smallest provincial legislative building in Canada. When Charles Dickens visited Province House in downtown Halifax in 1842, he labelled it "a gem of Georgian architecture." When our road team was seated in the gallery, we received a standing ovation when Premier Russell MacLellan introduced us to the House.

Province House is one of those Canadian landmarks steeped in history. When I toured the building, I sat in the chairs used by then U.S. President Bill Clinton and Russian President Boris Yeltsin at a meeting of G7 leaders in Halifax in June of 1995.

Following question period, the premier invited us to his office, where there was a cheque presentation and a photo op as the Province of Nova Scotia donated $500. As I shook hands with the premier while cameras flashed, I had no way of knowing Nova Scotia would be the only province to make a donation.

After Province House, we went to a junior high school to visit a boy in a wheelchair who had been collecting money for Jesse's Journey, but wasn't well enough to attend the news conference the day before. I signed my hat and traded it for a million-dollar smile from the boy, who was really happy we took the time to stop by.

The weekend was spent winding our way from the Halifax suburb of Bedford through city streets congested with traffic that had slowed to a crawl as people rolled down their windows to donate. Our volunteers were sweating as they scrambled from vehicle to vehicle and the road team asked me and our RCMP escort to slow down a bit to give the volunteers, who were still stuck in traffic, a chance to catch up.

It wasn't often I was asked to slow down because of the volume of work the volunteers had to contend with, so this was a nice problem. I eased my pace and the police officer behind me honked to get my attention and to point out the cemetery where many of those who drowned in the sinking of the Titanic are buried. Since the release of the movie Titanic, the City of Halifax has been working hard to make the cemetery a tourist attraction. The hero of the Hollywood movie was a young Irish passenger named Jack Dawson and the RCMP officer told me there actually is a gravestone marked "J. Dawson." But

*A MOMENT TO REFLECT – John Davidson looks out at the Atlantic Ocean
from Quidi Vidi, Newfoundland before taking his first steps on Day 1
of his solo walk across Canada in 1998. He knew Ireland was closer
than his destination of Victoria, British Columbia.*

*MAN OF MANY TALENTS – Newfoundlander Ed Coxworthy –
motorhome driver and jack-of-all-trades – was an invaluable member of
the Jesse's Journey team. He actually was a miner at one time but this outfit
is his costume as part of The Submarine Miners singing group.*

*BUNDLED UP – Neither wind nor rain nor sleet nor snow would
stop John Davidson's solo trek across Canada, although they all tried.
He is pictured here outside Deer Lake, Newfoundland, on April 28, 1998.*

the real J. Dawson was a stoker in the engine room of the doomed ship. That hadn't deterred those caught up in the romance of the film and the cemetery was having problems with people wanting to chip pieces of "J. Dawson's" gravestone to take home as souvenirs.

We were quickly approaching the harbour as we passed under the Angus L. MacDonald Bridge, linking Halifax and Dartmouth. Founded in 1749, Halifax has one of the world's largest harbours. Commercial shipping has long been a source of wealth for the city, which acts as Canada's gateway to commerce, particularly when the St. Lawrence River is frozen. The harbour also has played key naval and military roles and in 1917, during the First World War, it was site of the world's largest man-made explosion before Hiroshima. On that fateful day, the harbour was crowded with warships, troop transports and supply ships when a Belgian relief vessel and a French munitions carrier collided. The resulting explosion, fire and flooding killed more than 1,900, injured 9,000, destroyed 1,600 buildings and damaged 12,000 houses. In all, more than 30,000 people were left either homeless or with inadequate housing.

Throughout the afternoon of our 14th and final day on the road in Nova Scotia, traffic was tied up several times. People were in a buoyant mood as they honked horns and called out words of encouragement. At one point, traffic was moving slowly as it moved down a ramp that merged with where we were on Bedford Road. All of a sudden one vehicle ran into the back of another. It looked like there was little damage and as I turned to look at the RCMP officer right behind me to see if he wanted us to stop, he just smiled, wiped his hand across his mouth and looked off in the opposite direction. He seemed to be saying, "I didn't see that." His reaction told me that if you have a good idea and the right people on your team, they will overlook the inconsequential things to keep the whole project moving forward. We kept going and at the end of the day, a tired but happy group of volunteers were in the heart of Halifax with the day's 33 kilometres completed and hundreds of dollars in donations. Little box No. 44 had been shifted over to the "completed" pile.

GATEWAY TO A NEW WORLD

After the busy day on the road, I was enjoying the silence in my hotel room in downtown Halifax. The noises of the day were gone and as I wrote my journal notes, I could see from my eighth-floor window the flickering lights of Dartmouth across the harbour. Every now and then there was an opening in the clouds and the moon shone on the water.

Below me, through the darkness, I could make out a harbour shed alongside the dock. The building gave no hint of the role it had played in Canada's history. There were no signs indicating that during the war years, 368,000 troops had left from there. Too many would never return. There was nothing to acknowledge that two million people arriving in Canada had passed through its halls in the 43 years before the building was closed in 1971. When I was two years old, I passed through that building, the last standing immigration shed in the country. This was the arrival point, the gateway to Canada. This was Pier 21.

The wind and rain were back when we reached Caribou and boarded the ferry to make the 22-kilometre crossing to the picturesque island province made famous by Canada's best-known fictional character, the green-eyed and redheaded Anne of Green Gables. Signs along the road sometimes made me think Canada was a fictional place. There was the sign at Port Aux Basques informing travellers that it's illegal to take potatoes off Newfoundland. As we boarded the ferry leaving Nova Scotia, there was a sign telling us it is illegal to transport honeybees onto Prince Edward Island. Then there was the sign on a gate in Cape Breton that proudly boasted we were at "Young MacDonald's Farm." They didn't have to write EIEIO after it; we got it. In a fun way, all these signs made Canada seem rather comical.

As Nova Scotia slipped behind us in the wake of the ferry, my thoughts took me back to the Chapel Island Reserve on Cape Breton Island. The big brown eyes of a little six-year-old girl in a wheelchair and the donation from the kids at her school were among the things that would drive me on. It was two provinces down and eight to go.

· PRINCE EDWARD ISLAND ·

"With ordinary talents and extraordinary perseverance all things are possible."
~ T. F. Buxton

The ferry arrived at Wood Islands on the southernmost tip of Prince Edward Island and docked after its 75-minute journey from the Nova Scotia mainland. In a matter of minutes the ship had disgorged its cargo of cars, vans and cyclists. There was little fanfare attached to the arrival on Canada's smallest province. At most airports, train stations or even bus depots, you see businesspeople with briefcases and laptop computers meet and shake hands before scurrying off to waiting cabs or tears of joy as families are reunited. Husbands and wives kiss, grandparents hug children and grandchildren and lovers embrace. But at the Wood Islands ferry terminal, everyone and everything disappeared in a hurry.

It was Sunday, May 24, and after a lobster dinner with old friends and writing in my journal, I called home. I was happy to hear Sherene's voice as she told me how the boys were doing. Then it was time to sleep. The next day was the first of the six it would take to walk across Prince Edward Island.

Monday dawned sunny and cool as we reached our starting point. The island's red clay was waiting under a clear blue sky. The Trans-Canada Highway from Wood Islands wound through Belle River, Pinette, Flat Creek and Orwell as it led us toward Charlottetown. As I passed through the historic village of Orwell, I was just a kilometre east of St. Andrews Presbyterian Church, where they still hold services in English and Gaelic. This part of the Trans-Canada was a real treat because there was a very wide apron at the edge of the road. When I passed an elementary school at noon, I was swamped by about 300 kids clapping, cheering and chanting, "Go John Go!" I signed as many autographs as I could and then it was time to move on. After lunch, a CBC television crew from Charlottetown came out to the road to shoot a story about Jesse's Journey.

Before we finished our first full day on the island, we marked the road and went ahead into Charlottetown to take part in some special events. Charlottetown is often referred to as "The Cradle of Canadian Confederation." Our first stop was Province House, built in 1847, which is now the meeting place of the provincial legislature. The Speaker of the House greeted us and we were given a tour of the building. It was there in 1864 that a meeting of the Fathers of Confederation led to the British North America Act, creating the Dominion of Canada. The room where that meeting took place, the Confederation Chamber, has been restored to the way it looked when that historic gathering took place three years before Confederation. We were shown the long table where the idea of a Dominion of Canada was debated. Our tour guide was bubbling with enthusiasm and proud that she also had shown Terry Fox and Rick Hanson through Province House when they passed through Charlottetown.

Back on the road later in the day, as we were playing a little bit of catch-up in regard to time, the sun was sitting low in the sky and the shadows were long when Bevin Palmateer put his creative genius to work. With his video camera, he captured shots of my shadow moving across the red earth and fields of potatoes just beginning to sprout. It occurred to me that I would be a long way from Prince Edward Island by the time these potatoes were ready for harvesting. By then I would be looking at wheatfields on the Prairies. But on this day I was just enjoying the long shafts of light and the warmth of the sun as I finished another day on the road.

HELLO TORONTO – CAN YOU HEAR ME?

There were wisps of fog early the next morning as we travelled to our starting point and the air was cold until the sun made it over the horizon. The first glitch of the day found us outside of cellphone range for a radio interview with The Fan in Toronto. We finally found a phone booth and made the connection. The Fan is a sports-talk radio station and was interested not only in the fund-raising aspect of Jesse's Journey but also the athletic story of a 52-year-old who intended to walk more than 8,000 kilometres across Canada.

The program operator who took the call put me on hold and then put me on the air with the announcer. At the end of the interview, the operator came back on the line to say goodbye. I was surprised when he said, "Thanks a lot John. We love you for what you're doing." It was an uplifting comment from someone I'd never met and got my day off to a good start.

There was no shortage of people stopping to make donations as I moved closer to Charlottetown. As we entered the city, there were lots of flashing lights and sirens as both the police and fire departments provided us with an escort. An honour guard of police officers in their blue dress uniforms saluted as we entered the building where Charlottetown Mayor George McDonald welcomed us. When it was my turn to speak, I took full advantage of the opportunity to tell the audience our story.

Each day on the road there were more and more people who wanted to shake hands and donations were definitely picking up as we moved across the island. The rolling hills were offering some of the prettiest scenery imaginable. From the lawn of an Anglican church at the top of a hill in Bonshaw, where we were parked, the view out over the West River was a living postcard in the sunshine. The island reminded me of a model train set-up without the train. Everything seemed so well laid out. Wherever I looked, the green fields and English-looking hedgerows, along with the red soil and the ocean, made the island picturesque. People young and old were stopping their cars or walking down farm lanes to make donations to Jesse's Journey. Prince Edward Island had heard our story and islanders were responding.

As I looked into the sun and squinted through a late-afternoon haze, I caught my first glimpse of Confederation Bridge, which locals call "the span of Green Gables." We would be crossing the $840-million engineering marvel in a couple of days. The 13 kilometres of reinforced concrete that link Prince Edward Island to mainland Canada make this the world's longest multi-span bridge over ice-covered water and it had opened to traffic just the year before. The bridge crosses the Northumberland Strait and from a distance, it looks like some kind of giant centipede standing in the water.

At the end of the day, with another little box moved, I soaked my feet in saltwater while two little dogs at Molly's Bed and Breakfast made me laugh as they tripped over each other and bumped into furniture while slip-sliding across the floor. "Charlie" wanted to play all the time, but it was pretty obvious "Molly" was a senior citizen of the dog world.

Velma was the owner of Molly's Bed and Breakfast, which backs onto Malpeque Bay. The bay is famous for its oysters, which are in demand all over the world. A shy, determined woman, Velma was living a quiet life on Prince Edward Island, but conceded a piece of her heart was still back in Ontario, where she had been a hospital administrator for 16 years before moving to the island. In 1989 she had been seriously injured in a head-on car crash in Nova Scotia on her way to a food show in Halifax. It had been a rough 10 years. But her greatest strength was her positive attitude, which seemed to be fed by the easy pace of island life.

On the morning of our last day on the island, over a breakfast of pancakes and bacon, Velma summed her situation up when she said, "I just keep going." Given a choice, she would have had things turn out differently, but with Molly and Charlie added to the mix, she had found a contentment few people enjoy.

Velma was happy with her quiet life on the island, far from the fast pace of big cities. In these urban jungles, we can be blinded by greed we mask as opportunity in a chase for the dollar dragon, thinking it will make our dreams come true. How often do we roll the dice on the chance of financial reward, fooling ourselves into thinking this will bring success and with it, happiness? It is the antithesis of the quiet pace of life that unfolds for people like Velma and her words, "I just keep going," stayed with me for a long time.

The emerald-coloured fields of Prince Edward Island resembled a travel poster for Ireland. At Victoria-by-the-Sea, fields of green swept down to red sand curling around the inner harbour to the pier. At the end of the pier, awash in the morning sunshine, a white wooden lighthouse flew a Union Jack. The perfectly still backdrop of blue water beyond the harbour made this place an artist's delight.

As I admired Victoria-by-the-Sea, I was walking with 52-year-old Paul Naylor from Bonshaw, Prince Edward Island. He is what homegrown islanders call a "CFA," which means "comes from away." Paul had long known where he wanted his dream to take him. He was an employee of Air Canada for more than 26 years before he and his wife Wendy moved to the island in 1986. He told me how he scouted the island for a property that could be made into a bed and breakfast and found just what he was looking for in a sawmill reaching the end of its time. He spent the first six months clearing the land by hand of the scrap slabs of wood that littered most of the acreage. In hindsight, he said, the scrap wood was probably the reason nobody else wanted to buy the place. Paul and Wendy ended up with their bed-and-breakfast business and their own 27-acre woodlot.

Paul was a great example of someone who visualized his goal. His dream was meaningful to him and challenging. He had a plan in regard to how he was going to reach that goal, it was specific and measurable and in the end, he made his dream come true.

I listened with interest as he told me more about the island while I logged my final kilometres there. It didn't surprise me to learn there are no soft drinks sold in plastic bottles or cans in this pristine place. As I had crossed the province on foot, it was easy to see that restricting soft drinks to glass bottles had kept roadside litter to a minimum. When Paul and I reached Englewood School just outside Summerside, the students made a $100 donation. The school had won a National Science Award and it was easy talking with kids who had an appreciation for the importance for research.

By the end of the day we had reached Confederation Bridge and I had finished the Prince Edward Island portion of the walk across Canada. In the morning we would move on to New Brunswick, the only province I had never visited. It would be Day 50 on the road; just seven more provinces to cross.

· NEW BRUNSWICK ·

"Do what you can with what you have, where you are."
~ Theodore Roosevelt

Earlier in the journey, when we made the crossing from Newfoundland to Cape Breton, Marine Atlantic gave us a warm welcome and free passage. Getting from Prince Edward Island to New Brunswick was the exact opposite. We knew pedestrians are not permitted on the bridge, which is totally understandable, but the letter our home team sent outlining what Jesse's Journey was all about and requesting a "freebie" bridge crossing for the vehicles brought a negative response that made it clear nobody gets a free pass.

We made one last smiling appeal when the motorhome and escort vans, which had been on television and in the newspaper all week, rolled up to the ticket booth on the bridge. The cold response was, "That'll be $112." When we cleared the approach ramps on the New Brunswick side of the bridge and I stepped back onto the road, the drivers of Bridge Authority trucks seemed to be keeping a close eye. I figured they were making sure I didn't walk on any part of the roadway considered part of the bridge. As I left the mammoth structure behind, I felt sorry our experience with the people connected to that man-made marvel was as cold as the concrete itself.

It was almost June when I took my first steps in New Brunswick. The winter weather was supposed to be behind me, not to return until late fall in Saskatchewan. But on the first day in Province No. 4, a combination of high wind, rain and sleet was again tearing at my face.

Two Acadian Rotarians were in a parked car about two kilometres from the Confederation Bridge, waiting for me. They were our new volunteers, the next links in the chain, and were ready to play their part to make Jesse's Journey a success. My hands were cold, red and raw as I shook hands with the newcomers. Everyone had a cup of hot chocolate as the introductions were made and we quickly ran through the daily routine. As they listened to our list of "how to do" and "what to do" instructions, I felt a little sorry for the two volunteers, who looked like they were wondering what they had gotten themselves into. For us, the routine was familiar and it was easy to forget that what we were doing every day was brand new and maybe a bit intimidating to the uninitiated. I had seen that look on faces before but I knew that by the end of their time with us, they would be veterans and friends who wanted to stay longer.

Then it was back to the highway to finish our first 33 kilometres in New Brunswick. The provincial route would follow a zigzag pattern to take us through the major centres of Moncton, Saint John and Fredericton.

The following day, the wind was still blowing hard as we headed southwest along the highway toward Sackville, but the lupines were blooming and fiddleheads were growing along the roadside. I managed two stretches of 11 kilometres each before lunch. Only a handful of people stopped as traffic moved quickly along the Trans-Canada, which at this point was a four-lane divided highway. One woman who pulled over was very moved by the whole project. She asked to take a picture of "Jesse's dad" and donated $50 before driving away.

There's a long gentle slope to the Trans-Canada as it sweeps down into the wide expanse of the Tantramar Marshes east of Sackville. Acadian dikes reclaimed the wetlands three centuries ago and the meadowlands that resulted have been labelled "the world's largest hayfield." Off in the distance, the motorhome was parked almost a kilometre back from the highway, nestled at the base of the 12 signal towers of Radio Canada International. The wires connecting the towers seemed to be strung out in a criss-cross pattern over the marshes. The saltwater of the Tantramar Marshes acts as a giant reflector for the short-wave radio signals. There was a small museum exhibit about short-wave radio in one of the few buildings, but mostly this giant communications facility was strangely devoid of people.

In the motorhome, one of our new volunteers had produced large tins of frozen lobster for lunch. His family owns a lobster packing company in Shediac, New Brunswick that processes two million kilograms of lobster each year. Its customers are along the eastern seaboard and the West Coast of the United States. He smiled as he said, "There you can sell lobster, but not in Texas. There you sell steak."

The day ended in Sackville, home to the campus of Mount Allison University. The school has the distinction of being the first university in the British Empire to grant a degree to a woman – a Bachelor of Science to Grace Annie Lockhart in 1875. Tall oaks, Georgian architecture, fine older homes and a pond full of swans in the centre of town all enhanced Sackville's image as a university town.

It was May 31 and a quiet Sunday morning as we made our way along and away from the tree-lined streets of Sackville the next day.

The schedule called for what we referred to as a "site visit" at the end of the day, so after walking for more than seven hours, the Jesse's Journey caravan was off to Shediac for a parade and barbecue. There were hundreds of people on hand, along with the sound of sirens and sight of flashing lights, as we made our way through Shediac. A 14-metre-high, 80-tonne steel lobster gives weight to the town's boast of being "The Lobster Capital of the World."

Smoke was rising from the barbecues in a park, where Rotary Club of Shediac members were hard at work raising money for Jesse's Journey. I was impressed with the hospitality and generosity of the townspeople, who celebrated our arrival in both English and French. The wind and cold didn't let up as I spoke to the crowd and thanked them for their help. My French is terrible but nobody seemed to mind. When I finally got to bed, I thought about how diseases don't recognize language and how people who speak both English and French, people I'd never met, had come together to help. That, I decided, is how it's supposed to work. The people of Shediac were very generous. It was a good day.

NEW MONTH – NEW CHALLENGE

On the first day of June, fresh from our great reception in Shediac, we felt really pumped about how we were doing as I pounded the pavement leading into Moncton. Little did I know Jesse's Journey was about to make front-page headlines, but not with the kind of story we were looking for.

When we reached the heart of the city they call "The Gateway to Acadia," there was a formal welcome to Moncton in the foyer at city hall. True to their word, our friends from Manulife were on hand to make a $1,000 donation. Officials from the West Moncton Rotary Club presented the team with $250. And as we shook hands and posed for the cameras, the newly elected mayor of Moncton, Brian Murphy, made a donation on behalf of the city. As the mayor walked to the elevator immediately after the ceremony, a newspaper reporter from The Moncton Times and Transcript hurried after him to ask about the city's contribution.

The next morning, there was a newspaper story about the arrival of Jesse's Journey in Moncton and the city's donation of $10! I had no idea how the city decided on that amount but it became a public relations nightmare for the beleaguered mayor. I felt sorry for him and later in the week there was a front-page story headlined, "Red-Faced Mayor Admits $10 Donation a Rookie Mistake." The mayor promised the city would establish standards for making donations. I just looked at it as $10 we didn't have before we arrived in Moncton. The day after the events at city hall I was the guest speaker at a gathering of the Rotary Club, which donated $4,000. And so as my head hit the pillow and I moved little box No. 54, the roller-coaster ride continued.

From Moncton, the Trans-Canada Highway continues a zigzag pattern as it swings southwest, passing through Petitcodiac and Sussex before reaching Saint John. The daytime temperatures were now in the high teens and sometimes over 20 C. A steady flow of people stopped to make donations and the air horns of transport trucks regularly greeted us. We seemed to be getting a lot of attention in this part of the province. Maybe it had something to do with the media coverage in Moncton.

As the days flowed into each other, there were mornings I had to look at the schedule to find out where I was. Day 55 on the road would probably have been noted in my journal as a routine windy and wet day along the highway except for the story of one New Brunswicker who made it anything but routine.

The motorhome rolled to a stop on the shoulder of the Trans-Canada when we reached our marker to start the day's walk. The escort van moved into position behind me with its lights flashing and I finished stretching my legs and getting ready for another 33- kilometre chunk of highway. Like most other days, there was someone ready to walk with me and that day it was Armand Belliveau.

Armand and his family owned a kitchen cabinet business in Shediac. He told me they imported oak and maple from the United States because there were very few hardwoods in New Brunswick. The bulk of the finished products were shipped back to the United States and sold in Massachusetts and Maine.

Armand had lived an interesting life. For a number of years he resided in the United States and his children have dual citizenship. He served a year in Korea with the U. S. Army and as a younger man, he was a boxer. He had fought two fighters Muhammad Ali had defeated on his rise to glory. I could see Armand was still in great shape and was unlikely to fade as the day lengthened.

He was a little different from most of the people I had met along the road. As he talked, I could tell he had mellowed with the years. He had set aside the games of his youth and he and his wife were now ballroom dancers. The man who stepped into the ring in his younger days also was convinced boxing will be banned within his lifetime and thought it should be. "We don't let animals fight in a ring; why should we let humans do that?" he said.

As the day grew longer and people continued to stop or honk and wave as they passed by, Armand showed no sign of tiring as we counted the kilometres. Holding his arms out as if exaggerating the size of a fish, he shared with me his philosophy of physical life and his story of the two clocks.

"The human body should last for 120 years," he began. "On this side, there's the clock that is at zero that starts ticking when you're born," he said as he fully extended his left arm. Simulating life unfolding, his left hand went up and down in a series of little ticking motions as his arm moved slowly until it was directly in front of him. He then extended his other arm as far right as possible and said this represented the 120-year mark on a person's "body" clock. As he talked about how a person might smoke too much, drink too much, not eat properly or lack in exercise, his right hand moved up and down in the same little ticking and chopping motion as it came closer and closer to his left hand. When he eventually clapped his hands in front of him, Armand summed up life by saying, "When those two meet, you're out of here!" It was an interesting philosophy.

It was late afternoon when we heard the honk from the escort van indicating we were at the end of another day on the road; another day and another special moment as I shook hands with Armand and congratulated him on being the oldest person thus far to walk an entire 33 kilometres with me. He was 58 and, if his theory holds true, he was just barely halfway through his own journey of life.

SAINT JOHN – THE MODERN MARITIMES

As we left the Trans-Canada Highway, the switchover to Highway 1 was a little scary as a steady stream of vehicles poured south into Saint John. The place names along Highway 1 reflect the history of the area – French names such as Quispamsis, English names such as Bloomfield and native names such as Nauwigewauk.

The little town of Hampton donated $100, which was matched by the town's Rotary Club, and I ended the day at Rothesay on the outskirts of Saint John. It was cold and wet as we walked into Saint John, the oldest incorporated city in Canada (1785). When Samuel de Champlain arrived in the area on June 24, 1604, it was the feast day of St. John the Baptist and he christened the river the Saint John.

The rain and the spray from the tires of trucks and cars that whizzed by on the four-lane highway leading into the city made for a poor day financially. But like Newfoundland, New Brunswick's weather is unpredictable. Winds from the Bay of Fundy can bring quick changes and by the time I reached city hall in the centre of downtown, the sun was shining as I signed the city's guest book and the mayor presented pins to everyone on the road team.

The heart of Saint John is a model for any city seeking to preserve its heritage, while stepping into the future. A $250-million facelift has revitalized the core of the city. Brunswick Square and Market Square on the waterfront and the Saint John Trade and Convention Centre are all linked by "pedways." There's visible evidence of rejuvenation in a downtown that's full of people at the shops, restaurants and outdoor cafés of this historic seafaring city.

As I reflected on the places I'd seen, it was obvious how the most progressive cities and towns protect their heritage while envisioning their futures.

Whether the claim to fame is a striking geographic feature or a historic building, they build on what they have. It reminds me of the number of times I have heard hockey coaches talking about their playoff strategy with the words, "We're going to go with what got us here."

At night, we walked through the enclosed pedway system linking downtown buildings and the arena complex, where fans of the hometown Saint John Flames of the American Hockey League stood and applauded as I was introduced at ice level. Their cheers gave me a lift as we had been through some pretty lean days on the road. It was reassuring to know our message was getting through about the difference research can make.

After we left Saint John, I walked north for three days toward Fredericton, where we would rejoin the Trans-Canada. We looked a little different because the roof of one of our two mini-vans was now equipped with a pair of powerful strobe lights that faced back toward traffic coming from the rear. The lights were a gift from a police officer in Saint John who thought we should be a little more visible. From a distance, the lights made the van look as if it had ears, like the world's most famous mouse, and from that point on, this vehicle was nicknamed "the Mickey van" or just Mickey. By default, the second mini-van was simply called "the other van."

We were now in the rolling countryside of New Brunswick and one day I saw deer standing in a field not far from the side of the road. They turned their heads and their doleful brown eyes watched with passive curiosity as I walked along with the Mickey van and its new flashing lights behind me. Then in an instant, the deer disappeared into the woods.

BEARS AND BEERS

It was early in the morning on our way to Fredericton, with the tall grass along the roadside still wet with dew, when a huge black bear crossed the road about 100 feet in front of me. I decided quickly that he probably had the right of way. After emerging from the woods and padding through the soaked grass, the bear left big moist paw marks on the pavement before vanishing into the tall grass and trees on the other side of the road. When I reached the spot where I could see the prints on the pavement, I put my hand down to compare sizes. When my hand is spread out, I can span an entire octave of eight white keys on a piano. The paw mark on the road was about two inches bigger than my reach. My guess was that this bear probably weighed about 600 pounds and, standing on its hind legs, likely would have been about seven feet tall.

The narrow road to Fredericton eventually widened to four lanes, with a huge paved shoulder to walk on. Dozens of Canadian Forces vehicles were moving back and forth along the highway from the nearby military base at Gagetown. Little jeeps with long communications aerials whipping back and forth purred as they passed by. Big green army trucks with canvas tops growled along the highway in mini-convoys, driven by youngsters who looked like they were all about 15 years old. Some of them honked; some of them didn't; none of them stopped. It's probably military regulations.

From the highway I could hear to the sound of gunfire from the base shooting range. It was a little unnerving because we couldn't see the range. I didn't know if the small arms fire was live ammunition, but I made what I thought was a safe assumption that whatever was being fired wasn't aimed in the direction of the highway. It was also comforting to know that, in contrast to some other parts of the world, when you hear military weapons fired in Canada, it's either a practice session or something ceremonial.

In the afternoon, a single green army truck passed us with one end of a canoe sticking out from under a canvas tarpaulin. As the truck droned on down the highway I said to the crew, "There goes Canada's Army – and Navy!"

Just one day away from Fredericton, I was putting in a routine day on the highway and looking forward to the afternoon break to get some juice and fruit. I could see the motorhome parked a couple of kilometres ahead and someone walking toward me from that spot. It only took a minute to close the gap between us and then I was holding my wife in my arms. Sherene and I must have looked funny to passing motorists as we kissed in front of a small audience at the side of the highway. I didn't care. It was more than two months since we'd seen each other and in the 27 years we had been married, it was the longest we'd ever been apart.

Sherene was a welcome addition to our little band of road warriors. For the next few days she was part of the team, helping with whatever had to be done, quickly fitting into the rhythm of life on the motorhome and adjusting to the breakfast routine, a well-orchestrated dance in tight quarters. She brought mail and messages from the home team in London. She knew when to help and, probably even more importantly, when to stay out of the way.

Some people have a unique quality of being able to get things done without being intrusive. Sherene is one of those people gifted with quiet leadership. She didn't hesitate over any job that had to be done and at one point, even drove a news van for a CBC television crew while a cameraman sat facing out from a raised rear door at the back of the vehicle shooting a story on Jesse's Journey.

It was while he shot videotape of me walking into Fredericton that I realized how much the 33 kilometres a day was taking a toll in general wear and tear on my body. The road team was concerned. Every day we spent time working on my legs and icing my ankle. The crew wanted me to get a medical check-up, which I planned do when we reached Edmunston, New Brunswick. Sore muscles and banged-up feet were the price I was paying in pursuit of the goal, but having Sherene with me made the aches and pains seem a little easier for a few days.

Fredericton was where Sherene got to see her first of the many civic receptions I'd described in my phone calls home. It was also where she decided I should get a haircut. The last time I'd been to a barbershop was in Port Aux Basques, Newfoundland.

Usually when you go for a haircut, you're just asked how much you want off the top or the sides or the back. You're not often asked if you want a beer with that! I didn't know it beforehand but I had wandered into what is believed to be the only barbershop in the country with a liquor licence. I passed on the offer but was certainly curious about the operation. The story is that when a group of young guys from Camp Gagetown come into Fredericton for a night on the town, they want to be able to enjoy a cold beer while they wait for their buddies to get a haircut. It took a zoning change and because the city wanted to make sure haircutting would still be the shop's main business, there is no bar. The beer is merely a convenience kept in a fridge that's out of sight. Still, it was pretty novel and when it was time to leave, Jesse's Journey added one free haircut to its list of gifts in kind. That's just what people do in Canada.

Sherene left for home the morning we departed Fredericton and I began walking on to Woodstock. Along the Saint John River, the weather was starting to feel like a preview of what we could expect in Ontario. The river was smooth and for the first time, the day was hot and tiring. It was another day filled with vignettes to record in my journal. There was a man and his two young daughters who came to our table during dinner to make a donation, one of the few we received that day. There was a couple from Ilderton, Ontario, near London, our volunteers for the week, who returned from a visit to some New Brunswick friends with a donation of $409. The $9 came from their friends' two grandchildren. They had been saving for toys but said they wanted to give it to Jesse. Kids always amaze me.

IF WISHES WERE HORSES BEGGARS WOULD RIDE

In Woodstock, the Rotary Club had organized a parade through town. There were pins and another guest book to sign as the mayor welcomed us. Two little kids donated $10 to Jesse's Journey. They were busy looking at the map of Canada on the side of the escort van, so I pointed out London and told them, "That's where Jesse and I live." I guess they weren't too impressed because as they looked at the map, the next question was, "Where's Disneyland?" Everyone had a good laugh as we headed back out to the highway.

A lot of tourists from Ontario stopped to make donations as I made my way to Hartland, home of the world's longest covered bridge. Covered bridges are sometimes called "kissing bridges" because back in the days of the horse-and-buggy, the darkness of a covered bridge was the ideal place for lovers to steal a kiss.

The legend of the covered bridge at Hartland is that if you can hold your breath while you cross it, your wish will come true. As I walked across and thought about Jesse, I knew exactly what I would wish for. But even walking as fast as I could, 391 metres was too far to hold my breath. It didn't matter. Wishing and hoping were not part of my plan. My design didn't involve luck or waiting for wishes to come true. To me, a wish is an abstract you're not really involved with. You don't want to work for it; you just want to benefit from it happening. A dream on the other hand lends itself to personal involvement. I started with a dream that quickly evolved into a meaningful, challenging and measurable goal.

To generate $1 million a year for research, you don't cross bridges holding your breath. You take a lot of breaths, you get busy and you focus on going the distance.

Eighteen kilometres farther up the Trans-Canada, we reached the town of Florenceville. The Saint John River flows right through the town, which was renamed in 1855, during the Crimean War, to honour Florence Nightingale, the nursing heroine of the conflict. Before the change, the two little villages along the side of the river had the storybook names of Buckwheat Flats and Buttermilk Creek. No disrespect to Florence, but I liked the old names better.

The mayor of Florenceville was also the town crier and a good-hearted man whose daughter had cerebral palsy. We were greeted at the town hall by an honour guard of Beavers, Cubs and Scouts with flags and banners waving. Dressed in his full town-crier uniform, ringing his bell and in his best "oyez, oyez" voice, the mayor read an official proclamation of welcome. At a reception, the people of Florenceville presented us with more than $2,000 – more than $2 per person in this little New Brunswick town.

There was another reason Florenceville was a milestone for Jesse's Journey. As I broke through the honour guard's banner in front of a big part of the town's population, I knew I was now one-quarter of the way across Canada! We were exactly where we were supposed to be according to the plan. Florenceville was the quarter pole on our cross-Canada "racetrack" and we were picking up steam. We had been on the road for 66 days and 66 little boxes of work had been shifted over to the "completed" side.

North from Florenceville, the highway was quiet on a Sunday morning when my new friend the mayor and his wife brought their daughter out in her wheelchair to be part of the Journey experience. We transferred her to the front seat of the escort van because it was too dangerous to have her wheelchair on the highway. There was a lot of girl talk in the van and we had officially added one more member to the Jesse's Journey team, someone who may have been on a team for the first time in her life.

A short while later, one of our volunteers pointed out a grand house on the west side of the Saint John River that had been the home of one of the McCain brothers. Harrison and Wallace McCain built McCain Foods Limited into the world's french-fry king, producing one-third of the planet's fries.

A bitter succession feud rocked the family in the mid-1990s and eventually boiled over into the courts. The McCain brothers never reconciled. The Florenceville residents with me this spring morning told me the mansion was empty except for a gardener and a housekeeper. This knowledge made the house that once was a home look rather sad and the story was another example when wealth didn't guarantee happiness.

North toward Edmunston, the countryside in this part of New Brunswick was more rugged, with fir trees and green fields giving way to steeper hills. It was difficult to stay visible to motorists on the hills and we couldn't always keep the RCMP cruiser right behind me in the guard position. The officer sometimes moved well back where the cruiser could be seen easily. The idea was that the flashing lights on the cruiser would warn motorists there was something up ahead, even if they couldn't see what it was. The officers were great at playing this game of cat and mouse. I always felt comfortable having an RCMP escort behind me, the flashing red and white lights providing an extra margin of safety. Just a week before, the son of the RCMP officer behind me on this day had been killed in a motorcycle accident. Maybe it helped the officer cope to know he was assisting another father who was doing all he could for his son and children like him. His story became a part of the Journey as I moved the 67th little box.

GREEN LIGHT

It was getting warmer and the first day of summer was fast approaching as I walked through Perth-Andover and Grand Falls on the way to Edmunston, which would be the last stop in New Brunswick before we crossed into Quebec. I wasn't aware of it, but the end of New Brunswick and beginning of Quebec would signal the start of two remarkable stories involving two remarkable people.

There was to be a changing of the guard at Edmunston. Ted Eadinger from London would become part of the permanent road team, taking over for road manager Trish Federkow, who was heading home to St. Catharines, Ontario for a break. And a young teacher named Mario Chioini, born in Montreal and fluent in both French and English, would also arrive from London to help us for the 21 days we would be in Quebec. For Ted and Mario, Jesse's Journey would be a life-changing experience.

It was raining when Ted and I met and shook hands outside McDonald's in Edmunston. Sometimes I think things come along at just the right time for people and I believe that was true for my friend Ted. He grew up in Saskatchewan, where he'd been involved in all kinds of community work and volunteer projects. Our paths first crossed when he became general-manager of the television station where I worked in London. It was Ted who had OK'd my leave of absence in 1995 to push Jesse across Ontario. In January of 1998, three months before I left for Newfoundland to begin the solo walk, Ted's wife Chris died of cancer. At 58, Ted was on his own.

As I made my way through traffic with a police escort in downtown Edmunston, I was hoping our other new volunteer would arrive soon. Then behind me I spied a studious-looking young man in his 30s. He had steel-rimmed glasses, slightly long hair and was wearing a T-shirt, khaki shorts and hiking boots. When I asked, "Are you Mario?" he nodded and smiled, the smile that silently asks, "What am I getting myself into?" I handed Mario a collection bucket and a handful of brochures and said, "Just try to do what everybody else is doing." For the next three weeks that is exactly what he did, and a whole lot more. Before the year was over, there would be an international adventure for Jesse and Mario. But neither of us was aware of that as he began handing out brochures, collecting donations and speaking French with people on the streets of Edmunston.

At the end of our day on the road, Bevin Palmateer was standing by to make sure I kept my appointment with a local doctor for a medical check-up. After my final speech in New Brunswick, Bevin whisked me away to the doctor's office where, despite having rather chewed-up feet, I was given the green light to keep on going.

The sun was shining and it was getting warmer and even though I didn't have to wear my red jacket as often, it and my hat were pretty faded. Sometimes dreams also can fade. They can be pushed out of sight by mortgage payments, lost or new jobs, car repairs, braces for the kids. But waking dreams are pretty strong and have a unique quality. They may fade, but they never really go away. They are still there inside, just waiting for you to bring them alive.

· QUEBEC ·

"You win a few, you lose a few. Some get rained out.
But you got to dress for all of them."
~ Satchel Paige

On the day I stepped into Province No. 5, it felt like we'd all been together for a lifetime. In the middle of the day, as we neared the Quebec border, I could sense great team chemistry as people stopped along the road to donate. Mario Chioini walked the first 20 kilometres of the day with me and I enjoyed seeing his pride as we took his picture in front of the fleur-de-lis on the big royal blue sign that says, "Bonjour, welcome to Quebec." Mario was in his home province and ready to shine.

On the motorhome, we celebrated our arrival in Quebec with a lunch of hot pastrami sandwiches. Regardless of whether Mike Woodward, a friend and former colleague at CFPL-TV in London, was driving, making hot chocolate, cutting up fresh fruit, preparing peanut butter and jam sandwiches, writing and faxing news releases or charging batteries and changing the oil, he was a key member of the team. He once told me he always wanted to be a tugboat captain and I think Mike saw the motorhome as his boat. Even though this boat was on land, he definitely was the skipper. This was the first time since Newfoundland Jesse's Journey had an all-guy crew. Seven men would make for an interesting few days.

We were well into Quebec and Mario was paying for his enthusiasm on his first day on the road. As I struggled up and down steep hills leading to Degalis, Mario was confined to driving the escort van and nursing a badly blistered foot. But that didn't stop him from accomplishing other tasks. As the escort van crawled along behind me, I could hear him speaking in French, doing interviews with radio stations along the route, which would take us through Notre-Dame-du-Lac, Cabano and a village with the unforgettable name of St-Louis-du-Ha!-Ha! "Haha" is an archaic French word for an unexpected obstacle or abruptly ending path and it's believed the reference in the name is to a nearby lake.

Mario plunged himself into his work. He translated everything from media interviews to menus. He kept the trip smooth and free of any problems in the areas of accommodation, transportation and communication. He was pouring his heart into making the Quebec portion of Jesse's Journey a success and the results were evident.

Sweat was pouring from volunteers collecting donations and handing out brochures as we headed toward Rivière-du-Loup. Their T-shirts were soaking wet, partially because Mario was on overdrive with the media, getting us into parades and events wherever he could. More and more we saw people at their laneways with cameras in hand, waiting to shake hands with a father from English Canada.

Midday was hot and sticky but in the distance, we could see young children waiting with their mothers and fathers in all that heat to make a contribution and to offer, in French, their words of encouragement. At first we just thought they had seen the flashing lights and were curious to know what was going on. But we soon become aware that the message was passing from house to house and the children were waiting to become a part of Jesse's Journey.

At the side of the highway, lady luck was with us as unplanned medical help arrived for Mario. It was the same doctor I had seen in Edmunston! After stopping at the roadside with his wife and children, he brought out some ointment for my feet, but I decided Mario needed the attention more. The doctor's wife, who had met us the day before, was moved as she watched our road team in action. With her arms hugging her daughters' shoulders, she smiled and pretended she didn't have wet eyes as people stopped to make donations.

June 21, our third day in Quebec, was the longest day of the year and after finishing on the road, we moved up to Rivière-du-Loup. In the morning we would have to drive back to our starting point, but this night, from the balcony of the motel, we were looking north across the St. Lawrence River at a brilliant red sunset. We had finished 33 kilometres on a hot day in what had become a long string of hot days. But even with the heat and humidity, the all-guy team was in a good mood. I was glad because it helps make being a volunteer a rich experience and something you want to repeat.

A SMALL CLOUD OF DOUBT

Despite the road team's good feelings, I was struggling a bit and my emotions were colliding with reality. I was sweaty and tired and with the official arrival of summer, I was missing Sherene and the boys. I knew from the beginning this year would be different and it was beginning to sink in just how much. There would be no backyard barbecues this summer, no trips to the cottage, no swims in the lake, no Saturday mornings to take my time reading the paper, no walking the dog.

But even as I mourned the temporary loss of the comfortable routines of home and pondered the months still to come on the road, I realized that if this was the real cost of a dream, the price didn't matter. While I struggled with the thought that the effort might not be rewarded in the way I wanted, I could only hope the journey would bring us closer to a cure, if not for Jesse, then for someone else's little boy.

In my room, I ate by myself and tried to rest for a while. When you're tired it's easy to let negative thoughts cloud your mind and I'd made a mistake by letting myself think about the thousands of kilometres of road still to come and another winter ahead. Then, as I looked at the calendar in my room, I found a way to snap out of my mini- slump. I picked up the telephone and called my dad in Brantford, Ontario. I tried out the French Mario taught me earlier in the day. "Bonne fete des péres," I said. Happy Father's Day! That night, my mind was back on track as I moved little box No. 71 to the growing pile on the "completed" side.

HOT, HAZY, HUMID AND REAL

It was 18 years earlier that Terry Fox passed through Quebec and the response then was less than spectacular. I had been cautioned back in April, before leaving home for Newfoundland, not to expect great results in Quebec. As we headed into Rivière-du-Loup, we left the Trans-Canada Highway, which we would not rejoin until we reached Sudbury, Ontario in late August. For the next three weeks, we would be meeting Quebecers in villages and towns along the south shore of the St. Lawrence.

The Journey vans and motorhome were right behind me, along with police cars and fire trucks, as I made my way into downtown Rivière-du-Loup, holding up traffic all the way. I was surprised and quite relieved by the carnival-like atmosphere as people came out of houses, retail shops and businesses to make donations. Behind I could hear the growling engine of a tractor-trailer stuck behind the motorhome and I figured the driver must be fuming. But when he got a chance to pull out and pass us, he gave me a big wave and laid on the air horn, attracting even more attention to our little parade. When I left Rivière-du-Loup following another city hall reception, another guest book signing and with another pin to add to the collection, I was feeling good about Quebec and Quebecers.

Summer arrived with a breeze that was nothing more than hot sticky air blowing off the St. Lawrence. We were on Highway 132, which cuts through miles and miles of low-lying land reclaimed from the river. On both sides of the road, hayfields swished back and forth in the wind. The economy here is built on the eel fishery. We could see weir traps, which looked like rows and rows of wooden posts in the tidal water. This is where the eels were caught before being shipped around the world.

Up ahead there was a shimmering mirage where the road met the horizon and I could see the twin silver spires of the Catholic church in the village of Kamouraska. The farther I walked into Quebec, the more I felt the influence of the Catholic Church, both metaphysically and as a physical presence. The ever-present spires watch over farmers as they plough their fields and over all citizens as they go about their daily activities. Perhaps the spires inspire deep thoughts, ideas of change or serve as a reminder that dreams are waiting to be fulfilled.

Few people stopped along this sleepy two-lane road, where the air was hanging heavy. But sometimes, despite the heat, people got out of their cars to shake hands, take a picture and make a donation. The constant breeze from the St. Lawrence didn't blow away the haze or bring any relief. It was a bit difficult to breathe, with the air temperature beyond 30 C., and my feet felt like they were baking as the heat radiating from the pavement exceeded 40 C. But there was nothing to do except keep moving, bringing the big picture into clearer focus with each step. This is how character is built.

MURPHY STRIKES – AGAIN!

With 33 kilometres more behind us at the end of what felt like a day in an oven, Murphy's Law struck again. Exhausted and drenched in sweat, we got back to our motel to discover we had no luggage. Bevin and Mario had gone to Quebec City to begin their media blitz without realizing the van they were driving contained the road team's luggage. In the heat and humidity, probably no one was thinking clearly when the plans for the day were being worked out. When they returned that night to find us still tired, sweaty and dirty, we weren't sure whether we wanted to slug them or hug them.

June 24 is St. Jean Baptiste Day in Quebec and when we reached the little town of La Pocatière, we were less than 100 kilometres from Quebec City. In an effort to beat the heat we had started our day earlier, but it really didn't work. It was still a struggle to keep moving forward, to extend the unbroken line that began in Newfoundland. I was really battling with mental fatigue and the road team was working overtime to make sure I drank lots of water and stayed hydrated. As I watched the never-complaining volunteers do everything possible to keep us moving, I could see firsthand the extraordinary power of the human spirit. And it was about to be rewarded. On Day 77, the heat broke.

The wood-carving shops along the 40 kilometres of road between La Pocatière and Montmagny are a feast for the eyes. I walked past dozens of artisans' studios jammed with carvings and the aroma of freshly cut wood. Outside some of the shops were life-sized carvings, sometimes of a man holding an axe or of a woman with a broom. In front of one store was an entire wooden family, including children and a dog, all carved in typical Quebecois style.

Farther west we stopped in L'Islet-sur-Mer and the mayor welcomed us. We all signed our names in the town's guest book, where an entire page of beautifully scripted calligraphy honoured Jesse's Journey and our walk across Canada.

Across the square from city hall was a very old and historic church. I didn't usually go to see these kinds of things, opting instead to sleep before getting back on the road. But this time, the church was so close that I walked across the street with the rest of the road crew to have a look. An elderly couple was on volunteer duty as tour guides. The church is a masterpiece of stained glass, with a beautifully carved raised pulpit. The wooden pews, ornate statues and bronze plaques tell the story of the town's history through the families that have belonged to the church. The old people showing us around were proud Quebecers who spoke matter-of-factly about how the church was built in 1605. The main portion of the old church was no longer used for Sunday services as the congregation had dwindled, we were told. Services were now held in the smaller and newer part of the church. It was only 100 years old!

L'Islet-sur-Mer is where the Bras d'Or 400, a hydrofoil and perhaps the finest seagoing combat vehicle ever built in Canada, sits on shore as an exhibit at Canada's largest maritime museum. The Bras d'Or, the one and only hydrofoil of its type and built in the 1960s, suffered a fate similar to the Avro Arrow, a state-of-the-art warplane scrapped by the Diefenbaker government. The Bras d'Or 400, which was so fast on the water that it had difficulty training its guns on a target, now has a huge hole cut in its side to let tourists on-board to see what might have been. As I walked away from L'Islet-sur-Mer, I thought to myself that I would not let anyone cut a hole in the side of my dream.

LIFE IS A HIGHWAY AND SOMETIMES A BLUR

The days leading up to Quebec City were a ball of confusion. Maybe it was the anticipation of soon being in my home province that made the hours on the road seem longer than ever before. There'd been a big increase in people traffic, with volunteers and permanent road crew members shuttling in and out as some went home for a break. Sometimes at breakfast in the motorhome, I wasn't sure who was here for the day and who was leaving.

It was almost the end of June when we reached Montmagny, 50 kilometres east of Quebec City. Along this part of the river is one of Mother Nature's great transitions as the saltwater comes to an end and the St. Lawrence becomes fresh water. The mayor of Montmagny told us about the town's fall festival in October, which coincides with the arrival of 600,000 snow geese heading south. The geese feed on plants that thrive in the waters of the St. Lawrence, which at this point is about five per cent saltwater. The mayor said that in just one week, the geese eat all the plants and then they move on. Like the migrating geese, our road caravan moved on as I shifted little box No. 79.

By Montmagny, the rotation of road crew and volunteers had sorted itself out. Trish Federkow had returned from her furlough to St. Catharines. Ted Eadinger and Bevin Palmateer had left for the airport in Montreal, where they planned to park the Mickey van before catching flights home to London. Ann Hutchison, who is married to my friend Peter Garland, was bringing her infectious enthusiasm to our team and would drive the Mickey van back from Montreal to join us on the road.

In 1988, two years after Jesse was diagnosed with Duchenne muscular dystrophy, Ann had a bittersweet year. In July she got married and in October she was diagnosed with cancer. There was no doubt she knew, perhaps more than anyone who had been on the road with us, the value of research.

As I surveyed two other new recruits, I was again amazed at how people who had no connection to us would choose to leave behind their families and the comfort of their homes to join us for a week or even longer. We nicknamed André Trenqua "the gentle giant." He was from Drummondville, Quebec, and lost his left leg in a farm accident when he was four years old. Marc-Olivier Roy, also from Drummondville, was a handsome young man who, except for Jesse's Journey, probably would have been at home spending summer evenings with a girlfriend. Instead, André and Marc-Olivier became "the French connection" on the road with us.

The first thing we discovered is that neither of them spoke English. But we also learned it was incredible how much we could communicate with hand signals, the odd word here and there in French, a lot of smiles and a good dose of laughter. When those who spoke only English and those who spoke only French worked at it, few problems were left unsolved. And when there was a seemingly insurmountable hurdle to get over, bilingual Mario was there to assist. I think Mario secretly enjoyed watching us struggle for a bit, but eventually he would jump in with a translation. As we headed toward Lévis, across the river from Quebec City, the new road crew was comfortably in place.

On the Sunday of the July 1st weekend, I completed 15 kilometres of highway before we marked the road and everyone piled into Mickey for the short ferry ride from Lévis across the St. Lawrence to the Lower Town of Old Quebec

City. From there, motorcycle police escorted us up the steep hill to the Chateau Frontenac, the jewel in the crown of Quebec City. On the holiday weekend, Quebec City was alive with tourists taking in the city's atmosphere and history.

TWO SOLITUDES MADE ONE

Samuel de Champlain founded Quebec City in 1608. As you look east down the St. Lawrence River toward Ile D'Orleans, you can quickly understand why Quebec City is sometimes called the Gibraltar of North America and why, hundreds of years ago, it was clear that whoever controlled Quebec City controlled access to the continent. It was here in 1759, on the Plains of Abraham, that British forces surprised and defeated French forces in an ongoing struggle for control of North America. The battle lasted less than 20 minutes and claimed the lives of both the British commander, Sir James Wolfe, and the French commander, the Marquis de Montcalm. Now, with great pride on a Sunday afternoon almost 240 years later, English-and-French-speaking people sang, danced and made music together as they hosted tourists from around the world. It is in Quebec City that the marvel of Canada's cultural success is most evident.

On the south shore again the morning after our visit to Quebec City, people began making donations as soon as I was on the road. After supper in a restaurant that night, a man and his wife came to our table to meet us and shake my hand. They made a contribution of $500 before saying au revoir.

André, the gentle giant, left us at Quebec City. He was another of those volunteers who knew when to work and when to laugh and we had shared a couple of funny moments together. There was the day the knee on his artificial leg was squeaking and we had to get out the wrenches and a can of WD-40 to fix it. And I'll never forget the rainy day when three or four of us were lined up in the aisle of the motorhome stretching calves and thighs and doing knee bends before getting out on the road. André was sitting watching us with his artificial leg crossed over his other leg. Suddenly he picked up his metal leg and, mimicking our exercise routine, threw it over his shoulder! Needless to say, we all collapsed in a heap. That's when it hit me that laughter sounds the same in English as it does in French. When it was time to go, André hugged each of us and then, as quietly as he had arrived, slipped into the wake of the Journey as we moved westward.

Before he left the motorhome for the last time, Marc-Olivier Roy, who was only 18, made a short speech in his best attempt at English. He thanked us for a great week and, despite all he already contributed to our effort, he apologized that he didn't have much money to contribute. But with a smile that told us he knew he was speaking to friends, he reached into his pocket and pulled out a $10 bill for Jesse's Journey.

One of the most memorable moments in Quebec happened off the road. It was about 8 p.m. on the day we arrived in Quebec City when I heard a knock on the sliding glass door of my motel room. Standing there in the summer twilight with her mother was a little girl in her pajamas. Her mom explained that after they read our brochure, eight-year-old Michelle Gagnon said she wanted to donate something "to Jesse." Michelle then handed me $10. In the morning as we prepared to get underway again, I signed my name on a Jesse's Journey hat and left it at the front desk for the caring little girl.

HAPPY BIRTHDAY CANADA

On Canada Day, July 1, people began making donations as soon as we were on the road, back on the south shore of the St. Lawrence and walking west toward Montreal. At one point I heard the sound of a woman applauding from the veranda of her home as Jesse's Journey passed in the early-morning sunshine. But by mid-morning it was raining heavily. Donations dried up and we spent the rest of the day being washed by the spray of passing vehicles.

Highway 132 hugs the south shore as it winds through quiet villages where the scent of wild roses fills the air and painted window boxes overflow with flowers. The communities of Bernière-St-Nicolas, St-Antoine-de-Tilly, St-Pierre-les-Becquets and Ste-Angèle-de-Laval, on the way to Nicolet, are comprised of small houses, painted all colours of the rainbow. The houses appear to be dozing in the sun and are wedged shoulder to shoulder as they crowd right up to the roadway.

There's a tremendous sense of history in these European-looking villages, almost as if time has stopped. For days on end we looked out on the

St. Lawrence River, where Samuel de Champlain and Jacques Cartier sailed all those years ago.

It was a summer morning and the grass was still wet with dew when I saw stone ovens just off the side of the road up ahead. Smoke was drifting up and the air was filled with the smell of freshly baked bread. The ovens, round and about five feet high at the centre, were smooth and shaped like the igloos you see in children's books. In each there was a main shelf for baking. At ground level there was an orange glow from the coals, giving each oven a toasty Christmas-hearth look. Through the open doors of one we could see loaves of bread turning a golden brown as they slowly baked.

With a picture of hot buttered bread in my mind, I walked to a spot where an older woman was removing bread from an oven. She had a kerchief on her head and held a huge wooden paddle, which she used to lift the finished loaves from the shelf. She was so engaged in her task that when she finally looked up she seemed a little startled. "Bonjour monsieur?" she said, as if she was asking a question. This wasn't a commercial bread-making operation but a woman baking bread for her family. I handed her one of our brochures and her eyes lit up and a smile crossed her face when she saw it was printed in French. The brochures were in both official languages because Jesse's Journey is a national project and we wanted all Canadians to feel welcome to take part.

Between Sorel and Longueuil, the early-summer sky churned in shades of grey and black. Driving sheets of rain cut visibility to a minimum and jagged bolts of lightning ripped through the dark sky, lighting up the road and frequently forcing us to stop and take cover in the safety of the escort van. The rain finally eased and our soggy troupe, with running shoes that now made squishy noises, stepped back onto the road to complete the day's 33 kilometres.

WILLING TO GO IT ALONE

In the dismal weather, donations were few and far between as I trudged on toward Montreal. The weather had left me with a feeling of loneliness and it was time to call on the reserve of discipline I had built up in the seven months of training before I set out to walk across Canada. One of the bonuses of training at home was that each night I was able to see my family. I had now been away from them and home for almost three months. It wasn't self-doubt about my physical abilities that I was fighting, but I worried that maybe I was needed at home more than out on the road. This was my emotional tug-of-war.

I knew this was dangerous territory but I had made a commitment to the walk back on those dark, windy, wet and cold nights when I was training in London. I concluded that if I could just get through the times when I seemed to be alone, then maybe when the sun was shining and there was someone to say, "Keep going," I might be able to make it. The completion of the set distance of 33 kilometres of road each day was mandatory. The only thing that was optional was how fast or slow I got the job done. I'd have to go back to the basics of focusing on the almost mindless, constant repetition of moving my feet, to the exclusion of almost everything else. Again I told myself to stay the course.

The road team must have thought I had an obsessive need for routine but in stressful times, repetition was my way of coping. It wasn't always exciting but it worked for me. Through good days and bad days on the road, I tried to stick to the same routine as much as possible. I would start out every morning at the same time and while no two days on the road were alike, the basics of the pattern didn't vary. I knew I would have to maintain the pattern if I was going to survive almost 8,500 kilometres of highway and almost 10 months on the road. On the days when almost no one stopped it would have been easy to let my emotions take control. Staying with the same pattern helped prevent that from happening. The routine of mentally moving those little boxes was important because they measured how long it would be until I could go home.

On the road little things meant a lot. With the skyline of Montreal visible in the distance, there were two memorable moments. The first occurred when a truck driver pulled his big rig to the shoulder of the highway. He climbed down from the cab, made a donation, gripped my hand and said, "You're a good man." He probably never knew how much encouragement he gave me at a time when I really needed it.

The second was a visual moment. It had been raining heavily all day and it seemed like an eternity before we heard the honk from the escort van to let us know we had made our distance. When I looked beside me, I saw one of those pictures no camera can do justice to. It was Ann Hutchison, soaked to the skin, with water dripping from her chin and her hair wet and tangled. She was beaming with a smile that said, "I did it!" Ann, a cancer survivor, had just become the first woman to spend an entire day on the road with me, walking the full 33 kilometres and passing her own personal test with flying colours.

THE BIG 'O' AND AN EVEN BIGGER 'OH!'

The sight of the Olympic Stadium in Montreal brought back memories of the 1976 Summer Games as I looked at the distinctive landmark on the north side of the St. Lawrence, where the Jacques Cartier Bridge links Montreal and Longueuil. It was three months to the day since I had left home. As I was briefed on the mechanics of the next few days and getting through the second-biggest city in the country, I was cautioned not to expect a lot of donations while we made our way through Montreal. I wondered if the team was recalling our 1995 Toronto experience, when I pushed Jesse down Yonge Street in his wheelchair and people asked us for money!

The journey through Montreal was surprisingly smooth with few delays. There was one moment of chaos in the parking garage underneath Place Ville Marie, the day we went to the mayor's office. The parking garage had a minimum height clearance for vans and we failed to consider the extra couple of inches that had been added when the two strobe lights were mounted on the roof of Mickey. In the underground garage, the strobe lights scraped a couple of overhead pipes and that started alarms ringing. Suddenly, security people were running everywhere and before long they had surrounded us. We had no idea what all the excitement was about. When Mario Chioini translated, we tried hard not to laugh but we apologized to the security guards, who weren't very happy with us.

The whirlwind visit to downtown Montreal included signing the Golden Book at city hall and happily accepting donations from some corporate sponsors. On the streets there was a lot of media attention. As I made my way along a street where there were plenty of outdoor cafés, people were applauding and I found myself surrounded by television cameras from CBC, CTV and Global Television, along with still photographers from The Montreal Gazette and La Presse. But the most memorable contact made in Montreal happened – of all places – in the middle of a freeway in rush-hour traffic.

The freeway system in Montreal can be a little scary at the best of times and at rush hour it's downright frightening, especially when you're walking in the middle of the traffic. Even with police cars and lots of flashing lights both in front of and behind me, I was not comfortable. Transport trucks were just a few feet away as they moved past in the lanes on my right and left. Over my shoulder I saw a man of about 40, with dishevelled hair and a scruffy-looking salt-and-pepper beard, running to catch up with me through the traffic, which had slowed to a crawl. He had a leather satchel slung over his shoulder and I figured he was a journalist wanting to do an interview. It turned out the man was from Paris, France and he didn't want an interview. He had something bigger in mind.

Jean-Luc Robert was in Canada to ask if Jesse would go to Paris in December. I was caught off guard and this really was an "Oh!" kind of moment. I listened carefully to his proposition as I drank tea and ate fruit during my mid-morning break. In Canada, Jesse's Journey is not associated with Muscular Dystrophy Canada, which turned us down when we requested its participation in the 1995 crossing of Ontario. But it seemed the French Muscular Dystrophy Association – Association Francaise contra les Myopathies – was very impressed with what Jesse had accomplished and wanted him to take part in its annual telethon in Paris. The plan was to have a television crew from France visit Jesse in London and then join us on the road in Northern Ontario. The crew would shoot video to be shown when Jesse visited France to tell the story of Jesse's Journey. Jean-Luc asked me to think about it and then, slinging his leather bag over his shoulder, he disappeared as he dodged through the dense traffic.

We had a long drive to Valleyfield that night to attend a Rotary Club function, where $2,300 was donated. As we rode back to Montreal in the van, I thought about the events of the morning and Jean-Luc Robert. It was a lot to ponder. If Jesse decided he wanted to go and if we maintained our schedule on the road, I would be entering British Columbia about the time Jesse was going to Paris. I talked to Sherene about it on the phone that night and she broached the subject with Jesse. Needless to say, he was excited at the idea. On the road the following day, I took the next step.

'HEY MARIO, POUVEZ-VOUS ME FAIRE UNE FAVEUR?'

For almost three weeks I'd been watching Mario Chioini's dedication to Jesse's Journey and the ease with which he switched from English to French and back. Born in Montreal, his pride in his French heritage rang clear in his voice with every interview on radio and television. I'd enjoyed his sense of humour and his always-positive attitude. It was time to talk.

I asked Mario if he could do me a favour and it wasn't surprising to see the shocked look on his face when I got more specific: "Mario, do you think you could take my wife and son to Paris, France in December?" It took him a second to realize I was serious. Then his eyes began to sparkle as my question led to a lot more questions. As we walked we discussed some of the issues. As a teacher, could Mario leave school for a week in early December? What role would he play in Jesse's trip to France? Was Jesse up to making the trip? Obviously there were a lot of things to be worked out before December, but the bottom line was that Mario agreed to escort Jesse and Sherene if it could be worked out. The trip to Paris was looking like a go.

On his final day on the road with us, as we crossed the border from Quebec into Ontario, Mario walked the full 33 kilometres with me. Later in the year he would travel several thousand more kilometres for the Journey, only this time it would be with Jesse. The little box that represented Day 92 had turned into a very interesting package.

· ONTARIO ·

"I am a slow walker, but I never walk back."
~ Abraham Lincoln

It was mid-July when I took my first steps in Ontario. Towns and villages with distinctively French names such as Les Coteaux and Rivière Beaudette would soon become communities with decidedly English-sounding names, such as Lancaster and Summerstown. In a broad sense, I was home.

In the distance I heard the sound of bagpipes pumping some life into the humid summer air and by the time I reached the Ontario tourist information kiosk a kilometre or two from the border, young men and women in kilts had worked the pipes to a fever pitch. I heard the military snick of snare drums and the soft thump of a bass drum rattled in my chest as I broke through a banner held by my mom and dad. I was officially in Ontario, Province No. 6.

In front of the motorhome, escort vans and police cars were friends from home and several American tourists at the kiosk wondering what was happening. One family from Boston, Massachusetts stood patiently in the sunshine listening and learning about us. When the formal welcome ceremonies were over, the father came over to meet me, reached into his pocket and donated $60. "You're doing a good thing," he said as he shook my hand. That night, I wrote his words in my journal.

Corn on the cob is one of nature's sinful delights when the yellow rows of kernels are laced with butter and salt. And when you have your annual physical, you don't tell your doctor about it. It was the day's lunchtime treat and is one of those taste sensations that serves as a calendar in Ontario, like strawberries in June. As I enjoyed this summer pleasure, the calendar was on my mind. August was not that far away and we had just entered Ontario. While the heat was tolerable, I couldn't help thinking ahead to Manitoba, which we wouldn't reach until well into October. That would be followed by a dash across Saskatchewan and Alberta before winter closed in on us in the Rockies.

We were still on the north shore of the St. Lawrence River and on the road to Cornwall, donations were very good. The owner of a Petro-Canada station in Cornwall made it his first order of business to see that the motorhome and escort vans were washed and the gas tanks filled. That was just the start of his family's generosity. As we moved through Cornwall, the family's work ethic was demonstrated by the man's teenaged son, who spent his day on the run, handing out brochures and collecting donations for Jesse's Journey. At the end of the day, I watched him limp on a badly blistered foot toward home, where his mom had our supper organized and our laundry cleaned and folded.

On the Sunday night we were preparing to leave Cornwall and head toward Morrisburg, the same family gave us a special sendoff when they arrived at our motel with a giant picnic supper. They had fed us, serviced and fuelled our vehicles and even lent us a van to shuttle volunteers back and forth at the next changing of the guard in Ottawa. We were strangers being shown the kind of care Eastern Ontarians repeatedly exhibited during one of the toughest times in their history – the massive ice storm that crippled a huge portion of Eastern Canada late the previous winter.

Although our own advance team had been chased by the storm on its way to Newfoundland, stories about the event seemed remote and not quite real until we saw a front-page picture from an old newspaper. It showed collapsed hydro towers with wires dangling in the snow, cars with crushed roofs pinned under toppled trees and everything coated in a thick layer of ice. We suddenly realized the stunning magnitude of the storm.

When you're at home in another part of the country and can flip to the sports pages or the comics over a hot cup of tea or coffee, events such the ice storm don't seem real. Not until you're alerted to a need for food, blankets and generators do the calls for help begin to register. But when you're living through it, you have no choice but to get busy and help your neighbours and yourself. The ice storm had put the people of Eastern Ontario through a lot. They knew how to work hard, how to stick with it and they knew what it meant and how it felt to do something for others. Their response during and after the crisis showed the true strength of their character.

OTTAWA A SECOND TIME AROUND

From Cornwall I passed through the Eastern Ontario towns of Long Sault, Ingleside and Iroquois before we marked the road and made a detour to Ottawa. Besides being the nation's capital, Ottawa, which is at the same latitude as Moscow, is a city of contrasts. In spring it is home to the world-famous Tulip Festival and in winter it is renowned for the amount of snow it gets. It also has the world's largest skating rink when the Rideau Canal is iced over. But in the middle of July, it was sweltering. It was humid and the thermometer seemed stuck at 35 C.

Motorcycle police escorted Jesse's Journey to Parliament Hill. At the top of Wellington Street, I paused to look at the statue of Terry Fox. When reporters asked me what I thought about Terry, I said, "Terry was in a league all by himself and as Canadians, we were lucky to have had him for the time we did."

At the eternal flame in front of the Parliament Buildings, I gave a little boy a loonie to toss into the water around the flame so he could make a wish. As I watched him flip the coin into the water, I thought about how this was where Jesse and I ended our journey together in 1995. The rest of the way across Ontario, I would be tracing in reverse virtually the same route Jesse and I shared three years earlier.

The highlight in Ottawa was seeing Jesse on videotape and hearing him speak to researchers at the Ottawa Hospital Research Institute. This is the facility headed by Dr. Ron Worton, discoverer of the gene that causes DMD. As Sherene and I watched Jesse's image on the monitor, I felt very proud of my son, who was giving hope to so many people. After the video, Sherene and I and Dr. Worton unveiled a plaque officially dedicating the Jesse Davidson Laboratory at the institute.

As we toured the laboratory, we had plenty of questions for the technicians and researchers, who seemed glad to take the time to explain their work. As I scanned the lab full of equipment and watched researchers working at the bench, I knew exactly why I was making this trek across Canada. Maybe I didn't know a lot about research, but I knew one thing: Without money, it wouldn't happen.

In Ottawa there was a heavy media workload and everywhere we went there were cameras, microphones and relentless heat. The extreme humidity was making everything difficult, including breathing.

After Jesse and I had finished our wheelchair push, Jesse was honoured at centre ice at a hockey game between the Toronto Maple Leafs and Ottawa Senators – a thrill for someone who had never skated. This time around there was a lot more media attention, similar to when Jesse and I had visited Prime Minister Jean Chretien in his private office after being recognized by the House of Commons. My final flashback to that time was the thought of Jesse's smile as the prime minister of Canada donned a Jesse's Journey T-shirt and posed with my son, a youngster who had won so many hearts.

Jesse's goal on our journey across Ontario was both personally meaningful and measurable. With his efforts and his success, he touched hockey players and politicians. Even more important, he touched moms and dads across Ontario and Canada who wanted him to succeed. By following his plan, Jesse had raised $1.5 million for research.

THE 'KING' OF NEWFOUNDLAND RETURNS

As we prepared to leave Ottawa, it was time to say goodbye to Mike Woodward, who was heading home to London for a much-deserved rest, and to welcome back my friend from Bell Island, Newfoundland, Ed Coxworthy, who had rejoined us to drive the motorhome. It was good to know humour had reboarded our travelling road show. I've always believed you can go a long way if you don't take things too seriously and enjoy a few laughs along the way.

It didn't take Ed long to settle back in and to show his form. On his first day, with the temperature hovering around 35 C. and stifling humidity, Ed said, "By the Jesus, Johnny, it's like walking on a stove and breathing soup."

On Highway 2 at Iroquois, Jesse's Journey began moving west again, through Cardinal and on toward Brockville. There were people waiting along the road and at almost every stop there were town pins, hats, T-shirts to be presented, guest books to sign and pictures to be taken. The best news was there were lots of donations.

July 18 was my 100th day on the road and moving that 100th little box made the "completed" pile take on a different look. Ed said he could see my legs also had taken on a different look and weren't the same size anymore. He said the difference was obvious and when he measured my calves, he confirmed my right leg was now a full three centimetres bigger than my left leg. I assumed the right leg must be working harder because of the angle of the road. The difference hadn't affected performance, but it was decided we should increase the frequency and intensity of the stretching and massage routine.

The hot weather was still a strain for all of us and shimmering mirages kept us company as I made my way through Rockport and Gananoque on the road to Kingston, a city of many personalities. At different times in its history it was an Indian settlement, a French fort, a British citadel and for a brief period (1841-1843), Canada's capital.

The road crew for the next few days would be a bit of a family affair. My sister Dorothy and brother-in-law Peter from Brantford, Ontario had joined us, along with Grace Roca from London. Grace, who was in her mid-30s, was the most petite, quiet and energetic volunteer imaginable. She came to Canada from Portugal when she was 12 years old, left school at a very young age and was married when she was 17. She was only 19 when she and her husband John celebrated the birth of their son Rob. The heat didn't seem to bother Grace, whom Ed nicknamed Gracie. She had grown up working in the fields picking tomatoes and knew all about hard work. She barely said a word as she tackled every job she was assigned. With her Jesse's Journey T-shirt clinging in the heat, Gracie jogged from house to house, putting hundreds of brochures in mailboxes along the route.

BELIEVE IT OR NOT!

Kingston is where one of the most incredible stories I've ever heard unfolded when Jesse and I were crossing Ontario, but I didn't know anything about it until a year later. Jesse and I were making an appearance at a convention in London the year after we'd passed through Kingston. A woman whose name I never learned rushed over to greet Jesse and said she and her sister had met us a year earlier on a hot and sticky afternoon along the road just outside Kingston. She was clearly excited to meet us again and asked if Jesse and I could wait for just a few minutes while she went upstairs and brought her daughter, who had cystic fibrosis, downstairs to meet Jesse. While Jesse and the young girl chatted, I found out what had happened on the road in 1995.

This woman and her sister had been driving west when they passed Jesse and me heading east toward Ottawa. She said to her sister, "That's John and Jesse. That's Jesse's Journey. We have to turn around and make a donation." They turned around and as they got in line with other slow-moving drivers waiting to make a donation, the woman asked her sister to push the button to make the passenger window go down. She said her sister stared at her like she was from another planet because the automatic window hadn't worked for years. But this lady wasn't taking no for an answer.

She told me that while she fiddled with the master switch for the window, she urged her sister to keep flicking the switch for the passenger door power window. Nothing happened. Then all of a sudden, just as they pulled up beside Jesse and me, the power motor hummed and the window glided down. They made their donation and drove straight to the service station where the driver's husband worked as a mechanic. She was all smiles when she got out of the car and told him they'd fixed the window. But after her husband listened to the whole story, he said, "Honey, the window couldn't go down. It hasn't worked for years. I'll show you." With that he took a screwdriver and removed the door panel to show her that the wires that should have powered the window weren't connected!

It's a remarkable story, but I don't think for a second the woman was lying. I have never been a very religious person, but there are nights when I put my head down and ask myself, "What did make that window go down?"

On the road to Belleville, it seemed as if there was some kind of divine referee keeping the forces of good and bad in balance. The scale tipped toward the bad guys when one of our volunteers, who had driven all the way from London to take part in Jesse's Journey, had his car stolen. Police found the car later in the day with the driver's side window smashed and the steering column damaged where the car was hot-wired. But keeping things in balance, a woman stopped at the motorhome at lunchtime to make a $100 donation. Following her was a young couple from Quebec who were teaching their children what it means to give to others. The two little kids were very shy, but they wanted to make a donation to help other kids.

When we reached Trenton, I was able to add a new element to the daily description of where we were and what things looked like from the roadside in my morning radio interviews. I could now say the water we were looking at was Lake Ontario.

A large group of cadets marching inside the fence at the Canadian Forces Base in Trenton cheered and applauded as I walked by with the flashing lights of an Ontario Provincial Police car right behind me. CFB Trenton is Canada's largest military air base and there was an almost constant roar of what sounded like thunder as giant military cargo planes rumbled down the runway before lifting into the sky. At most airports you see brightly coloured planes from airlines around the world, but in Trenton, the aircraft are almost all the same dull shade of military green. Sadly, in the years since our adventures on the road, Trenton has become known as the place where the bodies of all those young people lost in Afghanistan come home to Canadian soil.

Along the road there were stories of courage and hope almost every day. There were also sad ones and I heard one of the most heart-wrenching accounts in Trenton while walking with a member of the Lions Club who had both a son and a grandson with Duchenne. Here was a man whose troubles I could not imagine and as we walked, the tragic tale that unfolded was almost beyond comprehension. This man was a paramedic whose twin grandchildren died of crib death 21 days apart, one at four months old and the other at five months. In both instances, the man beside me was the paramedic on duty who answered the call. Some days the painful stories are more than I can handle.

As we drank a cup of tea on the motorhome before bed, the emotional strain of the day made it difficult to share the story with Ed. When I finally finished, Ed paused, then said, "Johnny, if we could all throw our troubles into a hat, you'd want to draw your own back out." When I went to bed, I didn't want to dwell on the sadness I had seen that the day; I just wanted to get on to tomorrow. Some days were like that.

THE ROAD TO 'THE BIG SMOKE'

The next morning, I passed "The Big Apple," set back from the highway in one of the many orchards near Colborne. The world's largest apple was just one of the dozens of roadside attractions I would pass in the weeks and months ahead. More than 650,000 people a year visit the bright red, four-storey apple-shaped structure, inside which there are audio-visual displays about the local apple industry. Along the road there were lots of people who wanted to shake hands and motorists who gave me a thumbs-up and shouted, "Keep it going!" One motorist clapped with both hands as he drove by. I don't know how he was steering.

On the north shore of Lake Ontario, as we passed through Cobourg and Port Hope, media attention from Toronto was increasing. There were radio interviews to be done and television cameras were with us almost every day as I made my way through two of the prettiest lakeshore communities in Ontario.

For years, towns and cities across the province have wrestled with the question of how to save their downtowns from decline in the competition with suburban malls and big-box retailers. Cobourg and Port Hope both looked like they had found the winning formula. The two communities had managed to preserve the Victorian architecture of their stately homes, churches and public buildings. Gas lamps and hanging flower baskets completed the streetscapes that had captured the attention of film and television production companies in both Canada and the United States. The main streets of these two towns were thriving with a retail mix akin to "the butcher, the baker, the candlestick maker." There were bookstores, florists, barbershops and antique shops. All had the appearance of a long-term commitment to the downtown. There were no empty stores and local residents told me there was a waiting list to acquire a shop on the main streets.

People were making donations and traffic was stop-and-go as I climbed the hill leading out of Port Hope on another hot and hazy afternoon. As I moved toward Oshawa, I was leaving behind two confident little towns that had solved the riddle of keeping a vibrant core.

In the days leading up to Toronto, I spoke to city councils and provincial and federal politicians. Day after day through Whitby, Ajax, Pickering and Markham, I told the story of Jesse's Journey and our goal to provide the research community with $1 million a year, every year, forever. People might have thought it was easy to repeat the story over and over, but it wasn't. This was a story no father wants to talk about and every time I spoke, I struggled to keep my emotions in check. I was very aware that I was discussing a disease that marches on relentlessly. And this was my son I was talking about. We were a family like so many others, in a race with time, and I didn't know if we could win. There was no choice. I had to keep talking and walking.

Toronto was where I had marked one of the proudest days of my life when I saw my son receive the Order of Ontario at a ceremony at Queen's Park in 1995. As Jesse was being honoured, I thought about his life. Here was a youngster, just 15 at the time, who didn't walk or run. He had never been on a hockey or baseball team. He couldn't swim. He had never used a skateboard or ridden a bicycle. And yet this was an "all-star" moment when he received the Order of Ontario from Lieutenant-Governor Henry Jackman. When your dream involves helping others, their successes fill you with pride.

The kilometres clicked by one by one and along the road more and more people were eagerly waiting for their turns to be a part of Jesse's Journey. Near Toronto, a woman who operated a chip wagon at the side of the road made a heartfelt donation. She had lost three nephews to Duchenne.

The challenge of getting through Toronto or "The Big Smoke" – one of many nicknames ascribed to the metropolis – began in the pre-dawn darkness as we drove into the heart of the city to appear on Citytv's Breakfast Television. The show's host, Ann Rohmer, remembered Jesse and me from 1995. She was gracious in her comments even though the interview on the fast-paced morning show lasted only a few minutes. Bevin Palmateer told me later there was a touching moment after the interview wrapped up when Ann Rohmer went back inside, leaned her head on her producer's shoulder and said, "God, I love that man."

Toronto was a whirlwind of activity. On the 40th floor of the Royal Bank Building, I spoke to executives of the bank, people of power and influence. In the heart of Canada's financial district, businesspeople often portrayed as cold and aloof were moved by the story of Jesse's Journey and my reason for doing what I was doing.

Major television network cameras surrounded me as I headed back to the road after speaking to Toronto City Council. While there seemed to be media everywhere and a constant honking of horns, it was important for me to keep things in perspective. There would be days ahead in the remote parts of Northern Ontario, far from the steel canyons of Toronto, when once again I would be all alone on the road.

At night, inside Toronto's SkyDome, now called the Rogers Centre, the public address announcer introduced me at a Blue Jays game. Then at field level, with video footage on the giant Jumbotron showing Newfoundland and the early days of the cross-Canada journey, I rounded the bases Jesse and I had circled together three years earlier. Upstairs later in the broadcast booth, I was on the air with Tom Cheek, who has since passed away, and Jerry Howarth, the radio voices of Blue Jays baseball at that time.

But the most memorable moment at SkyDome wasn't seen or heard by the fans. It was one of the highlights of my marathon walk. In a private area deep inside SkyDome, a group of parents and kids gathered as three women from Oshawa and Whitby, mothers of children with Duchenne, made a very special donation. With their young sons in wheelchairs beside them, they presented a cheque for $60,000 in memory of another young man who had passed away in the spring of 1997 at the age of 20. Tears of joy and sadness mixed together in a very emotional moment. These three moms, part of a Toronto-based group of parents of children with Duchenne, had worked hundreds of hours in smoky bingo halls to make this moment possible. Since I had dipped my foot in the Atlantic Ocean and began the cross-country journey, this was the most shining example of philanthropy I had witnessed. In the days that followed, I thought of them often as I headed down a highway that had taken on a new kind of symbolism. It was the road to a better life.

IDIOTS, BUTTER TARTS AND POLITICIANS

As I made my way across the top of Toronto on Highway 7, the road team was working overtime as traffic backed up with people wanting to donate. It was just after 5 p.m. in the rush-hour chaos when our daily routine came to a screeching halt. Police cruisers with flashing lights were blocking the right lane in front of and behind us as they provided our escort. In the single lane beside me, westbound drivers, all staring into the glare of the afternoon sun, were whipping past with barely a car-length between vehicles. When one driver slowed down to see what was happening, there were five sudden and very loud bangs and everything behind me came to a stop. The hoods of five cars were bent like inverted Vs, with steam rising from their engine compartments and fluids spilling onto the road. Fortunately, no one was hurt.

The police officer behind me got out of her cruiser and said, "Hang on a minute. I just have to go and talk to these fools!" When I mentioned to the officer my concern about whether we would be considered to have been directly involved in the accident she said, "No. They're just being idiots. You can't go 90 kilometres an hour one car length apart and expect that everything will be OK." When she asked if I wanted her to radio for another cruiser so we could continue, I told her we had completed 32 of 33 kilometres and it probably would be best if we just quit for today and added one more kilometre to tomorrow's workload. For the sake of the road team and volunteers, this was one time I was glad to get off the road.

Again surrounded by police cruisers, it was a hot and sunny morning as I walked toward Brampton. I was surprised to see a middle-aged man in a shirt and tie and not-very-practical leather shoes ask for a bucket and a handful of brochures. It wasn't long before the man, who was the area's Member of Parliament, had loosened his tie and was soaked in sweat as he joined the rest of the volunteers dashing from vehicle to vehicle collecting donations. I'd stood in front of cameras shaking hands with a lot of politicians over the last few months, but this was the first time I had seen a politician literally roll up his sleeves and go to work for us. Back at his constituency office, he had lots of bottled water and juices waiting for us, along with a good supply of butter tarts, muffins and fruit and a floral arrangement that included all the provincial flowers.

HULK HOGAN MOVE OVER!

On the road I tried to stop and say hello to every person I met who was in a wheelchair. One morning I stopped to greet a little blonde-haired boy smiling as he struggled to catch up with me. He said he was in Grade 2 and wanted to be a wrestler! He was a really neat kid and despite the chest brace that held him straight in a standup walker designed to fit his tiny body, he had the heart and courage of a lion. He had a little kid's big smile and a twinkle in his eye as he handed me the donation he had saved. I bent down, kissed the top of his head and held his little arm in my hand as we shook hands and said goodbye.

The summer days were now with us and I was walking familiar roads. In this populous area of Ontario, the crowds were beginning to build. We were close enough to home that people could reach us by car and that meant the makeup of the road crew was changing almost daily. Suddenly it seemed like everyone wanted to help.

The air horns from tractor-trailers provided a steady sound of encouragement and many truck drivers pulled their rigs to the side of the road to make a donation. The Ontario Provincial Police had made Jesse's Journey a priority and police cruisers and motorcycles were with us throughout the day. As we left Toronto, one of the motorcycle officers chased a young male car driver who had ignored instructions and passed me on the right. On the motorhome at lunch, the officer told us the driver was a kid and he let him go with a seatbelt warning and a suggestion that it might be a good idea to "find some folding stuff and make a donation." The teenager apparently thought that was a pretty good deal and was quick to reach for his wallet. So on the day I moved little box No. 114, I had encountered a great little kid who will probably never be a wrestler and a not-so-little kid who found out cops can be nice guys too.

On the first day of August, I walked through Georgetown and Acton and there was a steady stream of people along the roadside who applauded, shook my hand and made donations. I thought it was a little funny when people called me "Sir" or sometimes even "Jesse." It really didn't matter. What was important was that they were taking part in Jesse's Journey. Sometimes the comments were a little embarrassing and I didn't know what to say. That was the case when one man pulled his car to the side of the road and walked back to meet me. As he made a donation, he said, "You're making us all proud to be Canadian."

My home province was responding and the days on the road were becoming chaotic. There were people with cameras waiting to include me in a family picture, people who wanted me to sign things and still others who wanted to press another "guardian angel" pin into my hand and tell me about a lost loved one. I was doing my best to try to accommodate everyone but was concerned about losing time and falling behind in distance. I think Ed Coxworthy was the first to realize this as I stepped onto the motorhome at break time a little later than I should have and looking a bit more tired than I should have been. He took it upon himself to begin managing my time.

VICTORY SALUTE – By the time John and Jesse Davidson reached their hometown of London in August 1995, they were well past the halfway mark of their journey across Ontario. John raises Jesse's arms as Jesse waves his Canadian flag at London's Victoria Park. This is one of John's favourite pictures. Photo courtesy of The London Free Press.

MULTITUDES – Huge crowds greet the inspirational father-son team of John and Jesse Davidson at Victoria Park in London, Ontario in 1995 on the original cross-Ontario trek known as Jesse's Journey. John pushed Jesse in his wheelchair more than 3,300 kilometres to raise money for research into Duchenne muscular dystrophy. Photo courtesy of The London Free Press.

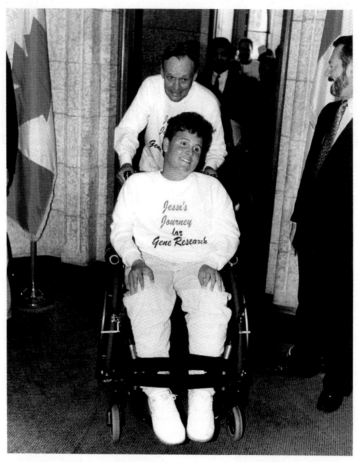

POLITICAL POWER – Prime Minister Jean Chretien, wearing a Jesse's Journey T-shirt, takes Jesse for a "run" in the corridor outside his office in 1995 after Jesse and his dad finished their four-month journey across Ontario.

ORDER OF ONTARIO – The Honourable Henry N. R. Jackman, Lieutenant-Governor of Ontario, right, shakes hands with Jesse Davidson as he presents the 16-year-old with the Order of Ontario at Queens Park in Toronto in 1996. Jesse's dad John, left, looks on proudly.

ROYAL REGARD – Jesse Davidson awaits his turn as his dad, John Davidson, left, shakes hands with Queen Elizabeth II in London during her visit to Ontario in June, 1997.

SAFETY FIRST – Rock cuts and blind corners on the Trans-Canada Highway along the north shore of Lake Superior require the team to be even more safety-conscious than usual. John Davidson gets a brief break from climbing at the crest of another hill.

TRADE-OFF – The hills from Wawa to Nipigon in Northern Ontario were the most physically punishing of the entire journey for John Davidson. But the view over Lake Superior was spectacular.

ART IMITATES LIFE – Canadian artist Ken Jackson's painting, Jesse's Journey,
captures the effort and intensity required for John Davidson to push Jesse up
Jackfish Hill north of Wawa, Ontario in 1995. The painting hangs in the
offices of /A\ London, formerly CFPL Television.

LOOKING BACK AND LOOKING FORWARD – In 1998, John Davidson stops
near the top of Jackfish Hill in Northern Ontario, wondering how he ever pushed
Jesse's wheelchair up the hill three years earlier. He's standing on
roughly the spot immortalized in Ken Jackson's painting.

JOHNNY COMES MARCHING HOME – A London Police colour guard and bagpipers usher the Davidsons – Jesse, Sherene and John – in the rain as John reached London, Ontario in August 1998 on his solo cross-Canada walk. Thousands lined the streets and more were waiting at a reception at Victoria Park.

SOLITARY MAN – The corn is as high as an elephant's eye as John Davidson makes his way through Central Ontario late in the summer of 1998. Some days lots of people stopped but on other days, it was a lonely walk.

Through Guelph and Kitchener, the roadside meetings continued. In Guelph, I posed for a newspaper picture with a nice young man who greeted me from his wheelchair. At 33, he was the oldest person I had ever met with Duchenne. It is hard to imagine how much hope that gave me. I thought of the picture from three years earlier of Jesse waving his flag as I held his arms up. He was 15 at the time. The man I'd just met was almost twice as old as Jesse was now. I didn't say anything to those who were with me but I think they understood how much this meeting meant to me.

Farther along the road we met the young couple from Cambridge who had stopped to contribute in Newfoundland on their way to St. John's to attend the funeral of the woman's father. I recalled telling the young woman there would be "better days ahead" and as she stood in the sunshine proudly holding their new baby, it was clear these were better days. As we shook hands, they felt like old friends and thanked me for what I was doing. It made me feel like I'd been on the road a long time.

A PASSION FOR PASTA

A chance meeting on a Sunday afternoon led to an unforgettable evening in Guelph. An Italian father and his son applauded as I passed the end of the road that led to their family business. The older man smiled proudly as he watched as his handsome son, a man in his mid-20s, come forward to make a donation on behalf of the family. At the same time, the father handed his business card to our road manager, Trish Federkow, and offered to feed us lunch at the family's banquet hall. I had just returned to the road after our lunch break, so she thanked the man for his offer but took a pass. When Trish caught up to me and told me about the offer, I said, "Trish, run back and see if they'd like to provide us with supper." She looked at me quizzically and said, "Really?" I answered, "Yes, because people don't make that kind of offer unless they really mean it."

As a hot and tired road crew of 12 was welcomed later at the banquet hall, the stage was set for another magical Jesse's Journey moment. A banquet table was set with silverware, china and red candles on a white tablecloth – not exactly what we were used to at night. After the introductions were made, we sat down to steaming bowls of pasta, spaghetti sauce and hot bread from the kitchen. I looked down the table at Bevin Palmateer and wondered if he was familiar with Italian custom. I really had to laugh when I saw how his eyes turned to saucers when the second course of chicken arrived. "There's more?" he said, making everyone laugh. It was good to see the team enjoying themselves as they mingled and talked with more new friends in the form of the family we chanced to meet along the road. The smell of freshly baked bread and wonderful homemade meal had clearly taken our minds away from the road for a while.

After dessert I stood up and thanked our hosts for their kindness and generosity to strangers. I told them about Jesse's Journey and shared a tale or two from the road. Then fresh glasses were produced and wine was opened to celebrate the occasion. When all the glasses were filled, we proposed a toast to Jesse's Journey and to new friends. It was one of just two occasions on the road when I drank a glass of wine. When good fortune shines on you and when you meet good people, that's what you do; you share your success.

In Kitchener, hospital workers in light blue uniforms joined me on the road. As we passed the Kitchener-Waterloo Hospital, I saw a teenage girl in a wheelchair, with her parents at her side, waiting to see the Jesse's Journey procession. Although it was a warm day, she had a blanket over her pajamas. There were tubes from her wrist to a plastic bag of clear fluid hanging from the metal pole beside her. A "halo" of steel rods held her head firmly in place. For a moment Jesse's Journey came to a halt as I jogged across the road to gently shake her hand and to thank the girl and her parents for coming out to see us. I didn't know if I had brightened her day, but I knew her smile certainly brightened mine.

With a clear sky and the road routine operating at pretty close to maximum efficiency we continued along the highway to New Hamburg and Stratford. More than ever we had OPP and fire engine escorts. Some of the fire engines were antiques, spewing out smoke as I walked on and shook as many hands as possible. As I listened to applause and heard comments like "Good work," I knew the words really belonged to Jesse, the young man who was the spark plug for all we had been able to accomplish, the young man I would see the next day for the first time in four months, on the day I would be moving little box No. 119.

'WHEN WE LOST DENNIS, DALE WAS OUR SUPPORT'

In a rural area of Southwestern Ontario we reached the small farm community of Embro, northwest of Woodstock. The owners of the village grocery store were both 21 when they were married, with their whole lives ahead of them. Thirty years later, on a hot summer afternoon, they were waiting to greet me, standing at the side of the road not far from the store. No one had to explain to the Mathesons what Jesse's Journey was all about. They'd already been there.

Their son Dale was born in 1974 and it was just two months before Christmas of 1978 when his parents learned their four-year-old had been diagnosed with Duchenne muscular dystrophy. "I knew about Duchenne," said Anne Matheson. "My brother, who died (from it) in 1972 at the age of 20, was three years younger than me. We were a family of seven and we never knew where it came from. The doctors always told my mother that it was a mutation at birth, but actually she must have, unknowingly, been the carrier."

Scientists now know DMD can be passed from mother to child, but in 35 per cent of cases, it occurs because of a random spontaneous mutation. Because the Duchenne gene is found on the X-chromosome, it primarily affects boys and it can occur in all races and cultures.

When Dale was diagnosed, the couple was referred to a genetics counsellor. Dennis, the couple's second child, was born the year Dale was diagnosed. The Mathesons waited until Dennis was six months old before having him tested, hoping against hope that he would be spared. Again, it was just before Christmas when they learned Dennis also had Duchenne.

"I know things have changed a lot since that time," Anne said. "But back then we didn't have a clue that I was a carrier. My sister never married or had any children, she was so afraid, even though tests showed she was not a carrier."

Al Matheson remembered driving back to Embro after Dennis was diagnosed and saying to Anne, "Well, I guess we won't have to worry about any more children because we won't have time. I'll be pushing one wheelchair and you'll have the other." It was a bitter statement born out of the shock of the moment but one that would eventually become reality in the lives of Anne and Al. At that moment, the knowledge that they had two sons with Duchenne was almost too much to bear and as they wondered what had hit them, the rest of the trip home was made in silence.

It was about this time Anne and Al realized all they could do was to take one day at time. "We decided that we wouldn't worry about what might happen 10 years down the road, because the future will look after itself. We can't control it, so why let it run our lives right now?" Anne recalled. The Mathesons began focusing on each new day as it came and concentrating on their sons. "We realized that whatever happened in the future, we still had each other,and we held tight to that," Anne said.

Dale and Dennis both went to high school, but only Dale was able to pursue a post-secondary education. When Dennis was in Grade 11 his health started to deteriorate, so he left school to help out at the family store. When he felt well enough, he handled the computer, which was something he enjoyed.

Then in 1995 the family received another blow when they learned Dennis had congestive heart failure. "We just couldn't believe it," Al said of the visit to the doctor and the trip home after the new diagnosis. "Dennis was pretty glum. He knew the consequences. He was an adult at 17 and the doctor laid it all out for the three of us. Basically they gave him just a few months. It was pretty difficult to cope with that." The couple did everything they could to help their son and in 1997, Dennis was hospitalized for the last time.

Anne described the night her youngest child lost his battle with the disease that had been with him for a lifetime. "I had already settled Dale for the night and was getting Dennis into bed when he began to have trouble breathing and telling me that he needed to go to Emergency right away. He knew what was happening, I'm sure of it."

They raced toward the hospital in Woodstock, taking Dennis on what would be his final journey down a familiar road. "I knew there was something seriously wrong because Dennis didn't caution me, as he always did, to slow down on the loose gravel, but instead he kept telling me to speed up," Anne said with a sad smile.

Dennis, with his parents at his side, as they had been for a lifetime, lost his valiant fight for life that night in 1997. He was 19 years old.

Dale, who turned 24 the August Jesse's Journey arrived in Embro, was the one who got the family through the hardest times when his brother died. "When we lost Dennis, Dale was our support," said Al. "He held us together."

Far from giving in to the disease that had been with him all his life, Dale was at the University of Western Ontario in London as a part-time student, studying genetics and working toward his B.Sc. "He loves it," smiled his proud dad. "He just showed us a mark he received on his last project, an 80 per cent."

"Sometimes," Anne said, "he asks 'Mom, why should I continue going to school?' and there are days when he just doesn't feel much like going. You can tell it's wearing on him, but he always bounces back and is determined to get his degree."

Sadly, the Mathesons lost their second son May 31, 2001. Dale was 26.

NO MUSHY STUFF

The green cornfields of Southwestern Ontario were standing tall in the summer sun. The sky was bright blue and there were families cheering us on at virtually every farm gate as Jesse's Journey moved south along Highway 19 toward Woodstock. From babies and little kids to grandparents sitting in lawn chairs waiting for our arrival, there were hundreds of hands to shake. While I greeted as many as I could, I was anxious to keep moving because I knew that after more than four months, Jesse was waiting just a little farther up the road.

Part of my early-morning routine included daily radio interviews and the rotation for radio stations in London meant I talked with each station's morning show hosts once a week. It was one thing for them to hear, on the air, about the expressions on the faces we saw along the road and some of the stories we'd been told. But it was quite different watching the reactions of the morning show hosts who joined us on the road, when they saw firsthand the excitement evident at the end of farm laneways and with every kilometre we completed.

All parents seem to come with the same flaw – we never really want to let go of our children, to recognize that they are no longer kids. We have a little trouble dealing with the reality, for example, of an 18-year-old who doesn't want his dad to hug him in public. Knowing there was a good chance the media would be present, Jesse had asked me not to make a big fuss when

I saw him. We had a deal: one hug, one pat on the head and a handshake. It was the best I could get from the young man who was making his own way in life. That aside, in my mind he would always be, just like his brothers, "my little boy."

Jesse had always sounded very strong when we spoke on the telephone but despite the buoyancy in his voice, I was concerned. I wondered if I would see a change in him. Would the disease he had lived with all his life have made a further advance? As we crested the hill leading into Woodstock, we could see a crowd of people, cameras and microphones, and in the middle of the gathering, sitting in his wheelchair, was Jesse.
I broke into a jog toward him and was relieved to see he didn't appear to have changed at all since I'd left home in April. Abiding by the terms of our deal, I gave him one hug, one pat on the head and shook his hand. With bagpipes, police cruisers and Jesse by my side, I had a feeling of being almost home. It was the second time Jesse and I had been welcomed by thousands of people on the streets of Woodstock, where I grew up.

Slowly we made our way through the huge crowd of parents, kids and thousands of balloons toward the stage set up in front of the Old Town Hall in downtown Woodstock. There were speeches and donations and I was in such a good mood when I spoke to the crowd that I actually confessed that when I was in high school, I once put soap in the fountain in the square where we were standing. The crowd laughed as I told them how huge clumps of bubbles had floated throughout downtown. It was a pretty harmless prank and I figured this was a safe moment to fess up.

It was raining by the time we left Woodstock but there still were people along the roadway as we walked west, ending our day in Beachville, where a letter in the village museum makes reference to the first recorded baseball game in North America. The game was played in Beachville in June of 1838, a year before Abner Doubleday was given credit for inventing the sport with a game in Cooperstown, New York.

It was raining heavily when we returned to Beachville the next morning to pick up the journey where we had left off the day before. Road conditions weren't good and we double-checked with the police escort to make sure it was safe to set out. When we were given the green light, I stepped onto the road to begin the walk that would take me home to London. It was going to be a wet homecoming.

All along the road through Ingersoll and Thamesford, hundreds of people waited in the rain. Sometimes, when it was pouring heavily, they sat in their cars. As I approached they'd step out to make a donation and offer words of encouragement. Although I was being slowed by the huge turnout, I tried my best to reach through car windows to shake hands with seniors and grandparents who were there because they were thankful they had healthy grandchildren.

The rain was still falling when I reached Thamesford, about 18 kilometres from downtown London. Service clubs donations there amounted to $4 a person for everyone living in the village. From the open back of a transport truck I spoke to a group of people who were all smiling, even though some of them had been standing in the rain most of the morning. Some had umbrellas; many didn't. Thamesford is the home of my friend Ron Calhoun, who, as national fund-raising chairman for the Canadian Cancer Society, had coined the phrase "Marathon of Hope" for Terry Fox in 1980. As I gave Ron a hug, it was hard to tell which one of us was the proudest of the people of Thamesford.

TAKE A DEEP BREATH – HERE WE GO!

When it was time to move on to London, I was cautioned about the crowds ahead and the need to keep moving as quickly as possible. But nothing had prepared me for the onslaught waiting on the streets of my hometown.

On the motorhome there was a lot of activity as we got set to greet the crowds. The vehicle had been our home away from home for more than four months. Besides providing transportation and shelter, it was everything from exercise room to laundromat. It was our first-aid post, bank and snack bar. But this day it was definitely a communications hub.

We were a little behind schedule as we left Thamesford just past midday. Although there were people waiting in the rain, Ed Coxworthy insisted I stop for a quick bite of lunch. Ed, the Newfie jack-of-all-trades, was doing his best to keep the chaos to a minimum. Normally, we welcomed people on-board but today access had to be limited to media people, the road crew and volunteers who were emptying donation buckets of the money they contained. Even so the motorhome was full of people and there would be no nap after lunch. As I looked at Ed, who knew the usual routine would have to be set aside, I said, "I don't want to keep these people waiting." With that I stepped off the vehicle, plunged into the crowd and got back to work.

If there was one thing Jesse and I accomplished in our adventures together on the road, it was bringing people a greater understanding of the need to fund research to create a better life for kids like him. As I began shaking the hands – young and old, big and small – reaching out to me, I knew the effort Jesse made when we were together in 1995 had struck a resounding chord with the people of London and Southwestern Ontario.

This stretch of road, which was lined with people, took a great deal out of me. It's difficult to imagine the effect it has when people are clapping as you pass by and how they well up as they say things like, "We love you, John. Good work. Congratulations. Keep it going. God bless you John." And all along the way people wanted to shake hands. While women may have been more overtly emotional, the men who said nothing seemed to send me messages in the way they squeezed my hand. It was as if their support for what I was doing was to be measured by the strength of their grips. In a matter of minutes, my hand was aching and it was a relief to stop to talk to a bunch of little kids in brightly coloured rain capes. "Are you really Jesse's dad?" they asked. That made me laugh and more than anything else it helped keep me focused as I moved along.

There were thousands and thousands of people in the streets. I was guided through the crowd at a Wal-Mart store where the employees and management donated $8,000 to Jesse's Journey. That donation marked the beginning of a continuing relationship with Wal-Mart in London.

THERE'S NO PLACE LIKE HOME

A line from a song written in 1822 and famously spoken in The Wizard of Oz says it best: "There's no place like home." And that was true, even though by the time we reached downtown London, I was physically and emotionally drained. Then when I looked up, Sherene and Jesse were coming toward me and I kissed my wife in the middle of the street in front of a huge crowd of people. Escorted by the London Police Pipe and Drum Band and its colour guard, Jesse and Sherene joined me on the road as our crew of volunteers worked hard scrambling along both sides of the road to collect donations. We made our way to city hall and I continued shaking hands along the street and waving to people high above me on the balconies of apartment buildings. It was still raining and the wet pavement reflected the colours of the umbrellas held by the crowd. With so many voices cheering, the sound of the pipes and drums and the flash of cameras, it was overwhelming and I sometimes seemed to be seeing and hearing these things in slow motion.

I had written my name in a lot of city guest books since the Journey began back in Newfoundland, but penning my signature in London was a little different. As Sherene and Jesse also signed their names in the city's guest book, I thought about how we were really signing on behalf of all the volunteers who had helped along the way.

Next we unveiled a plaque at the base of a sugar maple tree Jesse and I had planted with Queen Elizabeth in 1997 in Victoria Park. Hundreds of people standing in the rain welcomed us home. After speeches from the politicians, Mayor Dianne Haskett announced the city would be making a $25,000 donation to Jesse's Journey.

Media interviews were next and then, after more than four months on the road and with five more months ahead, I got to go home to spend the night with my family. A little white dog that looked like a floor mop with a wagging tail greeted me at the door and jumped onto my lap as soon as I sat down. In a matter of minutes, both Charlie and I were sound asleep. It was the end of our first day in London and I had moved little box No. 120. That meant close to half of those little boxes were no longer on the side where they'd started.

ONE JOURNEY, TWO TEAMS

While the road team was highly visible wherever we went, the home team operated away from the spotlight, making sure all the pieces fit together every day. Two women, whose only communication link was the telephone, could be credited with keeping Jesse's Journey on the move.

Maureen Golovchenko, our Journey director, had seen the road team in action for a couple of days in Eastern Ontario. But the road team had never seen the home team in operation. Maybe it was just as well. Wherever we were, road manager Trish Federkow made it clear to everyone that I was not to be bothered with any of the dozens of problems that had to be ironed out by the home team every day. "John's job," Trish said, "is to walk 33 kilometres a day."

Maureen was a shining example of the right person for the right job. She saw the project as a wheel, with the spokes representing the issues that had to be dealt with every day, things like transportation, accommodation, volunteers, sponsors and media. The home team was the hub. She also described the project as being like a big quilt. Everyone involved contributed their little patches and it was her job to sew them all together. She proved to be an expert "quilter" and her ability to sew the patches of Jesse's Journey together was directly linked to my ability to keep moving those little boxes.

The weekend schedule in hot and muggy London included a series of events and appearances and one of the highlights was a rally at the University of Western Ontario. There was plenty of live music and it made me humble to see a long lineup of supporters from various groups who had come out to make donations to Jesse's Journey. At a city mall we posed for a picture with the staff and management of a gift shop called The Brandy Tree. This was a group of people I'd never met but they presented Jesse's Journey with a cheque for $18,000 raised from the sale of "Beanie Babies." It was amazing to think about the amount of effort everyday people had put in to make sure Jesse's Journey was a success.

Our final appearance in London was at a "cruise night" car show, where nostalgia was the name of the game. Chrome polished to a fine lustre and tailfins from the '50s and '60s made up a large part of these regular get-togethers. For those walking through the rows and rows of classic cars and enjoying early rock 'n' roll, it was a trip down memory lane. The host of a radio talk show who was also a classic car buff presented Jesse's Journey with a cheque for $13,000 donated by his listeners.

SEE YOU NEXT YEAR

On August 10 in bright sunshine, the music of Willie Nelson was stuck in my head as I found myself "on the road again." By nightfall London had disappeared from view and I wouldn't see it again until early in the new year. The comfort of sleeping in my own bed for a couple of nights and the chance to spend time with my family and to see for myself that they were well was behind me. It was time to shift gears and resume the routine of life on the road. The rest of Canada beckoned.

As I smiled and shook hands with the people I passed, my mind was racing. While it was a gorgeous summer day in Southwestern Ontario, I knew fall was just around the corner. According to the schedule, we wouldn't reach Manitoba until October 9. That meant we'd be crossing the Prairies in November and the Rocky Mountains in December. I would just have to return to the pattern that had been successful so far, taking it one day at a time, starting with today.

Although Jesse wasn't with me, people donated as they had done when we were together on those hot summer days three years before. Sometimes they came from a distance to wait at the side of the road. When we passed through the village of Arva, just north of London, there was no fanfare when staff members from a machine shop that serviced the auto industry donated more than $4,000 to Jesse's Journey. That company was located miles from the route we were following.

The 30 kilometres from London to Lucan was a familiar piece of road. I walked it dozens of times in the seven months I trained before beginning the cross-Canada walk. On those days I was always alone. Now, provincial police were leading and following me and ahead, a tremendous show of support was waiting for us.

In Lucan, historic home to the notorious Black Donnellys, Jesse's Journey turned into a festival. By the time we reached the firehall, the crowd had spilled out onto Highway 4, which doubles as the main street and runs right through the centre of town. For the next hour, the road through Lucan was closed. It was a blistering hot afternoon and with microphone in hand, I stood on the hood of a car to speak to the crowd. My feet were baking from the heat of the hot metal, but I wanted to make sure I acknowledged all the service clubs in the community who had come out to participate. In the crowd I saw the proud faces of the men and women of the Royal Canadian Legion, some no longer young faces. Despite the temperature and humidity, they were dressed in navy blue blazers and some were wearing ribbons and medals from campaigns fought long ago. Also in the crowd were the gently wrinkled faces of grey-haired seniors and strong-looking fathers who worked with their hands, some with a "farmer's tan" from hours in the fields. There were teenagers hiding behind sunglasses and little kids in baseball hats, T-shirts, shorts and flip-flops darting in and out of the crowd. But most of all, there was a strong sense of community and caring. This was small-town Canada at its best. This was Lucan, a village that is part of a municipality with a population of only about 4,000 and which, on a steamy hot day in August, donated $20,000 to help researchers seek a cure for Duchenne muscular dystrophy.

At the end of the day we took a side-trip to Grand Bend, which had been very generous to Jesse and me in 1995. After I walked through the summer resort town, Sherene and I spent a few minutes together watching the sun set over Lake Huron. It would be more than a year before we had another chance to watch a sunset at the lake.

Corn-on-the-cob and tomatoes were both in plentiful supply at farm-gate stands along Highway 23 as we passed through Woodham and Kirkton on the way north to Mitchell. Families waiting along the highway to make a donation made sure the motorhome was well-stocked with fresh fruit and vegetables. The harvested crops were a sign that fall was not too far off. Although I tried to keep my mind within the space of the day I was in, it was difficult to avoid thinking ahead to the Prairies and the Rockies, wondering what I would face in the months ahead. It was impossible to keep winter and memories of the wind and sleet in Newfoundland from flashing through my mind. So far the team had managed to stay on track, but the unknown always looms, particularly when it comes to the weather. I just hoped we could stick to the timing of our plan. I kept thinking that if we could make it to Winnipeg by Day 200, we just might have a chance to complete the whole thing.

Mitchell was the hometown of hockey legend Howie Morenz of the Montreal Canadiens. When he played in Stratford, Ontario, he was nicknamed "the Stratford streak." Morenz was just 35 years old when he died of an embolism in 1937, after breaking his leg in a freak accident during a game in Montreal. His funeral at the Montreal Forum was attended by 12,000. With the medical knowledge available now, Morenz likely would have survived the on-ice collision that eventually took his life. As we walked into Mitchell and shook hands along the road, his story was a reminder of how the medical treatments available today came about as the result of research. Morenz gave me one more reason to keep moving ahead.

From Mitchell and thoughts of hockey, Jesse's Journey shifted sports as we took another side-trip, this time to St. Marys, home of the Canadian Baseball Hall of Fame. In-town quarries were the source of the limestone used to build the impressive town hall, opera house, museum and library, as well as several churches. Called "Stone Town," picturesque St. Marys, with a population of 6,000, is nestled in a beautifully treed valley where the Thames River flows over a dam in the heart of town.

IF YOU BUILD IT...

The Canadian Baseball Hall of Fame was housed in a temporary location at old Exhibition Stadium in Toronto before finding a permanent home in St. Marys in the mid-'90s. The baseball diamond at the Hall of Fame is every fan's dream of what a diamond should look like, with rich green grass, a well-manicured infield and crisp white chalk lines. There were thousands of people there on an unforgettable summer night when I was asked to walk the bases with hundreds of schoolchildren. The St. Marys stop provided one of the best nighttime opportunities I'd had to speak to a huge audience about the need for research to ensure that all children are able to play baseball and have a chance to chase their dreams.

At the end of the day, as Ed Coxworthy was stretching my legs, I realized that the rest I had hoped for in London hadn't materialized. I had no way to know how much gas was left in the tank. As I wrote in my journal that night, I noted that I felt I might be close to the limit of my endurance. But before I fell asleep at the end of Day 125, I had pretty much decided my limits were known only to someone much bigger than me. I would just keep going as long as I could and leave it in His hands.

In the morning, I tried to catch some extra sleep on the motorhome as we drove back to our starting point outside Mitchell. The road from there to Listowel took us through Bornholm, Monkton, Newry and Atwood and there were donations from each village and from service clubs and people we met along the road. It was nice to return to the routine of the road, with breaks and meals that fell at the right time, and I was looking forward to being able settle back into a comfortable groove of 125 paces to the minute.

At a shopping mall on the outskirts of Listowel, there were donations from the Zehrs and Zellers stores. Then the sound of pipes and drums broke the quiet of the hot August afternoon as police cruisers guided us to the town's clock tower on the main street for a civic reception. It was a good afternoon as I was joined on the road by employees of K-mart in Goderich, who had driven almost 100 kilometres to be part of Jesse's Journey. They were good people I hadn't met before and brought with them a cheque for $1,000.

There were few opportunities to enjoy a home-cooked meal on the road and we'd become so used to ordering from menus that most nights we made a game of it. Before anyone opened a menu, somebody on the road crew would describe, in his best The Price is Right voice, a hot beef sandwich with all the trimmings. It was then up to everyone at the table to "bid" on the sandwich to see who came closest to the actual retail value without going over the price! There was no prize, but we had all become experts on the pricing of hot beef sandwiches. The servers sometimes looked at us as if we had been on the road just a little too long but we didn't care. It was our way of unwinding at the end of a long day.

But in Listowel, we were able to skip the game when we were treated to a real home-cooked meal. Not since the mini-banquet with our Italian friends in Guelph had we had been able to sit down to a proper dinner with a tablecloth, china and silverware. But a generous family in Listowel served us a meal of chicken and rice with peach pie for dessert. As everyone talked during dinner, I sneaked a peek at my watch; the deadline for sleep never seemed to go away. Before we left, everyone enjoyed a glass of wine and we toasted the Journey. It was the second and last time I had a glass of wine during our time on the road. The routine was that demanding.

After we got back to our motel, Ed took the motorhome to be fuelled. In my room there was a brown paper package containing Jesse's Journey shirts that had been shipped from London to replace those looking a little tattered and worn. But there had been a mix-up in sizing. What was supposed to be a large-sized shirt for me turned out to be extra, extra, extra large. When I heard

Ed return, I stood in the open doorway of my room wearing one of the new shirts, which hung past my knees. The headlights of the motorhome captured the sight and I could hear Ed laughing before the vehicle stopped. As he stepped off the motorhome, he said, "By the Jesus, Johnny, you look like a sack of spuds without the spuds!"

Farm families with their cameras at the ready were a common sight through the rural areas of Palmerston and Harriston. Although stopping to shake hands and pose for pictures wasn't a problem, I still hadn't found the walking groove I was most comfortable with. I was sure I'd rediscover it, but it had been missing most days since we left London.

One day during our lunch break at a little roadside picnic area, I looked at some tabletop graffiti where someone had carved deep into the table the words, "What Would Jesus Do?" Right beside that someone else had very neatly responded in ink, "Well, for one thing He wouldn't have defaced this picnic table!"

From the high of the lunch-time laughs, the roller coaster took a dramatic plunge that afternoon when I spent time on the road with a man whose daughter had been diagnosed with cancer when she was one month old. He and his wife lost their little girl 11 months later. Now he organizes the annual Terry Fox Run in the area.

The same afternoon I found myself surrounded by an excited group of Beavers, Cubs and Brownies who had come out to the road with their leaders to make a donation and to march along the highway in front of a real police car. They wanted to be able to say they took part in Jesse's Journey. When I walked with children, I always hoped that somewhere down life's road, when they got involved in helping others, they would think back to Jesse's Journey as one of their first experiences with giving.

After the youngsters left and as the shadows started to get long, there was a woman with two canes standing at the end of a country road waiting to make a donation. When I stopped to shake her hand she said, "You're good stuff." I thanked her and walked on, thinking the exact same thing about her. She was one of the many people we met each day whose names I seldom learned. By nighttime even their faces began to fade. But as I wrote in my journal, I realized their spirit and generosity were fuel for my efforts. And so it went, day after day.

SIX ZEROS AND COUNTING!

It was the middle of August and Day 128 on the road when Sherene called during our afternoon break. Her message was brief: Jesse's Journey had just passed the $1-million mark in donations! It was fabulous news and I was thrilled and extremely proud of everyone involved, both on the road and back home in London, because we had all worked so hard to reach that mark.

What exactly does $1 million look like? To athletes with multimillion-dollar contracts, it may seem like pocket change. But those who earn megabucks to throw a baseball or shoot hoops may never actually get to feel $1 million. It's all just documents and electronic transfers handled by lawyers and accountants.

I, on the other hand, knew just what $1 million looked like. I saw it in bills of every denomination passed through the windows of cars vans, transport trucks and motorhomes; handed over by people on bicycles, motorcycles and horseback; donated by those who got down from construction equipment or left golf carts to come to the side of the road to be a part of something special. I saw it in the form of jars full of pennies and nickels and dimes handed to the volunteers by kids at the side of the road. That's what $1 million looks like. Day after day, ordinary people reached into their own pockets to make a difference, to help keep researchers in pursuit of a cure. That's what real philanthropy is all about. Many of those athletes who live in an artificial world of adulation and autographs have probably never experienced what I felt on the road every day.

When it comes to fulfilling a dream, there are few factors more important than perseverance, even if sometimes it seems the road is getting longer every day. I constantly told myself how important it was to stay focused and to stay the course without deviating. I had to trust that if we stuck to the plan, it would unfold as it should.

We knew we had a good plan in place and the right kind of people to see it through, including the volunteers who kept Jesse's Journey moving forward day after day. A week with us on the road was no picnic as the volunteers handed out brochures in all kinds of weather, did laundry, helped prepare and clean up after meals and sometimes drove the motorhome. They laughed and maybe cried and when it was all over, they didn't want to go home.

The entire crew was together in Harriston, about 100 kilometres north of London, when we celebrated Ed's 59th birthday at a dinner with the Lions Club. We gave Ed some fitting gifts, including a fly swatter and an apron, and in order to take a picture around the birthday cake, we had to squeeze together so tightly that some of the Lions in the back row were being pushed against a set of double doors behind them. At the moment we were ready to say "cheese" and have the picture snapped, the doors gave way and a club member nicknamed "the Lion king" flew into the adjoining room like he'd been shot out of a cannon. "Holy flying Lions," a volunteer beside me blurted out.

Donations from the windows of passing cars were pretty steady as we made our way through Mount Forest and on to the town of Flesherton, where I got caught in a type of storm I wasn't used to – a storm of tears. It was time for a trio of female volunteers to say goodbye and they were quite emotional about it. So there I was, sitting in a restaurant in Flesherton, with three dinners getting cold because all three women left the table to go to the ladies' room to have a good cry. When two of our new volunteers went to cheer them up, I was left with five dinners getting cold. As with so many volunteers before them and many more to follow, Jesse's Journey had affected them deeply.

Out on the road emotions were often raw because of the people we encountered and the stories we heard. On the way to Flesherton, I had noticed a pretty little girl wearing a bright green dress and sitting in a stroller on the other side of the road. Even from a distance I could see it was a stroller designed for special needs. Her mother and grandmother waved to me, perhaps just happy to say they had been there the day Jesse's Journey passed by. It was a hot afternoon and I knew we were running late, but I stopped and jogged across the road to meet the little girl, whom I was told had suffered severe brain damage. It was heart-breaking to think about but the fact that these three made the effort to come out to see us inspired us to go on.

ON THE BRINK

It was 131 days since we'd left the harbour at Quidi Vidi, Newfoundland and with 131 little boxes moved from one side of my mind to the other, we were nearing the halfway mark at Collingwood. I felt good as the day started because Jesse had come all the way from London to see me break through the banner that marked this important point in our journey across Canada. But while I looked like I was physically on top of my game, emotionally I was completely spent. When it was time for Jesse to go, I struggled to laugh and joke a bit, but as I watched him leave, it was almost more than I could handle. We were now through the most densely populated area of Ontario and after the gruelling pace of the last month, I'd hit the wall. This was the last day I would see Jesse for five months. As I sat on the edge of the bed in the motorhome, I was fighting my worst fears about the future and with my elbows resting on my knees and my head hanging down, I was pretty close to tears.

It was my Newfie friend Ed who came to the rescue. We were the only two people on the motorhome and he could tell I was feeling very low. He reached out, put his hand on my shoulder and said, "You know, Johnny, we'll make it. And when we do, they can never take that away from you. Whether we make $10 or $10 million, they can never take that away from you." Ed always seemed to have a way to pick just the right words at the right moment and there was no question in my mind that whatever power was watching over me on the road had brought Ed to join our Journey.

FACT AND FICTION

Red maple leaves, a sure sign of fall, were blowing along the sidewalk in Elmvale on the way to Midland. Crowds had thinned and, alone on the road, I had time to clear my mind after what had been a wild ride through Southern Ontario. I had time to think and it became clearer to me each day that life isn't about the cars we drive, the houses we live in, our bank accounts, the jobs we have or the toys we own. Life is about character and what we're willing to do and what we want our legacy to be. I'd already answered that question in my mind. I knew what I was willing to do.

But when it came to the word legacy, August 18 was the beginning of a bitter lesson in politics. That was the day I began to realize that whatever the legacy of Jesse's Journey would be, we would have to create it ourselves. In the middle of the afternoon, there was a buzz among the road crew when CBC Radio aired a story about the Government of Ontario and a possible $1-million donation to Jesse's Journey. It wasn't just out-of-the-blue speculation. The provincial minister of Energy, Science and Technology had been in Collingwood when I broke through the banner marking the halfway point in the walk. He'd said at the time, "The request for $1 million is before cabinet now. I'd hate to miss a chance to help." And from London, the provincial minister of Intergovernmental Affairs had said, "I'm very optimistic discussions will go favourably."

Until the commitment of dollars to a project turns into reality, it's really just a suggestion, but a valuable suggestion politically if the public is left thinking a commitment has been fulfilled. It's action that cuts through the smoke and mirrors to reveal the truth. I had walked and posed with enough politicians to know that what gets said, the impression the public is left with and what actually happens aren't always the same thing.

The end result was that when the headlines were forgotten and the media stories faded away, the Government of Ontario didn't make any kind of donation to Jesse's Journey. I thought back to the controversy and embarrassment created by the $10 donation from the City of Moncton in New Brunswick. That city was ridiculed over the amount of its gift, but it was $10 more than we ever received from the government of my home province. I know a lot of politicians and I like a lot of politicians. I just don't understand them. Politics is a strange business.

A LITTLE REST BEFORE CHURCH

We were in Midland and my reserve tank of energy was finally empty. Even though I was exhausted, I hadn't been sleeping well, so the previous night I had taken a sleeping pill. But as soon as I got on the motorhome for breakfast, Ed took one look at me and he knew something wasn't right. He could see I was struggling and we weren't even on the road yet. Six kilometres into the day's walk, road manager Trish Federkow decided she had seen enough. I was sluggish and for the first time in 134 days, I was taken off the road to get some rest. The crew was concerned as they whisked me back to our motel. The room was blacked out and the phone disconnected. After putting in a set of earplugs, I fell asleep almost instantly. When I woke up six hours later, I couldn't believe I'd slept so long. I guess my body and emotions had been in overdrive since London and the wear and tear had finally caught up with me. The next morning, after my long afternoon nap and a good night's sleep, I felt much better. I was up early, rested and ready to go.

Our starting point for the day was across the highway from the towers of the Martyrs' Shrine, just outside Midland. The morning air was noticeably colder as we waited for the OPP escort to arrive. As a youngster, I had vacationed in Midland with my family, so I had been to Martyrs' Shrine, but that was more than 35 years ago. While we were waiting, Ed and I climbed the stairs of the shrine, which contains the relics of Jean de Brébeuf and four other Jesuits who were martyred by the Iroquois. All five were canonized in 1930.

The building I remembered as a kid now seemed so much smaller and safety concerns had brought changes. When I was young, long wooden matches were used to light prayer candles in red glass containers at the front of the church. But there's a lot of wood in this place and wood and live flames are not a good combination. Visitors were now instructed to place their donations in a clear plastic collection box and then flip a switch to turn on an electric candle. But when Ed made his donation and flipped the switch to light his candle, nothing happened. For the rest of the day I was in stitches every time he said, "By the Jesus, Johnny, that's it, I'm writing to Rome. I'm telling the Pope that he owes me 10 bucks!"

We had been spoiled over the last month by visits of friends from home who not only helped collect donations but often brought homemade goodies for the road crew. But by the time we reached Parry Sound, it was too far for a day trip from London and there were fewer and fewer visits. Each time we said goodbye, we knew there was little chance we would meet again until we got home early the next year. That was assuming we made it to Victoria.

PAY ATTENTION; YOUR LIFE'S ON THE LINE

It was late summer as Jesse's Journey made its way up Highway 69 to Sudbury along one of the most dangerous stretches of road I'd been on so far. There was just a single lane in each direction and very little shoulder to work with on a highway jammed with tourist traffic. The cars, trucks, vans and campers, nearly all hauling boats on trailers, made it seem like everybody in Ontario owned a motor boat. In a funny way, it also looked like most of the boats in the province were being driven around on land. But in reality, this piece of road was no laughing matter.

Our provincial police escort was worried about the speed and volume of the traffic. There had been a fatal accident just the night before. A woman died when her car collided with a transport truck and the road was closed for several hours. The next afternoon the highway was closed again due to another accident. Bumper-to-bumper vehicles were at a standstill and for the first time I could remember, I was walking past traffic that usually zipped past me. Members of the road crew took advantage of the captive audience as they worked the long line of vehicles, filling their buckets with donations handed from the windows of just about every car and truck we passed as we moved along. It was a case of the motorists' lemons being our lemonade.

The 165 kilometres from Parry Sound to Sudbury is one of the most remote pieces of highway in Ontario. In this sparsely populated area of the province, there are only four villages – Nobel, Pointe au Baril Station, Bigwood and Estaire – along Highway 69. It was there that I started to recapture the pace I'd been looking for since leaving London.

As traffic started to move again, a man driving a Mercedes Benz called out, "Go for it man!" He was among the many people who gave us a thumbs-up sign. A couple from Ingersoll, Ontario who stopped to make a donation said, "It's a very courageous thing you're doing." And a man and his wife from St. Thomas, also near London, said, "Good luck, John. You make fathers proud." Messages like these drove me on, even when dollars were scarce. I never let go of the thought that I was doing what I feel fathers are supposed to do – everything in their power to provide their kids with the best possible quality of life.

South of Sudbury on my 139th road day, we reached the 4,000-kilometre mark. I settled back into a daily routine of playing leapfrog with the motorhome as we got close to rejoining the Trans-Canada, which we left back in Quebec when we reached Montreal. Before long, we would turn west toward Sault Ste. Marie for the next portion of the journey, which would take us around the top of Lake Superior.

A strange little incident happened on the way into Sudbury. After I jogged past a construction zone, one of the workers jumped on a front-end loader and drove down the highway to catch up with me to make a donation. There probably aren't too many people who can say they've been chased down the Trans-Canada Highway by a front-end loader!

At night in Sudbury, home of "The Big Nickel," a nine-metre-high replica of a 1951 Canadian coin, we could see red-hot slag from smelters creating a fiery glow against a backdrop of blackness. The terrain around parts of Sudbury makes it easy to understand why the Apollo astronauts used the area as a training site in preparation for landing on the moon in the 1960s.

The next morning we passed through Lively and donations continued to come from a variety of sources: members of a car club parked on a hilltop by the side of the road; people who stopped at the motorhome or met us at dinner; golfers who dropped their clubs to come up to the roadside. A man with two stainless steel knees joined me on the road awhile and there were others who wanted to walk along for a bit, perhaps just to know they were part of the Journey.

These days on the road were often long and I found myself anxious to reach Manitoba, where the real race to the far west would begin. But as I walked on the highway Jesse and I had shared three summers before, there was a touch of nostalgia. Sometimes I remembered road twists and turns before we got to them. Near Espanola we passed through Nairn Centre, where the sawmill produces enough finished timber annually to build 18,000 houses. At the end of another day, a familiar laneway took me back to one of the prettiest places Jesse and I had seen, the Anishinabe Spiritual Retreat on Lake Anderson, just south of Espanola.

In a way it seemed as if time had stood still. Sister Dorothy and Sister Pat welcomed us again with open arms and right beside the nuns, their slightly older golden retrievers, Frisky and Mooch, happily wagged their tails. It was another of the few moments along the way that felt like being home.

I had decided this was the right place to take a much-needed but unscheduled day off and I could see the road team also was in need of a break to recalibrate how we were doing things. We soon would have to shift our focus to a geographic zone very different from where we'd been for the last month. Sault Ste. Marie was not that far away and from past experience, I knew the area north of the Soo was the most physically demanding part of Ontario and perhaps all of Canada. I was certain the decision to stop for a day was the right one and despite the phone calls required to juggle events farther along the route, it would be a wise investment in time.

The weeks and months on the road had taught me to listen to my body and this is what separated me from the road crew. They were doing a great job attending to daily details, but I was the only person who could take true stock of how I was doing. I knew burnout was one thing that could stop me from realizing the dream. Pacing was very important and it was time to stop in order to ensure that we could go on.

The change of colour in the leaves was now more visible as Ed and I climbed a hill and sat on a tree stump overlooking Lake Anderson. The sky was clear blue and the sun warm on our faces as I enjoyed a morning without having to look at my watch to see if we were on time.

With a big chunk of Ontario behind, Manitoba still six weeks away, and three more provinces after that, Ed and I avoided talking about the road. We both knew what we faced. Instead, we talked about our families and the workload they faced at home while Jesse's Journey made its way across Canada. We talked about the gardens we didn't get to plant, the lawns other people were mowing and all the things that would have to be trimmed, fertilized, fixed, oiled, cleaned or painted when we got home. But those were just a bunch of things and in time, they all would be dealt with. It was our families we missed the most. We missed our wives, not just because they weren't there to share in the experiences, both good and bad, we were having, but because they brought the music of laughter and a sense of balance to our days. We missed seeing our kids and knew almost a complete year would forever be missing from our home lives. I even missed negotiating the parental minefield. I missed the noise kids make. The one Ed missed most was his pride and joy, grandson Scotty. The sunshine sparkling on the water made the missing just a little bit easier.

The decision to take the one-day break at Espanola proved to be a watershed. Sometimes in life we get so busy with what we're doing that we forget why we're doing it. The rest gave all of us a chance to remind ourselves why we were there.

Ontario was Province No. 6. The parts of Canada I had already walked told the story of struggles among the British, the French, the Americans and Canada's aboriginal people. Northern Ontario's history is rooted in stories of survival in the rough-and-tumble world of the fur trade, fir trees and mining. Beyond Espanola and the E. B. Eddy forest reserve (three times the size of Prince Edward Island), the countryside became more rugged as farmland disappeared and pulp and paper mills began to dominate.

THE TIPPING POINT

On the last day of August, on the Trans-Canada between the little towns of Massey and Spanish, Bevin Palmateer was waiting with his video camera. He had spray-painted a bright red line across the road, with arrows pointing east to St. John's and west to Victoria. Both distances read 4,151 kilometres. I was now officially halfway across Canada.

The road was starting to take on a different feel. The highway was quiet as I walked past Serpent River, where, if you go north from the Trans-Canada, you arrive in Elliot Lake. Beyond Spragge, Pronto and Algoma Mills is Blind River, named by voyageurs who couldn't find the river's outlet on Lake Huron. Among the few people along the road was a conservation officer who stopped to shake my hand and simply said, "I'm a dad, too."

I had to get used to an increase in the number of logging trucks and tractor-trailers hauling oversized loads of heavy-duty equipment. The police officer in the escort cruiser watched his rear-view mirror for trucks with wide loads coming up behind us. When I'd hear a honk from the escort vehicle, I'd move to my right, farther away from the road. That would a part of the routine for the next four months.

September 2, west of Blind River on the Trans-Canada between Iron Bridge and Thessalon, was the first day since the Maritimes I could see my breath in the air. That day's 33 kilometres resulted in a grand total of $60 in donations. The days ahead were looking lean.

It was raining when we passed through Thessalon and Bruce Mines. I worked the road in five-kilometre blocks on what was an "on again, off again" day for rain gear. There was a reception in Thessalon, where we received donations from the town and from area fire departments. Since things were pretty thin on the road, these were welcome.

I got a solid reminder that we were in Northern Ontario when a black bear crossed the highway in front of me just before we reached Bruce Mines. The catch-all signs on scarce retail outlets along the highway were another clue. In Bruce Mines, one store sign advertised "ice, lottery tickets and fishing licences." From my time on the road with Jesse, I knew that north of Sault Ste. Marie, these signs would become even more detailed. One boasted "firewood and fireworks, movies, hunting licences, ice cream and bait."

I don't know if it was the thought of ice cream and bait that did it, but somewhere along the road I lost my appetite. Although the restaurant meals we'd had were very good, for a few days I didn't feel much like eating. It seemed that every 10 or 11 days my body clock cycled around to a point at which I just couldn't eat another restaurant meal. That was when I'd have a light supper in my room or on the motorhome. The crew wanted me to change my diet and the decision was made to increase the amount of fruit I was eating. And with the days getting colder, my mornings would start with Ed's legendary Newfoundland porridge.

In Sault Ste. Marie on Day 150, laughter again reared its welcome head. It had been decided I should have a full physical and blood work and the appointment was arranged for the Saturday night of Labour Day weekend. After the usual poking and prodding, I was asked to make a fist while a needle was injected into a vein in my arm and three small vials were filled with blood. To pass the time, I asked the young doctor, "Do you ever take a look at somebody before you get started and think to yourself, 'Boy, I wouldn't be surprised if we find something wrong here.'" He was a good guy and said in a very matter-of-fact way, "Not very often. Besides, people who walk here from St. John's, Newfoundland aren't usually very sick!" We both had a good laugh and 30 minutes after the blood test, he gave me the OK to keep going and wished me luck. With that good news, box No. 150 was shifted in my mind and I was ready to carry on in the knowledge that the "completed" pile was now bigger than the other side.

As we left Sault Ste. Marie, we could see for miles into the distance from the top of One Mile Hill. The Trans-Canada takes a dramatic plunge there and runs off to the horizon in a straight line. Cars and trucks at the bottom of the hill looked tiny as I started my descent and I wondered for a moment how I had pushed Jesse up this hill when we were going the other way.

NEW HORIZONS

The early-morning September sun created an illusion of warmth as it glistened on the waters of Lake Superior, the coldest of the Great Lakes. Somewhere beyond the horizon was Victoria and the end of the journey. But in truth that would be just the end of the road portion of the Journey.

Life makes no promises and regardless of what was to come, I knew I had done my best. Thousands of good people had joined the walk at one time or another and supported our project. Thousands of ordinary Canadians had shown us their generosity. When I felt my spirits lag a little, I reminded myself why I was out there: Someone needed to convey the message about the need for research and I had a better reason than most for being that someone.

One of my toughest individual challenges in the walk across Canada was the steep climb at Montreal River Harbour, almost 120 kilometres north of Sault Ste. Marie and a long way from Montreal. We arrived at the foot of the hill at the end of the day and I knew my legs would get a serious test first thing in the morning.

On September 11 it took me almost an hour to get to the top of the hill. When I reached the peak, I was greeted by a couple from Kingston who applauded my arrival. I was a little rubber-kneed, but after pouring some cold water over my head and resting to catch my breath, I was rewarded with a spectacular view over Lake Superior. I thought for a moment about Terry Fox and said to the road crew, "I don't know how somebody with just one leg ever managed to climb up that hill."

The scenery was stunning no matter which direction we looked from the Trans-Canada north of Batchawana Bay. But at the same time the road started to become very difficult. Visibility was often limited by jagged rock cuts where the road had been blasted out of the Canadian Shield. The road had sharp twists and turns and very little shoulder and at times, the tight turns made life extremely dangerous. While the escort van stayed close behind me, our provincial police cruiser was sometimes out of sight a kilometre or so back with its lights flashing to let truckers know there was something to look out for on the road ahead.

The drivers of the logging trucks and tractor-trailers that own the highway in this part of Ontario were very good about giving us a wide berth when they passed. Lots gave us an encouraging blast of the air horn. They were likely using their CB radios to keep each other posted as to our location and at the point where the Trans-Canada passes through Lake Superior Provincial Park, a couple of truckers stopped right on the highway to warn me about bears up ahead. It had been a hot, dry summer and there were few berries, so the bears were on the move and they were hungry!

After marking the next day's starting point, we headed back to Montreal River Harbour and the Trail's End Lodge. Usually when I climbed onto the motorhome at the end of the day, I'd drape a towel over my head to soak up the sweat and close my eyes during the ride to wherever we were going. This time was different. This time Sherene was waiting for me.

We'd been so busy when we were in London that Sherene and I had very little time to talk. Although we hadn't done our usual 33 kilometres on those days, they were full with appearances, media interviews and a side trip to St. Thomas. But this time we were going to try to shut out the world for a couple of hours and have dinner together. We'd been apart a long time.

On the motorhome that night, we shared a quiet candlelight soup-and-sandwich supper. Near the lodge there was a rocky beach where the Montreal River spills into Lake Superior and as we walked down to the shore after dinner, the owner of the lodge cautioned us not to stray too far because of the number of bear sightings. We sat by the water and talked for a few minutes before heading back to our cabin. It was a toss-up as to which of us was most tired. Sherene's flight had been delayed and when it finally arrived in Sault Ste. Marie, there was a long drive to Montreal River Harbour. For me, another day on the hills of Northern Ontario had left me tired as well. We were both trying hard not to fall asleep but finally decided we had to call it a day. It was wonderful to see Sherene but not exactly a wild and crazy reunion.

THE REAL 'LONG AND WINDING ROAD'

I held Sherene's hand as we arrived together in Wawa, home of "The Big Goose," one of the most noted landmarks in Canada. The nine-metre-high steel Canada goose stands at the entrance to Wawa, an Ojibwa word that means "wild goose."

As we walked along the road together I was thinking this would be the last time I'd see Sherene for four months. After she left, I was feeling a bit lonely as I shifted another little unit of work at the end of Day 158.

I was facing the most difficult and perhaps the hardest part of the walk across Canada – Wawa to Nipigon on the north shore of Lake Superior. The hills are incredibly steep and seemingly endless and I knew they would really take their toll on my body. There was no doubt they would dictate the agenda for several days to come. I knew it would be important to listen to my body, although I suspected we would be pushing the endurance envelope dangerously close to its limit. I also knew it would be difficult to stay mentally focused on completing just one hill at a time and then one day at a time. If there was compensation, it would be spectacularly rugged and beautiful scenery.

From Wawa to White River, the Trans-Canada Highway is 100 kilometres of nothing but hills, rocks, trees and more hills. I slept at every opportunity and to ease my tired muscles, the work already being done on my legs three times a day was stepped up. The massages on my calves and thigh muscles became much deeper.

In White River there was a moment when the past and present seemed to meet. Jesse's Journey, a charity working to make life better for a special group of kids, received a donation at a unique location special to all kids. The gift was from the people of White River and the presentation was made in a park near a statue marking the birthplace of a storybook character that has delighted children for decades. White River, besides laying claim to being the coldest place in Canada, is also the birthplace of Winnie the Pooh.

Record-keepers say the part about White River being the coldest spot in Canada is not officially true as the thermometer that registered a temperature of -72 F. in 1937 had shattered. The town of Snag in the Yukon actually has the dubious distinction of Canada's lowest temperature with an official reading of -62.8 F. in February of 1947. But with 13.1 feet of snow in White River in 1937, I'll bet it was still pretty cold.

The part about Winnie the Pooh is true. In 1914, Captain Harry Colebourn was on a World War One troop train that stopped in White River. From a trapper, Colebourn bought a black bear cub that had wandered out of the woods. He named the bear Winnipeg after his hometown and then Colebourn and the bear, along with the rest of his unit, crossed the Atlantic to London, England. Before leaving for the fighting in Europe, Colebourn gave the bear cub to the London Zoo. When author A. A. Milne visited the zoo with his son, Christopher Robin, they saw the bear and he started writing stories about "Winnie" and his friends. The stories, first published in 1926, are classics and still in demand today.

White River to Marathon was another lonely stretch of road, with no towns or villages. We were halfway through September and the grey, rainy days made the sand and gravel at the side of the road quite soft. There was a close call while I was walking and it made it very clear how dangerous life on the road could be. Up ahead of me on the slick pavement, the motorhome was forced off the road by a tractor-trailer. Luckily no one was hurt, but the motorhome came to rest on an angle, up to its axles in soft sand. The transport driver stopped to help and with some heavy spade work, he and Ed eventually managed to rock the motorhome free without any damage. But it brought home the need to be even more careful.

The days on the way to Marathon were uneventful and it was funny the lengths we went to sometimes to make the time go faster. One afternoon the kilometres clicked by as we all searched our memory banks to recall things from our childhood. We talked about cap guns, peashooters, Dinky Toys, marbles, chestnuts, baseball cards and jackknives. We recalled black and white pictures of Toronto Maple Leaf and Montreal Canadien hockey heroes you could send away for with the labels from Beehive Corn Syrup. We talked about when we were 10 or 11-year-old hockey players and how accurately we could shoot hockey pucks through a hole where a board was missing on the side of the garage.

It was fun thinking back to a time when every kid we knew, boys and girls, played hockey or figure skated, rode bicycles and went swimming. It seemed then like we could run and play forever. But reality brought us back to Earth when a young American couple and their daughter pulled to the side of the road to make a donation. I got a cold reminder that not every child's youth is as easy as mine when they told me their young daughter was about to undergo the same operation as baseball player Dave Dravecky. It was in June of 1991 that cancer cut short the career of the 35-year-old Dravecky, a pitcher with the

San Francisco Giants. The former all-star had to have his left arm amputated after a cancerous lump was discovered. This little girl was scheduled to lose her arm in a month.

There is never any warning and nothing can prepare you for these intensely personal moments, when people share stories about their families and children. They wished me luck and drove off, but I was really rocked by the girl's story. There was nothing to do except keep moving. But it had become a lot quieter. Nobody was talking about childhood memories anymore. That's just the way it was on Day 163.

BONJOUR MESSIEURS

It seemed like a long time since Jean-Luc Robert, the man from the French Muscular Dystrophy Association, had talked to me in Montreal. In the light drizzle of a soggy wet morning outside Marathon, the television crew he had dispatched from France arrived to capture our story before Jesse was to fly to France with his mom and Mario Chioini. The television crew had already shot videotape of Jesse in London and now wanted to see Jesse's dad and the road team at work. While Northern Ontario can look breathtaking in the sunlight, it can be equally depressing when the sky is grey. Everywhere around us, water dripped from the sharp angles of wet rocks, but we'd have to make do.

As they began shooting video to be aired in December when Jesse was in France, I could tell it would be a long day. Television production work doesn't happen quickly and in order for the cameraman to get just the right shot, I was asked to repeat sections of the road several times. At one point, we needed two-way radios to co-ordinate just one shot as I walked across a long bridge spanning a wide valley of fir trees and railroad tracks snaking through the canyon far below me. The camera crew was more than a kilometre behind me, high on a lookout point that provided a panoramic view of Lake Superior, the valley below and the railroad tracks.

As the day unfolded, the camera lens probed our every move, from making sandwiches to changing shoes and the general small talk of the lunch-hour, capturing a behind-the-scenes look at Jesse's Journey. After lunch the producer with the French crew asked if he could interview me. I'd been asked a lot of questions in the months on the road, but this man penetrated my mind in a way that hadn't happened before.

When an interview starts off with, "How many pairs of shoes have you gone through?" I know it's not going to be a difficult interview. But the French producer's tactic was completely different. He knew that for me and every other Duchenne parent, it isn't easy to talk about your child and the future. It's a subject we don't really want to talk about and if forced to, we know we run the risk of crossing an emotional line no one wants to approach. With great sensitivity and insightful questions, the producer did a wonderful job of taking me up to that line and a little beyond, showing respect and without making me crack. It is one of the best interviews I've ever had.

We were in Marathon having a tea and fruit break when it started to pour rain. To keep my feet dry, they were wrapped in plastic bags before I put on my running shoes. Ed Coxworthy called them "Newfie mukluks." To keep my feet tough and to prevent blisters, I was still soaking them three times a day in sea salt and water. I guess it was working because when Ed was stretching my legs, he said, "By the Jesus, Johnny, you've got feet like pig's ears."

The pulp and paper town of Marathon was established in 1944 when Marathon Paper of Wisconsin set up shop in Ontario. It really boomed in the 1980s when gold was discovered at nearby Hemlo, which at that time was the site of Canada's three largest gold mines.

At times it seemed like the motorhome had a revolving door and the cast of characters changed again at Marathon. The television crew left for Winnipeg to head home to France. Bevin Palmateer returned from doing advance work with the media and police in Thunder Bay. Trish Federkow left to go home for a break and Ted Eadinger, who was with us in Quebec, arrived to take Trish's place as road manager. It was surprising how easily people switched places but because they all knew the routine, the well-oiled Journey machine never missed a beat. When I arrived for breakfast, Ted looked up from a bowl of Ed's porridge, smiled and said, "Hi, it's me again."

MOTORCYCLES AND MISCONCEPTIONS

There weren't many people along the road as we made our way across the top of Lake Superior to Terrace Bay, where we arrived on the first day of fall. Jesse and I had experienced one of our most memorable moments in 1995 at the same roadside motel where we were staying in Terrace Bay – another pulp and paper town, this one built by Kimberly-Clark in the 1940s.

1995 was the hottest summer on record at the time. Before returning to the road for the afternoon, I was resting after lunch. My motel room was at ground level and looked right out at the parking lot and the Trans-Canada Highway. When I looked up, Jesse was at the door in his wheelchair. "Dad," he said, "there's 12 guys out here on motorcycles." When I asked what they were like, Jesse said, "They're big! You know, they have big beards, big leather outfits and big tattoos. They're just big dad, trust me." When I asked what they wanted, Jesse said, "They want to have their picture taken with me."

My immediate thoughts had been something like, "Big tattooed guys on motorcycles; probably drug dealers; probably involved with a strip club; probably bad news." But Jesse had his picture taken with them anyway and the big guys handed him $500 in cash. I didn't know where the money might have come from but I was still thinking the worst. I was wrong. It turned out the bikers were on their way to Thunder Bay to take part in a "Ride for Sight" program. It wasn't even close to what I assumed they were all about. But ever since then, when I see someone on a big bike I don't see the same person I used to see. Jesse's experience had reminded me we should never judge a book by its cover.

I added a town pin from Terrace Bay to the collection that had begun in Newfoundland and walked on to the neighbouring town of Schreiber, where half of the population is of Italian descent. Most residents can trace their roots to the southern Italian town of Siderno Marina. Their ancestors began arriving in Canada in 1883 and settling in Schreiber, where they went to work on the Canadian Pacific Railway.

From Schreiber west to Rossport, the trade-off continued. The hills were steep and demanding, but the view from the top of each one was its own reward. At this point the Trans-Canada Highway hugs the north shore of Lake Superior. The dramatic rise and fall of the Canadian Shield had given engineers a huge challenge in carving a roadway through the rock and the result is a road that plunges, climbs and twists, offering spectacular scenery at almost every turn. Villages that aren't right on the highway are sometimes missed in the rush to bigger cities and Rossport is one of the north shore's little secrets.

Before we doubled back to the Rossport Inn, the day ended with a long, steep climb. I never liked ending my day at the bottom of a hill; I always wanted to start the next day at the top. I was halfway up the hill when I heard the honk from the escort van, letting me know we had reached our distance for the day. I kept on going and was glad I did. At the top of the hill I met a couple from Aylmer, in Southern Ontario, who donated $200. It made it all worthwhile, especially on a day when only three cars had stopped. I shifted little box No. 168.

The Rossport Inn, which opened in 1884, is the oldest operating hotel on Lake Superior's north shore. It sits on a hill with a view of the water and the islands that protect the bay. Just below the inn, railroad tracks run along the shoreline. The motorhome was parked across from the inn, just beyond the point where the tracks bent with the shoreline. Sitting in the motorhome in the dark, we could have sworn from the angle of the high-powered headlights coming toward us that the freight trains were about to rip right through the motorhome. Then at the last second, the trains would veer off. The noise and vibration made things a little too exciting for Ed, who was sleeping on board the motorhome during the stop at Rossport. In the morning he looked groggy and a little shell-shocked. "By the Jesus, Johnny, I dreamt the engine of the train tore the arse-end right off the motorhome!" he told us at breakfast.

The dawn was beautiful on the morning we left Rossport. As the sun climbed into the sky, I started climbing the hills that led to Nipigon, the western end of the challenging stretch of road that started at Wawa. There were a lot more hills still to climb but in just over a week we would be in Thunder Bay and I knew that from there, as we headed northwest to Kenora, the road would begin to flatten out and would be much more manageable. I tried hard not to think about any province other than one I was in, but I also knew the schedule showed Winnipeg was still a month away. Then there would be a whole new problem. Prairie roads would be very flat for a very long time and the physical challenges would be replaced by mental challenges.

A SPECIAL PIECE OF ROAD

One day when the shadows were getting long in the late afternoon, I jogged across what seemed to be an endless expanse of bridge high above the Nipigon River. Police sometimes call the bridge the "Nipigon net" because virtually everything on rubber that moves across Canada has to cross the bridge at Nipigon and that's where police set up when they're looking for people trying to make a dash to the West after a major crime in Eastern Canada. Nipigon also marks the beginning of 100 kilometres of the Trans-Canada known as The Terry Fox Courage Highway.

On the day we reached the edge of Thunder Bay, an odd thing happened early in the morning. About a kilometre ahead of us, a motorist stopped on the shoulder of the road, stepped out of his car, waved to us and pointed at the ground. He drove off before we reached the spot where he'd parked but there on the ground, pinned under a rock, was a donation in an envelope and a day-old copy of The London Free Press. That was pretty special, but not as special as what we were about to see.

Right after our lunch break, I got a mental boost as I passed the 5,000-kilometre mark and then late in the afternoon, we reached the Terry Fox Monument. The monument looks out over Lake Superior and is close to the point on the Trans-Canada where the one-legged runner was forced to suspend his Marathon of Hope in September of 1980 when he was told his cancer had returned. The sun was shining and even though it was fall, there were still a few tour buses in the parking lot.

This stop was like no other. It was quiet and people seemed lost in their thoughts as they gazed up at the larger-than-life bronze statue of the courageous young Canadian whose contribution to cancer research lives on. Their faces were solemn as they remembered the curly-haired runner with the hippity-hop stride and the huge smile. Some people took pictures; others just stared and wiped their eyes. There was a feeling of respect, tinged with awe. The words carved in the stone base of the monument recount the story of Terry's 5,432-kilometre run for cancer research. Looking at the word "research," I felt a sense of kinship. Perhaps just a little more than others, I understood what drove Terry on, day after day. It was time to shift little box No. 173 and move on.

In Thunder Bay, there was a lot of media attention and we received major donations at receptions hosted by both Manulife and the Royal Bank. On the first day of October, at Shebaqua Corners northwest of Thunder Bay, it snowed. It was the first time I had seen snow since leaving Newfoundland. I thought about how long we had been out here and how much farther we had to go. The 180 kilometres from Shebaqua Corners to Ignace was another lonely stretch of highway, which meant long drives in the mornings to reach our starting point and long drives back at night.

As we made our way toward Ignace, we passed through just three widely separated villages, Raith, Upsala and English River. The bit of snow that fell in the morning disappeared quickly but was a reminder about what was ahead. Now in the mornings, it was still dark when I headed out to the motorhome. With the engine running, the lights on and the windows steamed up, it always looked warm and inviting. I almost wished I could just stay in it for the day.

On-board, Ed's famous porridge, with raisins and cinnamon, simmered on the stove. In a matter of minutes the orange juice, porridge, toast, jam, coffee and tea were finished. The dishes were cleaned up, fresh water loaded and everything secured. The morning radio interviews were done and the Ontario Provincial Police contacted. Before the sun was up, we were on our way again.

The frosty mornings were another sign that the clock marking the change of the seasons was ticking even louder. The landscape was morphing from a carpet of green to lighter shades of green and yellow. There were only a few maple trees to provide the brilliant splashes of red and orange we are accustomed to seeing in abundance in Southern Ontario. The road was starting to flatten out, which gave my back a chance to recover from the pounding it had taken on the hills between Sault Ste. Marie and Thunder Bay.

On most days, there was still some warmth in the afternoon sun. On the road, I shared with volunteers some of the highway trivia I had picked up. I told them about the little silver and green diamond-shaped signs located at the beginning and end of sections of guardrail. At the front end of the guardrail, the top half of the diamond is green and at the end of the guardrail, the bottom half of the diamond is green. This was a little quiz for volunteers, most of whom had driven past these signs for years without ever giving them a thought. The purpose of the signs is to tell snowplough drivers when to pick the blade up and when to put it down to prevent shearing off the guardrails in deep snow. It wasn't a great mystery, but it helped pass time as the kilometre count continued.

On the outskirts of Upsala we passed the official time marker and reset our watches back an hour to Central Time. We were thinking we were pretty smart with all our highway trivia and that we had an extra hour to nap because of the time change. That all went out the window when we actually reached Upsala and discovered everyone there operates on Eastern Time. Score another one for Murphy!

THE TIMES THEY ARE A CHANGING

Summer was over and there wasn't much traffic on the highway. From the CPR tracks that ran parallel to the road, freight train engineers sounded their horns and waved. From the industrial heartland of Canada, flatcars carrying stacked containers rolled west. Trains moving in the opposite direction seemed to be an endless stream of brown grain cars with yellow lettering. Painted on the side of each car were the words Canadian Wheat Board and its yellow logo of a sheaf of wheat. The Prairie gold was bound for ships waiting in Thunder Bay. Those ships, carrying just a part of Canada's annual harvest of 50 million metric tonnes of wheat, would be racing to reach the Atlantic Ocean before the winter freeze locked the Great Lakes in ice.

Ed and the motorhome were waiting for us in a wide-open area beside the highway just south of English River. The ground, which looked like it had been smoothed with a grader, was covered with wood chips. Set back from the highway, not far from the motorhome, were two white wooden crosses. The crosses, about three feet high, were side by side, with flowers at the base of each. The police officer escorting us said there had been a double fatality at this spot a few weeks earlier. The drivers of two tractor-trailers hauling wood chips were killed when their vehicles collided head on. The officer looked surprised when Ed told him exactly what time the accident happened. Ed then held up a wristwatch he had found buried among the wood chips while he was waiting for us to arrive for lunch. The crystal was shattered and the hands of the watch were stopped at 8:45, the exact time of the crash. Before we moved on in the afternoon, Ed took some clear packing tape and attached the watch to one of the crosses. It just seemed to belong there.

Before going to bed at night, I usually turned on the television to check the weather for the next day. As I flipped through the channels, I saw a picture of Gene Autry. "The singing cowboy" had died at his home in California at the age of 91. It had been a bad year for cowboy heroes from the days of black and white television. Earlier in the summer, Roy Rogers, "the king of the cowboys," had died at 86. "Buffalo Bob" Smith from the Howdy Doody Show of the 1950s also had died earlier in the year, as had singer Frank Sinatra, who was 82.

For a few days we were stuck in an area without cellphone service. When we finally cleared this dead zone, I was able to talk to Sherene, although I almost wished I hadn't because she told me Jesse was feeling a bit down. It was at moments like this that I wished with all my heart I could be at home just for an hour to try to make things right and to try to make him laugh. It was hard to come to terms with not being able to be in two places at one time. Such thoughts made me realize how long I'd been away. I headed back to the road feeling a little down myself.

I've often heard that "When God shuts a door, He opens a window" and in the strange life I was living on the edge of the highway, things seemed to have a way of balancing out. The morning after I talked to Sherene, I saw a bumper sticker on a pickup truck that made me laugh hard to enough to chase away any lingering blues. It said, "If you're opposed to logging, try using plastic toilet paper!" And so it went.

As we set off for Dryden, we noticed the jet trails in the sky were very short. We used these trails as a barometer to tell us how much moisture was in the air. Short trails signalled what would likely be a dry day and our forecast was right. We were now past the first week of October and enjoying the sun and the heat from these bonus days of Indian summer. After a couple of wet days in and out of the fluorescent orange rain suit, I was, for the moment, back to wearing a T-shirt and shorts. I wondered how much longer our luck would last.

When we arrived in Dryden, another pulp and paper town, a group of Wal-Mart employees met us at a shopping mall on the edge of town. Among the group who joined us for the walk downtown was a young couple, both doctors in Dryden, whose four-year-old son had Duchenne. After the police escorted us to the Royal Bank branch in town, the little boy sat on my knee and we posed for pictures as we cut a big chocolate cake together. I couldn't help thinking how much this little guy looked like Jesse at the same age.

Sometimes I'd forget we were surrounded by wilderness, but then we'd see a moose or signs of other wildlife. In Dryden, when I looked out the window of our motel in the morning, I found a coyote staring at me from the top of a pile of railroad ties.

At Vermillion Bay on the road to Kenora, which was still a couple of days away, I had to go back and repeat a four-kilometre section of road to make up for a construction zone. After I finished the section of road for the second time, a young woman directing traffic with a flag at the start of the area made a donation and wished me luck. Beyond the construction zone, one of dozens that forced us to retrace ground to make sure our distance was accurate, people heading east and heading west continued to stop.

One transport truck cab contained an older couple and their collie dog. They were seeing Canada and the United States together. The lady used a cane and had difficulty walking. Her husband said he didn't want to be worrying about her while he was out on the road, so she travelled with him. I had never really looked inside the cab of a transport before. This rig had a stove, microwave oven, bathroom facilities, a bed and even a television. These folks were on their way to Vancouver with a load of furniture. From there, they would carry something else to Kansas City and then they'd pick up a different load and head home to London, Ontario.

Later we met a man from Poplar Hill, just outside London. He was doing pipeline work between Ignace and Dryden. For him it was an emotional moment as he shook my hand and apologized for not having much money. Then he gave us $100.

GIVE US THIS DAY OUR DAILY BREAD

It was Thanksgiving Sunday and raining steadily at the end of our day west of Vermillion Bay. Only two people had stopped all day. After lunch Ed had taken the motorhome back to Vermillion Bay to start preparing our

Thanksgiving dinner while I moved on down the road. When we all returned to our base, the light from the steamed-up windows gave a warm glow to the larger-than-life picture of Jesse's smiling face on the side of the motorhome. From inside I could hear the voices of people who had gone from road crew to road family.

They had started out as strangers and I'm sure each of them thought long and hard before deciding to get involved in our unusual, one-of-a-kind adventure. Through the ups and downs, some disagreements were inevitable. But it had been decided at the very beginning that I was to be kept outside of this loop so I could focus solely on completing my 33 kilometres each day. So why did they join us and why did they stay on? The answer was in that picture on the side of the motorhome. Jesse was the impetus for all we were doing, the reason these people were here. He was the inspiration. Even if he didn't realize the number of people he was inspiring, I knew and for that reason, I had a lot to be thankful for.

When I opened the door of the motorhome, I was met by the wonderful smell of a turkey cooking in the oven. Everyone was in a really good mood and they all seemed to be busy getting ready for dinner. I climbed aboard to the usual chorus of friendly insults suggesting I hurry up and shut the door, along with the standard inquiry about whether or not I was born in a barn.

The turkey was served up with Newfoundland dressing made with summer savory. We had ham, potatoes, turnip, carrots, cabbage, yellow pease pudding and gravy. We even had little packages of cranberry sauce somebody managed to borrow from a restaurant along the way. And we had an apple crisp Trish Federkow made for dessert. Life on the motorhome seemed pretty good. Twenty-four hours later it would be a different story.

Thanksgiving Monday, Mother Nature decided to throw everything she had at us. It was raining at the start of the day and it just kept getting worse. By midday the wind was blowing hard. Before lunch, I completed 22 kilometres in a combination of rain, sleet, ice pellets and snow. To make matters worse, there was no solid shoulder on the road and trying to get through the wet sand and gravel at the edge of the pavement was like slogging through Ed's porridge. Finally the snow stopped, but it was still windy and raining. Fortunately, we had a police escort and lots of flashing lights.

Even though the truckers slowed down as they passed, I was blown off the road twice by a combination of high wind and tire spray. I finished my 33 kilometres just after 5 p.m. Soaking wet and just happy to be alive, I heaved a sigh of relief at the end of Day 188. I didn't know things were about to get a lot worse.

Ed was waiting for me at the motorhome but everyone else had gone ahead to a pre-arranged dinner in Kenora. As Ed and I drove toward town, a gauge on the instrument panel showed the engine was overheating. That diagnosis was confirmed within seconds when we saw steam coming from the engine compartment. With the emergency lights flashing, Ed slowed the motorhome to a crawl, but when he heard the lifters in the engine start to make a noise, he immediately pulled to the side of the road and stopped.

We were out of cell range and couldn't reach our crew so we did the only thing we could do. We waited. After the engine cooled, we started it up again and but we travelled only about a kilometre before we had to stop. Now we were within cell range, but Murphy's Law was playing games with us. It was the end of the day and the crew members who had gone to Kenora had turned their cellphones off.

WHEN THINGS ARE OUT OF FOCUS – REFOCUS

After talking over our options, we decided to call the police. When we were asked if we wanted to declare an emergency, we said yes. There was very little shoulder to park on and although we had our emergency lights flashing, the back part of the motorhome extended out over the surface of the road. When we didn't show up for supper, the crew finally called to find out what had happened. We told them to stay where they were and within half an hour, we limped into Kenora in the dark, hooked to a tow truck. To add insult to injury, we hadn't collected a penny all day. We arrived late at our motel in Kenora, licking our wounds from the weather, from the mechanical problems that would force us to work without the support of the motorhome for at least part of the next day, and from our less than successful returns on the road. I wasn't sure which to be the most upset about.

Then I realized I might be overreacting. The weather we couldn't do anything about other than pray. As for the motorhome, we were probably due for something to go wrong. It had performed flawlessly all the way from St.

John's. Finally, the fact that we hadn't collected a penny all day could be turned into a lesson much more valuable than money. Life can't always be about the money. If you can keep going when you're discouraged, you gain something money can't buy. You add to who you are as a person by building your character. Some of the personal assets we have, like determination, are worth more than cash at the end of a day like today. This was just one day and it didn't represent our whole project. To say it another way, I told myself, "Don't sweat the small stuff!" When my head finally hit the pillow, I mentally moved the box that represented Day 188. I knew this little package was empty financially, but in other ways, it was like moving a chunk of solid gold.

I was never so happy to see the motorhome as late the next morning when Ed rejoined us on the highway. Once again, he looked a little the worse for wear, having spent the night parked beside a refrigeration transport that had to have its motor running all night to keep the truck contents cold. He said the problem with the motorhome's 10-cylinder engine was a blown frost plug. All the frost plugs had been replaced and we were back in business. I didn't know why it had happened but maybe that's what you get when you forget to say grace at dinner on Thanksgiving Day!

It was almost the middle of October when we arrived in Kenora, the largest town on Lake of the Woods. Workers at the pulp mill there had been on strike since June. When the Canadian Pacific Railway arrived at Kenora in 1879, so did the lumber industry. More than 100 years later, Kenora is still reliant on the wealth of the forests. Some of the people on the streets appeared to be hanging around with nothing to do. There would be few donations from individuals. The strike had crippled the town's major industry and was eating at the town's greatest strength, its people.

At the town hall the mayor presented everyone on the team with pins and despite the tough economic times, there were cheque presentations from men's and women's groups, showing that generosity knows no bounds and that even people facing hard times want to share what they have.

To the west, the Manitoba border was just over 50 kilometres away. The sun was shining as I walked on to Kenora and past one of the most famous pieces of "highway art" in North America. "Huskie the Muskie" champions Kenora as a sport fishing paradise. It joined a long list of highway art that brightened our journey, including the Worlds Biggest Axe at Nackawic and the 80-tonne lobster at Shediac, both in New Brunswick. In Ontario we had seen Wawa's Big Goose, Colborne's Big Apple, Sudbury's Big Nickel, The World's Biggest Chair at Varney, between Durham and Mount Forest, and Jumbo the Elephant in St. Thomas.

The last two people to stop to make a donation in Ontario were two young men from Newfoundland heading west to seek their fortunes in the Alberta oil patch. They seemed to have everything they owned strapped to the roof of their car. They gave $10 to Jesse's Journey, then the two young men shook my hand and wished me well before driving off down the road with high hopes for their own adventure. I had a funny feeling they couldn't afford to give $10 to anybody. But then again, these were Newfoundlanders and typical of the island that leads Canada when it comes to giving.

· MANITOBA ·

"Perseverance is not a long race; it is many short races one after the other."
~ *Walter Elliott*

On the afternoon of October 15, I took my final steps in Ontario and strode into Manitoba. I had been on the road for 191 days since dipping my shoes in the Atlantic Ocean at Quidi Vidi, Newfoundland and it took 98 of those to walk the entire length of my home province. We had successfully crossed six provinces and were now facing the Prairies, the Rockies and another Canadian winter. But as I kept moving those little boxes, we had fewer than 100 days until we reached the finish line.

As I reflected on that first day in Newfoundland, I thought about how, in the pursuit of a dream, you to have to have an actual starting point. What you see when you're finished might not be anything like what you imagined at the beginning, but you must make a start.

I couldn't get over how quickly the terrain had become flat. After we crossed the Ontario-Manitoba border, there were a couple of little hills followed by a big valley and then suddenly we were on the Prairies. It was that fast.

My daily routine required some adjustments because we had moved into the Central Time Zone. The radio interviews in Ontario, for example, had to be done an hour earlier by our watches and this would only become more difficult as we moved farther west. We stayed in Falcon Lake for two nights and I tried to catch up on sleep. The last weeks in Ontario had been physically trying and as we nudged close to 200 days of walking, my back was reminding me that I wasn't 22 years old anymore. The flat land of Manitoba was a welcome sight.

I called home from Hadashville, a little Manitoba community about halfway between the Ontario border and Winnipeg. It seemed like it had been a long time since I'd talked to Sherene, Jesse and Tim. Jesse seemed very "up" as he told me a couple of his marks from school. I told Tim I had been interviewed in Kenora by a reporter named Tim Davidson! I told Sherene I missed her.

I was and am very proud of all my boys. As I was working my way toward Winnipeg, Tyler, our oldest son, was 20 and studying lighting and set design at the Centre for the Arts in Banff. After graduation he spent a couple of seasons at the Stratford Festival and he is now with Cirque de Soleil and travelling the world in their employ.

Tim, the youngest, was in Grade 10 in 1998 but he eventually followed his brother to The Banff Centre. His interests also were technical but he leaned more toward audio and now does theatre work in Toronto.

Jesse was 18 at the time of my walk, president of his Junior Achievement company and in his final year of high school. The following year he went to Fanshawe College in London to study hotel-restaurant management. He used to introduce Ty and Tim by saying, "These are my brothers, light and sound."

The day following my conversation with Sherene and the boys, I reported to the road crew that Jesse had earned an 89 in English and a 97 in marketing. Our newest volunteers, two retired teachers, smiled and seemed pleased. Once a teacher, always a teacher, I guess. I knew these two women were special because when the all the socks and underwear, road shirts and shorts came back after being laundered, they were not just in a pile, but neatly folded.

On the road I needed to shift gears mentally. In previous provinces, we never knew what we'd see around the next corner and it kept things interesting. Here there were no corners on the highway running straight all the way to Winnipeg. I saw quickly how boredom could become a problem.

People who were on the move across Canada were among those who stopped. There was a young couple making the long haul from Peterborough, Ontario to Victoria, four young guys helping a friend move across Manitoba from Falcon Lake to Winnipeg and a mother and daughter from London, Ontario relocating to Jasper, Alberta. They all made donations before driving off and their vehicles remained visible for a long time on the flat road.

In the last few days, there had been a dramatic increase in the amount of wildlife along the highway. Just before we left Ontario, two deer crossed the road in front of us. There was no traffic at the time and in the silence, their hooves clicked and clacked on the hard surface of the highway, as if the deer were tap-dancing. As quickly as they had appeared, they vanished into the woods on the opposite side of the road.

The critters didn't seem to be nearly as shy in Manitoba. Outside Hadashville, a white-tailed deer stood close to us for the longest time, just watching us walk down the road. When Ed was up ahead preparing lunch, seven deer – two bucks, two does and three fawns – came right up to the motorhome to see what was happening.

GOING IT ALONE – WITH OTHERS

We still hadn't reached Winnipeg when the unrestrained power of the weather seemingly decided to ask me again just how much I was willing to take. I was back to wearing the fluorescent orange gear as rain mixed with ice pellets stung my face. High winds sweeping across the open fields sometimes stopped me from moving forward at all. Leaning into the wind that was rocking the motorhome, I had to fight just to get the door open. As I got safely on-board for my first break, the wind slammed the door behind me. My fingers were numb, my eyes were red and it wasn't until I was shedding the rain suit that I realized we had visitors.

I slumped into my seat at the kitchen table, rain dripping from my chin, as Ed set a cup of steaming hot chocolate in front of me before fetching a pair of clean, dry socks that had been warming on the heat vent. Then I was introduced to a man and his wife who had driven out from Steinbach, Manitoba to make a donation. They understood why I was there.

They had three children, two girls and a boy, and their son had died of Duchenne in 1995, when he was just 21. Cold and wet, I listened in silence as another father told me the story of the final hours of his son's life. It was April when their boy was taken to hospital in Steinbach for the last time. Near the end, he could barely speak. The father said he was at his son's bedside when he awoke from a broken sleep and heard his son say, "Cool." He thought his son was cold and wanted a blanket so he tucked a cover around him. Then he heard the young man whisper, "Neat."

"Son, what are you talking about?" the father asked. His son was very weak and perhaps mistook his father's voice for that of his mother. "Mom," he said, "you have to see this. Come with me." He died shortly after that, in the early morning hours of April 19.

Before they left, the couple made a generous donation to Jesse's Journey. As they stepped down the stairs of the motorhome, the father smiled at me and said he was sure his son was in a better place. He said his son was the kind of kid who was always happy and never complained. I was close to tears as we shook hands again and said goodbye. As I watched them drive away in the rain, the weather didn't seem to be such a problem anymore.

I know I met other people along the road that day but I can't remember any of them. By the time we drove into Winnipeg at the end of the day, there was a long thin line of red sky running across the horizon, giving a hint that maybe we would have better weather tomorrow. I can still see that sky and will always remember the day I moved little box No. 195.

MAYBE WE HAVE A CHANCE

When it came to our plan and the way we had designed it so we could win, I always felt that getting to Winnipeg would be a key milestone and positive indicator of our ability to complete the whole journey. For the next four nights Winnipeg would be home as we shuttled out to the Trans-Canada Highway at the beginning of each day and back again at night.

Fortunately for us, Winnipeg has what is probably the country's most efficient ring road. Getting back and forth to the highway was fairly easy, which was good because there is always an extra workload in the bigger centres with radio, television and newspaper interviews. For Jesse's Journey, these were great opportunities to speak to people about the value of research. The ring road allowed us get back to work as quickly as possible.

As the road team slowly made its way across the country, the home team back in London continued to oil the machinery from a distance, making sure everything ran as smoothly as possible. In Winnipeg the home team had arrangements for us to acquire heavy-duty winter clothing and the proper footwear to withstand the sub-zero temperatures we would face in the weeks ahead.

Through Winnipeg and beyond, the mornings started out very foggy. After the sun burned off the fog, I walked the Trans-Canada toward Portage la Prairie under a big blue Manitoba sky. On a couple of days the afternoon temperature reached 22 C. It was October 23 and in a T-shirt and short pants, I again was wondering how much longer our luck could last with this kind of weather.

THE SMALLEST MOUNTIE

Day 200 on the road was a raw, cold Saturday morning. At Portage la Prairie, the mayor and members of the Lions Club were waiting for us at city hall. The mayor presented us with pins and, like so many of their cohorts before, the Lions of Portage la Prairie presented us with a cheque.

On the main street we experienced another of those moments we'd remember for a long time. Our RCMP escort brought along his son, who was about three and a half. The little boy, whose name was Justice, was dressed in his own miniature red serge RCMP uniform, complete in every detail, down to the brown Boy Scout-type hat. He had come to walk through town with me, so we set off together with his dad right behind us in the RCMP cruiser, lights flashing. The little guy got tired so I picked him up and carried him awhile before he decided he'd like to ride in the police car with his dad, undoubtedly the proudest father in Portage la Prairie on this Saturday morning.

On the Monday of the last week of October, there was very little traffic on the road as we made our way through the Manitoba communities of Holland, Glenboro and Wawanesa on the way to Brandon. In Glenboro, I felt like the Pied Piper again as the kids from the local public school listened to our story and then joined me on the walk back out to the highway.

Through Manitoba I learned a lot about wheat, canola and flax. A retired farmer from Holland, Manitoba who joined us on the road for the day said farmers in this part of the province were getting about $4 a bushel for wheat. The system involved an initial payment of perhaps $3.25 a bushel, with a subsequent payment of about 75 cents a bushel, depending on the final price the government was able to negotiate with its customers. Farmers were paid about double that price for canola, which is used for margarine. Flax is also grown in Manitoba and is used for making linseed oil and linoleum products. Another thing I learned is that wheat farmers in Manitoba get a larger yield per acre than farmers in Saskatchewan because Manitoba generally gets more rain.

Just after our agricultural lesson, we received a donation that arrived in a most unusual manner. Coming toward me was a tractor-trailer hauling grain and the driver was flashing his lights as he approached. At first I thought maybe he was in some kind of trouble and we should be prepared to jump out of the way. But as he drove by, he threw something from the window of the cab and yelled, "Good luck." It turned out to be a $5 bill attached by a rubber band to a neatly wrapped muffin. It was the first time we could say research dollars had arrived by air-mail.

It was getting on in the fall and sometimes I could see storm clouds gathering on the horizon. Through Brandon, Manitoba's second-largest city, and toward the Saskatchewan border, traffic had thinned to a trickle. Vacationers were long gone and it seemed the only people travelling the Trans-Canada were those who had to be there.

Two-thirds of the farmland in Manitoba lies within 130 kilometres of Brandon, another Canadian city that owes its birth in 1881 to the arrival of the railroad. The mayor was in a celebratory mood when we arrived because he had been re-elected just the night before. At a reception for the road crew, the mayor said how much he personally appreciated our efforts to raise money for research. His grandson had benefited from research after being diagnosed with leukemia.

For several days I had been expecting to be rudely awakened by a blast of winter, but in the last days of October, the daytime temperature was still hovering around 15 or 16 C. Even though the wind made it feel colder, our luck with the weather was holding. I had a feeling someone was watching over us.

When you pack your bags for a journey, you include all the things you think you'll need for the trip. But some of them can't be seen. Strength and determination, manners and a sense of humour won't show up on an airport scanner, but you know you have them with you. Whatever belief you have in something bigger than all of us, your spiritual beliefs, also travel with you. Just as our parents taught us as youngsters, I found myself saying "thank you" at the end of every day.

It may sound like a contradiction, but as the days grew shorter, they also seemed to grow longer. There was less daylight but a lot more boredom. I

LOST HORIZON – Telephone poles stretch in a straight line as far as the eye can see as John Davidson makes his way across the flat Prairies. This photo, used as the cover art for The Right Road, is one of photographer and road crew member Bevin Palmateer's favourites. Photo by Bevin Palmateer

MILES TO GO – The Prairies did not present John Davidson with the physical challenges of other parts of Canada but it was a constant battle to remain focused and to defeat boredom across the miles and miles of flat roads. This scene is in Saskatchewan.

END OF THE PRAIRIES - START OF THE ROCKIES – There was no question winter had arrived by the time John Davidson got to Banff, Alberta in December 1998. The challenging Rockies lay ahead.

still faced another six weeks of being able to look in every direction across flat land that meets the sky at the horizon. If necessity is the mother of invention, I needed to invent something quickly to keep me from sinking into chronic boredom. On the road to Virdon we came up with "truck hockey."

Tractor-trailers now made up the majority of the traffic on the Trans-Canada. What we called truck hockey operated a bit like the NHL player draft. We put the names of the most popular trucking companies we'd seen on the road on slips of paper and every morning at breakfast, we each drew a name. Each player was given a point for every one of his or her trucks that passed us on the highway. It may sound juvenile, but it helped fill in the hours as we moved toward Saskatchewan.

THE EIGHTH MONTH

On the first day of November, we adjusted our starting time to begin a half-hour earlier, at 8 a.m., to take full advantage of the available daylight. People continued to make donations as I walked through Virdon, one of the last towns on the Trans-Canada before you exit Manitoba. Virdon was the home of two people whose interests couldn't have been more opposite and yet both their creations have become part of society's fabric. Bob Rockola made his mark as the inventor of the modern day jukebox and Virdon's other notable was Dr. Ballard of pet food fame.

Sherene's dad, Mowbray Sifton, left us at Virdon after spending a week on the road doing the things all the volunteers before him had done. Ed Coxworthy had nicknamed Mowbray "the skipper." Ed told me that in Newfoundland, the title of "skipper" goes to the oldest person on board, regardless of whether he is the captain. Mowbray, who had joined us a week before in Portage la Prairie, had the distinction of being the oldest walker to date on the road crew. He said he'd be happy to shoot a golf score equal to his age but when it came to walking the highway, he topped that. During his week on the road, 74-year-old Mowbray "the skipper" Sifton logged 81 kilometres.

The walk through Hargrave, Elkhorn, Kirkella and finally Fleming, the last town in Manitoba on the Trans-Canada Highway, gave me many entries for my journal. One day when we were in a restaurant having lunch, someone left a donation of $40 pinned under a windshield wiper on one of the vans.

There was no note, just two $20 bills flapping in the wind, left by a person or persons who would always know they had taken part in Jesse's Journey. Maybe it's a Canadian thing, but no one had taken the money, which was very visible and had been there for a while.

The day after moving little box No. 208, I stepped into Saskatchewan and Province No. 8.

· SASKATCHEWAN ·

"I don't even know what street Canada is on."
- Al Capone

As I pushed Jesse across Ontario in his wheelchair in 1995 and walked across Canada in 1998, children all across the country kept amazing me with their straightforward "Let's help" attitude. They seemed to relate to the boy pictured on the sides of the motorhome and vans. To them, Jesse was a kid who represented a lot of kids who couldn't play hockey or baseball, who weren't able to ride a bike or go swimming. Kids understood that and they took action.

During a morning radio interview, I heard how the pupils and teachers at a London public school were working together to sell paper footprints. Their project had raised $1,100 and was also teaching a priceless lesson about the true value of giving back by helping others.

Back on the Trans-Canada a little later that morning, my first day in Saskatchewan, I was surrounded by kids when we stopped at the public school at Wapella. The 100 pupils at this little rural school had never met Jesse but had raised $40 with their "let's help" attitude. They had a good laugh when a reporter asked me to choose one of the kids to pose with me for a picture. As I stood in the middle of the entire school population, I said, "How about this little boy right here?" They roared because they knew the "little boy" was actually a little girl! Such moments always served as a pressure valve to release the stress of long days on the road.

Early in the morning in the Sweet Dreams Motel in Broadview, I found myself pulling on long underwear for the first time since the previous winter. We were still managing to dodge the snow bullet but the temperature had dropped to -9 C. At breakfast I realized how far west we were when I turned on the television and saw a reporter doing a live report from Ottawa in broad daylight. Outside the Sweet Dreams Motel, it was still dark.

Radio played a large part in Jesse's Journey and the powerful draw of the airwaves was demonstrated near Regina. Along the one metre of pavement I called "my office," I was on the telephone doing a live interview with CBC Radio in Regina and drivers who were listening to it began stopping along the highway. In the cold weather they didn't stay long. A couple of transport truck drivers pulled over to make a donation and so did a man driving east from Regina. Dressed in a shirt and tie and without a coat, he didn't seem bothered by the cold as he came across a wide expanse of median and highway to shake hands. A woman who stopped asked, "Are you the father?" She wanted to shake my hand. She mentioned a niece who had been taken to Toronto for surgery and encouraged me to keep going with the words, "Don't give up." I had decided a long time ago, as far back as Newfoundland, that wasn't going to happen.

Her words took me back to Collingwood, Ontario, and the day I was feeling down after saying goodbye to Jesse, who I wouldn't see again until the new year. Ed Coxworthy comforted me then. He knew that with this type of project, there would always be critics and those who questioned my commitment, even my sanity. He told me to hold the hammer down. Those critics wouldn't be able to tarnish my efforts once they knew I had stuck with the job and completed it.

GOING ONCE, GOING TWICE...

When we reached Wolseley, there were snow flurries in the air. Morning radio show host and good buddy Peter Garland was back on the road with us and through the magic of radio, he conducted an auction in London from on-board the motorhome in Saskatchewan. Peter was working very hard but made it all look so easy and by the end of the show, Jesse's Journey had received a $5,000 boost.

At Indian Head, in the heart of Saskatchewan's wheat-growing district, we met a First Nations family, a mom, dad and two young girls who stopped to help. Each girl made a $20 donation and I could see their father was deeply moved as he hugged me and wished us well.

It was in Saskatchewan that the bitter cold finally got us in its grip again. By nightfall on November 9 we were in Regina and into a deep freeze. The temperature the next morning was -28 C. I made the rounds to a series of pre-arranged early-morning radio interviews and then it was back to the road, where the cold air made it difficult to get the muscles warmed up and humming smoothly. The day was sluggish, but not just because of the temperature. It was interrupted at noon when we had to drive back to Regina, where I spoke to a combined meeting of five Rotary Clubs. Then it was back to the highway and more cold air before I reached 33 kilometres.

Even though the sun was been shining, it was a long cold day and I finished in the dark. The real warmth came when we got back to our motel and I heard the faraway voices of my family in London. Sometimes we think conversation is only meaningful if there is big news to share. On this night I was missing what might be called family music, the sounds we too often call noise. I wanted to hear voices saying, "Did somebody get the mail? Hey Jesse, look at this! Are the Leafs playing tonight? Just a minute I'll be right there. Did you take Charlie for a walk? Is there any more, Mom? I can't, I've got homework. Pass the milk, will ya?" In the silence of motel rooms night after night, I wanted to hear all that beautiful noise a family generates, the noise that's gone too soon when kids grow up and move away.

After talking with Sherene and the younger boys at home, I dialled the phone number of Tyler, our oldest son, at The Banff Centre. It was his birthday. My pictures of Tyler's past birthdays included a whole bunch of kids with balloons, candles and chocolate cake that always ended up everywhere. The cake eventually became pizza with the gang and then grew into going out for dinner to mark the occasion. We never really know where the time goes, but I realized that night that Sherene and I had now been parents for 21 years.

TWO MINUTES TO REMEMBER

Ed Coxworthy hadn't missed a Remembrance Day service in 39 years and though thousands of miles from his home on Bell Island, Newfoundland, he wasn't about to miss one this year. On November 11, he made his way to the cenotaph in Regina. They think ahead in Regina, where the bone-chilling cold of November can make some things impossible, especially for older people.

To accommodate the veterans and seniors who want to pay their respects, two services are held, one at the cenotaph and the other indoors at the Agrodome.

Out on the highway in the early morning, I was wearing a balaclava for the first time since April in Newfoundland. It was -27 C. and the wind chill was making me numb. On the motorhome at my break, we tuned in the Remembrance Day service from Ottawa and joined the rest of the country with two minutes of silence to mark the 11th hour of the 11th day of the 11th month, when the armistice was signed ending the First World War.

Before we got back to work, a boy of about 11 or 12 came across the highway to make a donation. On the road, a man who stopped to make a contribution said, "This is a story that fits into Remembrance Day." Another person who shook my hand told me, "Keep it going."

We were now west of Regina, where the railway tracks run parallel to the highway. Toward sunset, the sky put on a real Prairie show, lighting up the tracks like two bands of silver running to the horizon. In the morning, when you looked east, those same tracks were often a brilliant orange as they reflected the sunrise. There are plenty of these visual jewels in illusive Saskatchewan, but you have to know where to look. Anyone who has dismissed the province as flat and boring just hasn't taken the time to look beyond the obvious.

The weather had been frigid for almost a week, with the temperature hovering around -28 C. Finally, it warmed as we approached Moose Jaw. It would be natural to assume that in all the months I'd been on the road, I would have found some interesting treasures. But the truth was I hadn't really seen anything of value on the shoulders or in the ditches. Once we found about $5 in quarters, which we guessed had been in an ashtray that was dumped out, since the coins were scattered on the ground with a bunch of cigarettes butts. One day I found a small hammer, but by far the most common finds were bungee cords, those stretchy pieces of rubber with hooks on each end for holding things in place. Hubcaps were a close second.

Just outside Moose Jaw, I found one of those pouches people tie around their waists. Inside was a wallet with a driver's licence and other pieces of identification. There were a few coins but if there had been any folding money, it was gone. There was a news crew from Moose Jaw with us and, by coincidence, the cameraman said he knew the person whose name was on the licence. We found out later the person's car had been stolen the night before. The fanny-pack was probably thrown out the window after the money was removed from the wallet. It wasn't any big mystery solved, but it was more exciting than another bungee cord.

LUNCH ON THE RUN!

In Moose Jaw, home of the Snowbirds, Canada's most famous aerobatics team, I fell asleep on the motorhome before lunch was ready. When I woke up, I realized we were inside a truck wash. It must have looked pretty funny as five of us ate lasagna while high-powered jets of water blasted away the layers of dirt that had been splashed onto the side of the motorhome by passing trucks. As I used a cellphone to return a call to The London Free Press, I told the guys I was willing to bet that at that very moment, there probably weren't too many Canadians doing interviews with newspapers from motorhomes inside truck washes while eating lasagna!

That night, Jesse's Journey was in the spotlight at the arena in Moose Jaw. I was introduced at centre ice and presented with a hockey sweater before dropping the ceremonial puck as the Moose Jaw Warriors hosted the Prince Albert Raiders. A week before, I'd done the same thing in Regina at a game between the Western Hockey League's Regina Pats and the Spokane Chiefs. The only difference was that in Regina, they ask you to take your hat off before the national anthem.

From Moose Jaw, we moved toward Swift Current. While we were struggling with the severe cold, the snow I dreaded had yet to cause a serious problem and I was beginning to wonder if we might make it to Alberta before the heavy snow started. Late in the afternoon, the Prairies put on an amazing show as the sun began to set and long shafts of light shone on the area around us. The yellow stubble of the harvested wheat fields, running as far as the eye could see, seemed to be lit from beneath as rural Saskatchewan took on an amber glow.

After marking the highway at the end of the day, we made the long drive back to our motel in Moose Jaw. In the lobby, the newspaper box confirmed that Bevin Palmateer had been hard at work. Jesse's Journey was a front-page story.

The following morning, the winter we'd been trying to beat in our race across the Prairies finally struck. There isn't usually a lot of activity at seven o'clock on a Sunday morning in Moose Jaw and this Sunday was no exception. On the motorhome I could hear the usual sounds – the purring of the engine as it warmed up for the day's work, Ed stirring the porridge he had heating on the stove and the hiss of the tea-kettle shooting steam into the air. The sliding blinds at the breakfast-table window were pulled down to keep out the cold. As I stowed my red duffel bag, I could make out a taxicab idling in front of the doughnut shop next door in the yellowish glow from the streetlights. Down the street, a few Christmas tree lights were blinking in the dark as they danced in the wind. The rest of the bags were being loaded onto the motorhome and into the vans with the knowledge that there would be snow along the highway. By the end of the day we would be in Chaplin, halfway between Moose Jaw and Swift Current, and still 160 kilometres short of the Alberta border.

During the long drive in the dark out to our starting point, I saw there was an accumulation of snow at the side of the highway. Walking would be difficult, but the snow was not that heavy and I hoped it would ease off. When daylight came, I thought I was hallucinating when I looked across the highway and saw nothing but water. The mystery was solved at the end of the day when the mayor of Chaplin told me that what looked to me like a lake was actually one of six sodium sulfate pools in the area. Each pool covers about 17 acres and is about 15 centimetres deep. The mayor worked at the plant where the sodium sulfate from the pools is spun in a centrifuge and separated from the dirt scooped up in the harvesting process. The end product is shipped to Lever Brothers and Procter and Gamble to be made into laundry soap. This part of Saskatchewan also produces seed potatoes, which are trucked to Idaho, where they're planted and grow to become famous as "Idaho" potatoes. But I think it's sort of like being born in Canada and raised somewhere else. You're still Canadian.

A PENNY FOR YOUR THOUGHTS

The 107 pupils of the public school in Chaplin had decided they would each bring in a roll of pennies for Jesse's Journey. But what should have been a donation of just over $50 turned out to be three times that amount. Once again kids amaze me with how much they want to be a part of something special. I wonder where and why some people seem to lose that "let's help" attitude later in life.

When our three-vehicle convoy rolled back into town that night, there wasn't anyone on the streets of Chaplin. It was getting dark and snow was piling up in drifts in front of the combination hotel, restaurant and bar where we were spending the night. It was warm inside and about a dozen people, some with their kids, had come out on this cold night to make us feel welcome. We gave Jesse's Journey hats to the kids and there was plenty of western hospitality. We were asked lots of questions about our travels across the country and I had the feeling Jesse's Journey was probably pretty big news in Chaplin, population 292.

Before daybreak, Ed left us to take the motorhome west to Swift Current for an oil change. Alone on the highway, with the escort van crawling along behind me, it was bitterly cold and somewhat lonely. I sipped tea from a flask in the van at noon after completing 15 kilometres in the snow. I desperately missed Ed and the motorhome, our home away from home and what we called "the mother ship." Once again, no one had stopped all morning.

By nightfall Ed had returned and in one of the most desolate and remote areas of Saskatchewan, we met at our motel, located right on the Trans-Canada in the little town of Morse. On nights like this, after completing 33 difficult kilometres, research was a distant thought as we shovelled snow away from the doors of our motel rooms just to get inside. The rooms were freezing cold as we waited for the little oil stoves in the corner of each room to generate some warmth. There would be no warm shower but at least the phone was working.

When I talked to Sherene, she told me she and Jesse had received their invitations to go to Paris to take part in the telethon to raise money for muscular dystrophy research. I also talked to Mario Chioini, the high school teacher from London who would accompany Jesse and Sherene to France and serve as translator and Jesse's assistant. Mario, who I first met on the streets of Edmunston, New Brunswick, when he had that "What have I got myself into?" look in his eyes, saw the trip as a dream come true. It's funny how you meet some people and realize very quickly that they are trusted friends who can be counted on. Still, the trip to France wouldn't be easy.

A LONG WAY FROM HOME

It was snowing heavily the morning we reached Swift Current. Firefighters helped us collect money along the road into town and to make up for lost time, I did some radio interviews by cellphone as I walked. Once we left Swift Current, I worked the road until after dark to finish the final 14 kilometres of the day and I was physically and mentally tired. It was another day when no one stopped on the Trans-Canada. But my mind wasn't on Swift Current. I was just anxious to get to a telephone because there was alarming news from back home: Jesse was fighting a cold.

For most people a cold is just an inconvenience in life. You might miss a few days of work. You have to listen to everybody's advice about getting rest, drinking plenty of orange juice and ginger ale and eating lots of chicken soup. It's more of a nuisance than anything else. But for kids like Jesse, a cold can quickly become a life-threatening situation and I was worried. I knew Sherene was keeping a close watch on Jesse, but so far away from home, I felt helpless. After Ed worked on my legs, he gave me a pat on the back before he left. He always seemed to know when something was wrong.

The morning of Day 225, I did something I'd never done before – I called home very early, as soon as I knew it was breakfast-time in Ontario. Sherene told me Jesse was sleeping after a reasonably comfortable night. She never complains but I could tell by her voice that it had been a sleepless night for her. At that moment, the long-range goals of the Journey didn't seem important. Jesse's health was the only thing on my mind. "Don't worry, honey. He'll be fine," Sherene said. But when I hung up the phone and stepped out onto the highway, for the first time since I dipped my shoes in the Atlantic Ocean back in Newfoundland, I thought about going home.

This was the toughest day I had faced since Day 1. If an instrument existed to measure the emotional strain I felt, the needle would have been buried deep into the red danger zone. But I tried to draw on my resolve of earlier days. There was nothing I could do except carry on and hope I had made the right choice.

The wind was driving thin streamers of snow across the highway at right angles and the frigid temperature made it a miserable day for walking. Visibility was limited and transport trucks swung well into the passing lane when they came upon us. But not much of this registered with me. I was worried about my son and my mind was back in Ontario. I asked myself what Jesse would want me to do. Knowing how he felt about the value of research, I kept moving.

We reached Gull Lake the next day and at suppertime there was good news from home. Jesse was feeling better! Sherene said he'd slept for a large part of the day and that Charlie, Jesse's faithful little white dog, had kept him company all day at the foot of the bed.

In Gull Lake we found ourselves roughing it again. My motel room was ice cold and this time there was no little oil stove to warm things up. I was at one end of a line of rooms and the thermostat controlling the heat for the whole row was in a room at the other end. My room had two single beds so I took all the blankets off one, piled them on the other one and then crawled underneath. The good news from home about Jesse made all the difference in the world. I was sound asleep in minutes but not before little box No. 226 was moved to the "completed" side.

Saskatchewan wasn't going to let us escape without making us feel the power of its November winds. From Gull Lake to Maple Creek, the last town in Saskatchewan before we reached the Alberta border, I put my head down and leaned into it. It was blowing hard and gave no sign of letting up. Parked well off the side of the highway, the motorhome swayed as it was buffeted. It's incredible how much energy it takes to fight the wind and by the time I climbed into the motorhome at break time, I was exhausted. For days the wind kept blowing, sometimes pushing me backward. In all the time we'd been on the road, I had never encountered anything like these winds in Saskatchewan. I just concentrated on taking one windblown step at a time as we moved closer to Alberta.

"They" say that, "When the going gets tough, the tough get going." "They" forgot to add that a sense of humour helps and that laughter can make a tough job a whole lot easier. Near Maple Creek, Bevin Palmateer put on an impromptu skit that looked like a meeting of the Wild West and the NHL. His timing was perfect because a good laugh was just what we needed on our final days in Province No. 8.

It was lunchtime and outside the motorhome, Bevin was standing in the wind, shooting video for one of his weekly television reports back east.

Beyond where he stood and running parallel to the highway was a five-foot-high wire fence extending as far as you could see. The fence was covered from top to bottom with tumbleweeds driven by the wind, making it look like a shaggy woollen wall. The tumbleweeds were bigger than beach balls and some were blowing past Bevin as he finished his camera work. Giving us a nod that said, "Hey, watch this," he put on his best goalkeeper moves and tried to stop the tumbleweeds flying by. He looked like a cross between a goalie and rodeo steer wrestler. Maybe you had to be there, but it was pretty funny.

FOUR-LEGGED COWBOY

During our time in Saskatchewan, the motorhome was almost always visible to me. Day after day, Ed would drive seven or eight kilometres ahead, park and wait for me to catch up. Then he'd repeat the pattern. But he was seldom out of sight. Space is something they have plenty of in Western Canada. The landscape is flat and the highway is a lesson in perspective in both directions. To the east and to the west, the road and the accompanying line of telephone poles run to the horizon, where they disappear. On the Trans-Canada Highway, even the median is sometimes more than 30 metres wide.

Slowly, the landscape began to change as the brown and yellow wheat stubble was replaced by fields of grazing cattle. At lunch one day we watched a couple of cowboys on horseback rounding up some cattle that had strayed onto the railway tracks after slipping through an open gate. The cowboys had to work hard to get the cattle under control. But the most remarkable herding job I saw on the Prairies wasn't done by cowboys but by a dog!

The mother ship was parked at a right angle to the highway and backed into a bit of a laneway to nowhere, where it stood out like a sore thumb on the wide-open Prairie expanse. Beyond the motorhome there were about 100 sheep grazing. They seemed to be free to wander wherever they wanted, except in the mind of the black and white sheepdog watching them. The spot where the sheep and the dog staged their version of a Prairie showdown was well back from the road. The sheepdog looked over at us once in a while with no more than casual interest. We weren't her responsibility. But the sheep were and it was fascinating to see.

As she lay in the grass and looked back and forth, the dog kept a close eye on the flock. There seemed to be a line in the dog's mind that the sheep were not to cross. It was obvious the dog was well-trained and it was like watching a game. The sheep would wander closer and closer to the imaginary line that ran parallel to the highway. All the dog had to do was stand up and the sheep would turn and retreat back into the field. There was no question who was in charge.

The monotony of flat land, straight road and the endless line of telephone poles was often broken by the movement of freight trains. They may joke that Saskatchewan is so flat you can watch your dog run away from home for three days, but it was true that when we looked to the horizon, we could sometimes see as many as three trains approaching. They crawled toward us on the tracks beside the highway like long black snakes slithering in straight lines.

We'd see a train's three powerful headlights long before we could hear any sound. Then, about 30 seconds before the train reached us, we'd begin to hear it rumble along the tracks. The engineers would send a greeting with a blast of the whistle and the authoritative sound would roll out across the open expanse until silence dominated the landscape once more.

After leaving Maple Creek, we logged our final kilometres in Saskatchewan on Sunday, November 22. It was the 35th anniversary of the assassination of U.S. President John F. Kennedy. Everyone in my generation knows exactly where they were and what they were doing when they heard the news that he had been shot. Bevin was 10 months old at the time. I guess that's why my legs were suddenly telling me that maybe I should have walked across Canada 30 years earlier. But then I again asked myself, "What wouldn't you do for your kids?" and I moved the box labelled No. 230. The next day I walked into Alberta.

· ALBERTA ·

"Be yourself; who else is better qualified?"
~ Frank J. Giblin

A steady stream of people came into our lives on the road to Medicine Hat. The mother of a boy with cerebral palsy stopped to give me a big hug. At break time, another mom approached with her young son, a boy she had been told would never be able to walk or talk. I was happy to see he could do both very well. In the town of Irvine, the Lions Club made a donation of $500 and after lunch, a man who stopped to make a contribution said, "That's in memory of my son." He left without further explanation.

At city hall in Medicine Hat we were greeted by employees of the Royal Bank, who donated $7,500 to Jesse's Journey. That night in Redcliff, members of the Lions and Lioness Clubs proudly showed off their red vests covered with pins gathered from other clubs. After they also welcomed us to Alberta, I spoke about our journey across Canada and our hopes for research as the audience listened intently. The red vests reminded me of our earliest days on the road when the yellow-vested Lions and Lioness Clubs of Whitbourne, Newfoundland treated us to a fish and brewis dinner. Almost nine months later, more members of this family of clubs were reaching out to help a father they'd never met in a cause many of them were learning about for the first time. They had raised more than $4,000, taking the dream a step closer to the day when we would be able to give the research community $1 million a year for as long as it takes to find a cure.

Back at our motel in Medicine Hat, it was late when I called home to Ontario. A weight was lifted when Sherene told me Jesse was much better and that she and the boys were doing fine. The news that Jesse was feeling very positive and looking forward to the trip to France would let me sleep well. I wrote in my journal and went to bed. It had been a very good day.

Life's rewards aren't always big and they most assuredly aren't always financial. That little bit of news from home wouldn't have registered a blip on the radar screen of the universe but it brought a mountain of joy to me. We could all learn something if we took a few seconds as we looked in the mirror each morning to inventory "what really matters." If we did that, our days might be a lot different.

LAST DAYS ON THE PRAIRIES

It was late November and the foothills of the Rockies would soon dominate the landscape. Our first sight of the mountains was still a few days away but there was a sense of anticipation. More than six weeks of looking at a bald, treeless landscape, even one saved by the magic of a big sky, were coming to an end.

From Medicine Hat to Brooks, it was sunny but very cold and the Trans-Canada Highway shifted away from being a truly east-west corridor as it bent to the northwest. There were still 120 kilometres of telephone poles, 80-kilometre-an-hour winds and not much else between us and Calgary. When we left Saskatchewan we had moved from Central to Mountain Time but at the eastern side of the new time zone, it hadn't affected the brightness of the days: 7 a.m. in eastern Alberta was as bright as 8 a.m. in western Saskatchewan. However, the time change meant getting up even earlier for morning radio interviews in Ontario and as far back as the Maritimes. In the outdoor space of "my office," one metre wide and 33 kilometres long, I felt like my blood was beginning to thicken for winter and I was slowly getting used to the bitter cold that would be with us for at least a month.

We were on the road with just the Mickey van as Ed had taken the motorhome on to Calgary to be serviced. In the morning, we received a call from Ed's wife Kay back in Newfoundland. She was calling from a live concert on Bell Island and as I shivered at the side of an Alberta road on my way into Bassano, I listened to the voices of Newfoundlanders thousands of kilometres away singing Jingle Bells for me. It was another moment for the memory bank.

Because we didn't have the motorhome, we didn't have any milk for tea, but at least we had some fruit. Then two truck drivers stopped to make a donation and one made our day when he gave us a box of shortbread cookies, along with my first Christmas card. It wasn't the first time and it wouldn't be the last that something arrived just when we needed it. It was another of those times when it felt like someone was looking out for us.

Our arrival in Brooks meant we were less than a week away from Calgary. On the last Sunday of November I spoke to a group of Rotarians and firefighters. After hearing what I had to say, a young physiotherapist reached into her purse for her chequebook and donated $1,000. She too believed in research and she and I shared a passion for getting things done.

The community of Bassano bills itself as "the best in the West by a dam site." This is where you find the Bow River dams, which provide irrigation to more than 800 square kilometres of land. Farmers here raise cattle or grow wheat, oats and canola, as Bassano enjoys Alberta's longest growing season.

Early on the last day of November, I called home to London to say goodbye to Sherene, Jesse and my friend Mario Chioini. This was the day they were leaving for France. I told them I knew they would all do a good job. The media was at our house as I talked to Jesse and wished him a safe trip. Sherene told me Air France had scheduled a news conference at the airport. Jesse, no longer a little boy but a young man now, was going to help others in a country he had never visited. When I pushed the "end" button on the cellphone in the van and stepped back onto the road, there was a brief feeling of loneliness. Home felt like a long way away. But there was an even greater feeling of pride. I was proud of Jesse, who always measured life not by the things he couldn't do but by the things he did.

Between Bassano and Strathmore the highway runs north before making a 90-degree turn toward Calgary. On foot, you can see things you might easily miss in a car. Just before the highway made its big sweeping curve, there was a long slow grade. As I made the climb, off in the distance beyond the foothills, the snow-capped beginnings of the Rocky Mountains came into view for the first time. The blue sky and morning sun made it an even more dramatic moment. It meant the Prairies were behind us and we were well into "Wild Rose Country," as Alberta calls itself. Our goal had been to cross the flattest part of Canada in six weeks and we had achieved it, proving again the value of designing your plan so you can win and then sticking with it. Our final and perhaps biggest challenge awaited – the Great Divide.

JUST HANG ON FOR ONE MORE MONTH

The thrill of seeing the Rockies dulled a bit when I finally had to admit I wasn't nearly as mentally sharp as I had been earlier in the Journey. There were times I just wasn't alert. My timing had slowed and I was struggling more each day to make my distance. I seemed to be tiring earlier each day and to complicate matters, my back had been sore for several days. If there was ever a time to dig deeper into whatever reserves I had left, this was it.

I took stock of my situation in relation to the big picture. It was December and we were into our ninth month on the road. A total of 240 imaginary boxes of work had been marked "completed." With just over a month to go, we were 200 kilometres from the British Columbia border and Province number 10. But the tougher things had become, the more I knew how personally meaningful this journey was for me. The road seemed to challenge me by repeatedly asking how much I wanted this, how much I wanted to finish what I started so many months ago. The plan was unfolding the way it was designed but I had become more aware of how it was punishing my 52-year-old body. I needed to refocus because now, as always, quitting was not an option.

Ed took the lead role as the road crew turned its attention to working on my back and legs at every opportunity. There wasn't any panic, but if I was to finish at all, the road crew would have to keep me going.

Sometimes people stopped when the motorhome was parked beside the highway, not just to make a donation but to take a break from the snow and cold for a few minutes. At noon one day, a little girl came on-board with her dad to make a donation and to have a look at what she called my "house." On another occasion, Ed shared coffee with a fellow Newfoundlander, a transport truck driver who stopped to make a contribution while hauling Christmas trees from Wisconsin to Calgary and Edmonton.

In Strathmore, east of Calgary, they know what hard work is all about. This town of 6,000 was where history was made July 28, 1883, the day Canadian Pacific Railway workers set a record by laying more than 10 miles of track in a single day, ending in what would become Strathmore. At the time, the CPR was in charge of naming the hamlets that sprung up at its sidings as the steel rails spread west. There's no record of who named Strathmore, but a Scot named James Ross was in charge of the project and he had a tendency to give the sidings Scottish names.

Strathmore still exhibits a solid work ethic more than 100 years later. On the Trans-Canada, which passes right through town, the thriving and energetic community gave us a tremendous welcome. It was humbling to have firefighters say it was an honour to meet me as they escorted us into town with sirens screaming. Beside the road, 400 kids from the local public school were chanting, "Go, John, go." As I shook hands, one teenage girl said she was proud of me and that she thought what I was doing was really important. That night I spoke to the Lions Club of Strathmore at its last dinner meeting before Christmas. The turkey and all the trimmings reminded me we wouldn't be home for Christmas. It was a clear night and freezing cold as we drove back to the motel. Looking up at the stars in the black sky, I wondered how Jesse was making out in France.

Calgary and hospitality go hand in hand. In earlier times, the home of the world-famous stampede conjured up images of cowboys and cattle ranching, but the riches that lie beneath Alberta's soil, oil and natural gas, have moved the city that hosted the 1988 Winter Olympics onto the world stage. In true western fashion, I was presented with a white Stetson hat when I reached Calgary. The official welcome to "Cowtown" took place in the sunshine and frosty air at the city limits sign. Wearing my Stetson and feeling very much like a westerner, I was sworn in at the roadside as an official Calgarian. As I faced a battery of microphones, cameras and newspaper reporters, I was asked a lot of questions about the walk across Canada, questions about what I was doing and why. I welcomed every chance to talk about how funding research is an investment in our future and I stressed how research would provide the answers to make life better for kids like Jesse.

After the crowd dispersed back into the city and the warmth of wherever they were going, we got back to work on the Trans-Canada. Although the sun was shining, it was freezing cold and the crew cautioned me to keep checking my face for frostbite. At the end of the day, Jesse's Journey was in the heart of Calgary.

There was a real buzz of excitement in the city as everywhere we looked, people were getting ready for Christmas. For our crew, the festivities included taking part in the Santa Claus parade. Those who lined the streets applauded when they saw the Jesse's Journey banner and we really got into the spirit of things as we tossed some early Christmas presents into the crowd – Jesse's Journey T-shirts, rolled up tightly and bound by an elastic. I kept scanning the crowd and made a point to say hello and give a T-shirt to every child or young person in a wheelchair. Too often, some children only get to watch life's parade pass by. Along the route, the smiles I received from kids in wheelchairs were the gifts I received in return.

There were lots of group pictures taken in the afternoon as a delegation representing Rotary Clubs in the Calgary area stopped by our hotel. As cameras flashed, one Rotarian talked to me about the difficulties that lay ahead in the Rockies. Then he patted me on the back and said, "Give 'em hell, John!"

At the Saddledome we were guests of the NHL's Calgary Flames, who were playing Phoenix that night. During an interview as part of the television broadcast, I was given a Calgary Flames shirt with Jesse's Journey stitched on the back and at the Flames' post-game radio show, I met the team coach. I didn't expect him to be in a very good mood because his team had lost 3-2, but he knew it was just one game. He told me he thought I was a good dad and said he was amazed at what I had been able to accomplish. As I introduced the members of the road crew, I told the coach that just as in hockey, it was the efforts of the whole team that had led to our success. I was just the lucky guy with the highest profile.

TRIUMPHANT RETURN

Our time in Calgary gave me a brief chance to rest both my lower back and my legs before we set out for Banff, Lake Louise and the British Columbia border. As I thought about the Rockies, it suddenly dawned on me that at that moment, Jesse, his mom and Mario were on their way home from France. I hoped things had gone well and that we hadn't asked Jesse to take on too much. I decided to give the group a day to adjust to the time change before I called home.

West of Calgary, Ed had picked a most unusual place to park the motorhome at lunchtime. At the crest of a hill, the vehicle sat in the middle of the enormous median dividing the four lanes of the Trans-Canada. Our mother ship was facing west and through the windshield, the lanes converged as they disappeared in the distance. Under a clear blue sky, with just a few wisps of cloud to add to the picture, we had a spectacular, panoramic view of the Rocky Mountains.

Back out on the highway leading to Canmore, two transport truck drivers, a man and a woman, stopped to make a donation. The man said he had passed me several times as he'd driven back and forth across the western provinces. "Week after week I've watched you making your way across the Prairies and now here you are," he said.

Three teenagers, two boys and a girl, came running up the highway to make a donation. One of the boys had on a Toronto Maple Leafs jersey and all three had pierced ears and lots of earrings. They wanted to shake my hand. "This is a good thing that you're doing," the girl said. Just as it was getting dark, a woman from a farmhouse in the distance walked down the road to make the final donation of Day 243. On the motorhome as we headed back to Calgary for our final night there, I heard that Jesse, Sherene and Mario were safely home. I was tired but it was a good kind of tired and I knew I'd sleep well.

We had packed up the duffel bags for another move and there was only one piece of business left to attend to before driving out to our starting point, which was now well west of Calgary. I had one last medical check-up scheduled before we set out to cross the Rocky Mountains en route to Vancouver. I knew my body had taken quite a pounding since leaving Newfoundland in April and was a little concerned about this final check-up. The doctor took a long time looking me over before finally giving me the OK to keep going.

Back on the road, just as I was ready to set out toward Canmore, I received a call from home. With their body clocks back on Canadian time, Sherene and Jesse wanted me to know the telethon in France was a tremendous success. It raised $116 million for research! And yes, Jesse did get to go up the Eiffel Tower. That was just the kind of news I needed to hear on the day a vicious wind ushered in the challenge of crossing the Rocky Mountains.

THE START OF THE FINISH

The flat land that started as soon as we crossed the border from Ontario into Manitoba ended just as quickly about 60 kilometres west of Calgary. As we headed into the mountains, there was a definite divide, when we could look back and define the end of the flat expanses back toward Calgary.

The wind rushing through the gap felt like it was ripping right through me. It was cold and another day when I had to lean into the wind to keep moving forward. And there was a new problem. The coarse sand that had been spread on the road during earlier snowfalls felt like buckshot as it stung my face in the gusts created by passing trucks. I spent most of the day on the road by myself because I wanted our volunteers to be well-rested for what was ahead. They were our most valuable asset and while we had managed to avoid colds and the flu, this wasn't the time to push our luck. I was going to need all of these people in top condition to get us across the Rockies.

I thought back to the inventory I had done a few days earlier. I wouldn't make it without the volunteers, but the responsibility of taking one step at a time was squarely on me. I realized again that some things in life you just have to do on your own. This was quite literally where my shoe rubber had to meet the road. British Columbia was not that far away, but I expected getting there would be character-building, to say the least. Our itinerary for the following days sounded pretty intimidating: the Rocky Mountains, the Monashee Mountains, the Cascade Mountains and the Coast Mountains. Despite the wind and cold, I was glad to be there, even though I had no idea of the challenges these mountains would throw our way.

A young couple on a ski trip to Banff stopped to make a donation. They couldn't believe how long I had been on the road. An older woman who handed me an envelope of money said, "God bless you and thank you for what you're doing." A tall, bearded tractor-trailer driver wanted me to know he had three kids at home and how thankful he was that they were all healthy. He looked like he had tears in his eyes, or maybe it was just the wind making his eyes water. I didn't really know; I was just glad he stopped.

Canmore started in the 1880s as a railway and coal mining town. Now it has cashed in on its proximity to the mountains to become a paradise for yuppies.

The stylish condominiums, trendy shops and motels were decked out in clear white Christmas lights. For the ski crowd, Canmore is a fashion statement. But like all the other towns across Canada, it's the people who make the real difference.

At the edge of town, a smiling group of Royal Bank employees joined us for the walk into Canmore. We shared stories about our travels across Canada and they told us about the choices in their lives that had led them to call this place home. Each had a different story but all had asked themselves what was important and where did they really want to live. In Canmore, the mayor and representatives of both the Lions Club and the Rotary Club made contributions to Jesse's Journey.

At Banff National Park, there was no charge for the motorhome or the vans as park employees welcomed us to one of the most beautiful places in Alberta and waved us through the park gates. At one of our breaks, Ed told us that using his binoculars, he had seen a bear going into a cave on a mountain side. I was sorry I'd missed seeing that, but I'd had my own special moment. On the road, a cute little girl of about seven or eight had run back from her mom's pickup truck to meet me. She wanted to make a donation and as she shook my hand she said, "I hope your son is going to be OK." As I guided her back to her mom's truck, it hit me again how kids don't have an agenda. They just want to help.

I'm not sure whether I was looking for some magic elixir or just a chance to rest my tired muscles, but in Banff, we all went for a soothing soak in the hot springs. In Newfoundland, I was too early to see icebergs and in Ontario, too early to enjoy the autumn leaves in their full glory. On the Prairies, I was too late to see the yellow fields of grain blowing in the wind. But in scenic Banff, a town of 8,000 that plays host to as many as five million tourists a year, the hot springs are always waiting, no matter when you arrive.

A lot of strange things had happened over the last nine months on the road, so I suppose I shouldn't have been surprised by something I saw in in Banff. But then again... In a small bookshop on the main street, a little girl was getting her book "pawtographed" by a dog. The story was that the owner of the shop had written a book about his dog, which was a kind of mascot for the store, and if you bought a copy of the book, you could get it signed by the dog. The owner would touch the dog's paw on an inkpad and then press the paw on one of the inside pages of the book and presto – a "pawtograph." Only in Canada.

The only disappointing thing about Banff was that I didn't get to see Tyler, my oldest son, who was going to school there. He was in Vancouver at the time.

A GREAT DAY FOR KODAK!

It was dark when we took up our starting position on the shoulder of the Trans-Canada as we left Banff for Lake Louise. From the escort van, Ted Eadinger honked the horn to get my attention so he could point out the sunrise in the eastern sky. As I moved west, I didn't often turn around to see the arrival of dawn, but on this day, it was worth it. The black of the Alberta sky was being pushed aside by a rich red and lavender colour. It was one of those scenes that, despite its grandeur, looked almost gaudy, a bit like those paintings you see on television commercials promoting a starving artists' show and sale – too fantastic to be real.

The wind had died down and in the sunshine, the kilometres between Banff and Lake Louise were sheer magic as light and shadow played like a giant kaleidoscope on the green of the fir trees and the snow-capped mountains. But like a kaleidoscope, the picture soon changed.

Lake Louise, Canada's most famous lake because of its turquoise waters and magnificent setting, is named for Princess Louise Caroline Alberta, a daughter of Queen Victoria. It has been photographed by millions of tourists and is emblazoned on postcards mailed all over the world. We were a day away from Lake Louise when the weather suddenly changed. The Trans-Canada soon became covered in a sheet of ice and a steady rain from low clouds kept polishing the slippery road with another coating of water. Getting a foothold was as difficult as trying to walk on a freshly waxed and polished wood floor wearing new woollen socks. The ice made the fir trees and everything that could be seen from the road look like they were coated with glass.

Up and down the icy two-lane road, trucks moved forward just a few feet at a time. The dripping wet tires just a couple of feet from me were turning so slowly I could easily read the manufacturers' names on them. One by one the tractor-trailers crept slowly past, each with all its hazard lights flashing. Then

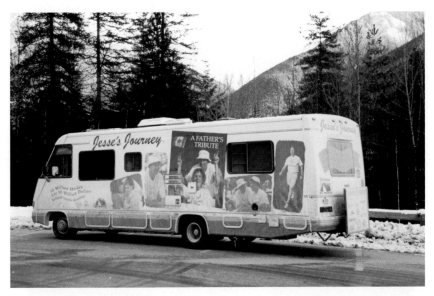

MOTHER SHIP – The Jesse's Journey motorhome, or the mother ship, as the road team called it, waits along the side of a British Columbia highway for John Davidson to catch up. This game of leap-frog was played for almost 8,300 kilometres across Canada.

286 DAYS LATER – John Davidson dips his running shoes into the Pacific Ocean at the foot of Beacon Hill in Victoria, British Columbia on January 20, 1999, the final day of his epic journey across Canada and his 53rd birthday.

PROUD MOMENT – Jesse Davidson, then 16, is shown following his investiture into the Order of Ontario in 1996 – a recognition of his heroic efforts to raise money for research into Duchenne muscular dystrophy.

we passed trucks that had slid off the road. The day was a real nail-biter for me and the volunteers in the escort van behind me. We weren't worried about donations, just safety.

From Chateau Lake Louise, which was built in 1928 to replace the original CPR hotel built in 1890, the lake probably looks very pretty under a fresh blanket of snow. Although our rooms were on the lake side of the chateau, I wouldn't know. By the time our little snow-covered convoy arrived in the dark, there was nothing to see. A dozen floors below our rooms, there was a yellow glow from the light standards in the empty parking lot, where the motorhome and vans look like children's toys. Otherwise, we could see nothing from our windows but black night. Snow clouds hid the moon and there was no way to confirm Lake Louise was even there. In the morning, the same blackness was all we saw as we left in the dark to reach our starting point.

BELIEVE IT OR NOT... AGAIN!

There's really no way to explain luck or the lack of it, but one of our strangest stories, involving both good and bad luck, materialized on the snow-covered Trans-Canada on our last day in Alberta. Our jack-of-all-trades, Ed Coxworthy, had moved the motorhome ahead and was waiting for us to catch up. He had taken one of the flashing lights from the top of one of the escort vans because it was broken and he was going to try to repair it. The trouble turned out to be the plug on the end of the wire, a piece of black plastic that plugged into what used to be called a cigarette lighter. These ports are now called utility outlets because they can power everything from CD players to air pumps. When Ed examined the plug, he saw that the black plastic piece was broken beyond repair and concluded we would have to have to make do without the light until we reached someplace where the broken piece could be replaced.

The bad luck part of the story was that when Ed pulled to the side of the road, the motorhome got stuck in the snow – not badly, but still it was stuck. Part of the good luck was that when we were in Ontario, Ed had the foresight to buy two things in anticipation of bad weather. First, he bought an all-weather snowsuit at a place called The Trading Post in Northern Ontario. I kidded him because it was one of about 50 places we passed all called The Trading Post. The second thing Ed bought was a shovel for each vehicle.

After they shovelled the snow out from under the motorhome tires, Ed and Bevin managed to rock the vehicle back and forth until they freed it from the snow. That's when the good luck really happened. Ed spotted a piece of wire sticking out of the fresh snow, right where the doorsteps opened out from the motorhome. Curious, he pulled the wire to see what was on the other end. After a couple of tugs the wire came free and on the previously hidden end was the exact type of plug Ed needed to plug into the utility outlet to operate the rotating light! We didn't know whether to believe Ed and Bevin but Ed swore it was a true story. What are the odds? In any case, Ed fixed the flashing light and we were back in business.

It was snowing heavily in the afternoon and it took me a long time to finish the final 11 kilometres of the day. The fresh snow made it a bit like walking in sludge and I was hit a couple of times by stones kicked up by passing trucks. It was as if I was standing next to a welder and feeling the sting of tiny bits of hot metal hitting my skin.

The shortest day of the year was just over a week away and it was dark as I approached the escort vehicles. The headlights of one of vans were shining on Bevin, who was standing at the roadside with the lens of his video camera up to his eye. If it hadn't been for him, I wouldn't have seen the huge stone cairn marker that sits back from the side of the road and reads "Welcome to British Columbia." It was just past 5 p.m. on Sunday, December 13 and we had just entered Province No. 10. Tomorrow would be Day 250 and the end was almost in sight.

· BRITISH COLUMBIA ·

"Do not let what you cannot do interfere with what you can do."
~ John Wooden

From the beginning I had thought that if we made it to Winnipeg, we might have a chance to complete the journey. But I was convinced that if I stepped into British Columbia, we would definitely make it to Victoria. I didn't come this far not to finish.

The Canadian Pacific Railways' spiral tunnels at Kicking Horse Pass, between Lake Louise, Alberta and Field, British Columbia, are an engineering marvel. About 700,000 people a year stop in British Columbia's Yoho National Park, many of them just to watch trains wind through the tunnels, which are even more amazing when you consider they were completed in 1909. Over a distance of 7.4 kilometres, the tunnels permit trains travelling east or west to iron out the 130-metre difference in height between the top and bottom of Kicking Horse Pass.

The pattern for the spiral tunnels came from a railway design in Switzerland, where switchbacks and looping tunnels cut through the Alps to eliminate steep grades. At Kicking Horse Pass, the lower spiral tunnel circles through Mount Ogden before switching back to where the upper spiral tunnel curves through Cathedral Crags. As many as 30 trains a day make the 47-minute journey through the tunnels. As we walked the Trans-Canada, we were just in time to see the engine of a freight train emerge from one end of the lower tunnel while the last of the freight cars it was pulling had yet to disappear into the other end of the same tunnel.

From Field, the highway rose and fell as it wound through the mountains to Golden. The government of British Columbia had advised us that I would not be allowed to walk the final 16 kilometres of precipitous road leading into Golden. When I had a chance to look at this piece of road, which was under construction and full of tight turns, I was not surprised by the ban.

I sat in the front passenger seat as the motorhome began to descend into Golden on the narrow road and the reasons we couldn't walk it became apparent. On my right, the jagged rock face, about 75 metres high at times, was draped with netting to prevent falling rock from hitting vehicles below. On the opposite side of the two-lane road beyond the concrete guardrail, the drop was too steep to let me see the lights of Golden in the darkness far below. Tractor-trailers and logging trucks heading east were in low gear as they made the slow climb up the hill out of town. The following morning, as we made the hair-raising drive east and back to the starting point, the road reminded me of every story I had ever read about buses tumbling down the sides of mountains in South America. From the starting point I walked until I reached the beginning of the "banned" road leading down into Golden. Then we went back toward our day's starting point and I repeated the 16 kilometres I had just finished in order to "patch in" the section of road I wasn't permitted to walk. That's what we'd done all across Canada when we encountered impassable roads.

In Golden, where the Columbia and Kicking Horse Rivers converge, we were greeted by firefighters, the mayor and representatives from the Rotary Club, Kinette Club and Shriners. We had supper on the motorhome, where Ed had made a traditional Newfoundland "Jigg's dinner" of salt beef and pease pudding, a combination of yellow split peas, turnip, carrots and potatoes all cooked in one big pot. Ann Hutchison, in her sixth province with us, had decorated a cake for dessert. It had the "less than" symbol and the number 1,000. The countdown was on. On the night I moved box No. 252 to the "completed" side, the ledger read 7,300 kilometres down and less than 1,000 to go.

THE REAL ROCKY MOUNTAIN HIGH

From the very beginning, when I began to sketch the plan for the journey in my mind, one obstacle loomed large: I knew I would have to make the trek through Rogers Pass in December. Even when the final route was selected, no one talked about what we all thought would be the toughest part of the Trans-Canada Highway.

The highway through Rogers Pass was completed in 1962 and runs parallel to the railway tracks but the incredible story of the railway unfolded long before anyone ever thought about building a road. In 1881, the Canadian Pacific Railway directed one of its surveyors, an American from Massachusetts named Major A. B. Rogers, to find a route for railroad tracks through the uninhabited and uninhabitable Selkirk Mountains. Rogers was 52 years old when he discovered the pass late that year. Historians have noted that he was a foul-mouthed man who chewed tobacco and that he didn't care about the $5,000 he would earn for finding a passage through the mountains. More than anything else, he wanted his name attached to the route that would lead to the Pacific.

Rogers Pass was the linchpin to the completion of the tracks that would unite Canada. But laying those tracks was no easy job. Ravines on the east side of the pass had to be bridged and on the west side were steep grades that necessitated construction of a long series of loops. In all, 13 bridges were built over the Illecillewait River between Rogers Pass and Revelstoke. Unbelievably, the tracks were completed by 1885, but in its first winter of operation, the railway line was closed by snow. The following year, 31 snow sheds were built right over the rail lines, a cumulative distance of about 6.5 kilometres, to protect the tracks from avalanches and keep the trains moving through the pass. Nevertheless, deadly avalanches along the tracks were not unknown in subsequent years. It would be another 77 years before there was a road to parallel the tracks.

NOT SO FAST

I couldn't decide whether our volunteers were simply in a hurry to get through Rogers Pass or whether I was just feeling the effects of being on the road for so long, but for the first time I could remember, I had to ask everybody on the crew to slow down a bit when they were walking with me. I was well aware that I was sluggish on the climb to the summit and I was having trouble keeping up with them. The good news was the weather. Our fears about having to battle heavy snow were so far unfounded. Indeed our biggest problem through Rogers Pass was thick clouds of gritty dust sent swirling into the air by passing transport trucks. The sand got in our eyes and teeth.

Breathing was difficult and we needed a lot of bottled water to rinse the dust from our eyes and to stop the coughing that came with every new cloud of dirt.

Although we had moved into the Pacific Time Zone, we had decided to keep the team on Alberta time until we reached Revelstoke, to make radio interviews in Eastern Canada easier.

It was just one week until Christmas and we were close to the summit of Rogers Pass in Glacier National Park. It had been a difficult climb in bone-chilling temperatures. The pass had taken a long time to complete because I had to go back and repeat some sections three times to make up distance lost because it wasn't safe to walk through the snow sheds that covered the highway in spots. It was too dark inside the sheds, with only a single lane in each direction.

On the final push to the top of Rogers Pass, Ed left the motorhome and for the first time in our travels together, he joined me on the road. Ed, who was a smoker, had only one lung. No one was allowed to smoke on the motorhome or any of the vehicles and I was willing to bet it wouldn't be long before Ed gave up cigarettes. I figured anyone with the stamina to walk through Rogers Pass in the winter probably had what it takes to quit smoking. I was soon proved right. Ed stopped smoking a month later and hasn't had a cigarette since.

When I called home December 18, Sherene told me Jesse was feeling a little down. He was a handsome young man, but a handsome young man in a wheelchair, and Sherene said she thought he was feeling low because he didn't have a girlfriend. Although life doesn't make any promises, it still seems pretty unfair sometimes. I knew Jesse would bounce back because he was that kind of kid. But as I was shifting box No. 254 and thinking there were just a couple of dozen more to go, I was wishing I could be home.

It was -20 C. when we took Mickey back east through the snow sheds to our morning starting point. We'd catch up with the motorhome at lunchtime at one of the snowplough turnarounds. In the cold, I had to keep checking the skin on my face for frostbite. By midday we were in the sunshine and had finally reached the marker at the summit of Rogers Pass. We stopped to take some pictures and by early afternoon we caught up with the motorhome, where Ed had hot soup and toasted bacon sandwiches waiting for us. As my back and legs were being worked on, I fell asleep knowing that when we returned to the road, we'd be moving downhill.

We lost daylight sooner than expected as we descended into a valley and I finish my distance for the day in the dark. Then we drove back to the summit for our final night in Glacier National Park, before moving on to Revelstoke. Our passage through Rogers Pass and a part of British Columbia where there are more than 400 glaciers had been relatively smooth. Other than having to deal with extreme cold, we had escaped unscathed from one of the country's most active areas for avalanches, where the annual snowfall has been known to reach 23 metres. But our luck was about to run out.

NEWFIE INGENUITY AT ITS BEST!

Five days before Christmas, one of the most memorable stories of the entire journey unfolded high in the Rockies. The scene was Glacier National Park on the day we were scheduled to move ahead to Revelstroke. The temperature was -27 C. and the motorhome and both vans were covered in a thick layer of frost. It was just after 6 a.m. and Ed had his famous Newfoundland porridge bubbling on the stove. The motorhome engine was running and it was warming up inside, but the vans had yet to be started. After scraping frost from the windows and getting the engines started, we left the mini-vans to warm up and retreated to the motorhome for breakfast. Suddenly we heard a loud bang and a strange grinding sound. We didn't know what it was but we knew it couldn't be good.

It took only a second for Ed to realize the sound was coming from the Mickey van and he immediately sprung into action. Without stopping to put on his coat, he was out the door of the motorhome and ran to shut off the engine of the van. When he lifted the hood, he found the source of the grinding sound. It wasn't serious damage, but we'd lost a fan belt. Unfortunately, we were a long way from help and on this stretch of road, we needed both vans. Ed, the jack-of-all-trades, was in for another test.

He decided there might be a solution. After removing the matching rubber fan belt from the other van, Ed took a fish-filleting knife and very carefully sliced through the middle of the good fan belt, all the way around, to make two slightly thinner fan belts out of one thick one. In the bitter cold, as Ed looped these half-belts back onto their respective pulleys, we crossed our fingers. When he started the engines, both belts held and, for the moment at least, both vans were operational.

However, the windshield-washer hose on the Mickey van had been severed by the shredded fan belt as it whipped around inside the engine compartment, meaning we couldn't get washer fluid onto the windshield. Ed went to work again.

The windshield-washer hose on the motorhome was long enough that Ed was able to cut a piece of it to repair the damaged hose on the Mickey van. The motorhome hose was smaller in diameter than the van hose so after heating each end of the thin hose he had appropriated from the motorhome, Ed used a ballpoint pen to enlarge it. With the help of some duct tape, he worked his magic to create a makeshift windshield-washer hose for the van. It wasn't perfect but we thought if we were lucky, it would probably last the day until we reached Revelstoke, where we could get everything repaired.

Back in the warmth of the motorhome as I was having breakfast, I smiled at Ed as I thought about his many talents and his impressive ingenuity. I felt proud of him and was thinking, "Not bad Coxworthy; not bad for a guy with a Grade 4 education!" The lesson was pretty simple and Ed was a perfect example of it. It doesn't matter how many titles you have in front of your name or how many initials you have after it but what you're willing and able to do in any given situation that defines a man.

The whole episode reminded me of Ed's wife Kay, who had told me back in Newfoundland, "You take my Ed with you. He can fix anything. He can even weld the rear end back onto a cat from the inside!" Kay was meeting us in Revelstoke the next morning and I was looking forward to telling her how close to the truth she was with her description of Ed's handyman talents.

'HOME' FOR THE HOLIDAYS

The approach of Christmas in the Rocky Mountains found everyone trying to stay busy, mostly to keep from thinking about family and friends back home. The holidays can be stressful but little things helped us survive and thrive. In

Revelstoke, Ann Hutchison, who was back on the road with us, this time with her husband Peter Garland, switched our usual healthy dessert of fruit to ice-cream topped with melted caramel, bananas and peanuts. Over tea and coffee, we decorated a tiny 15-centimetre Christmas tree. It was a gift from Peter and Ann who also brought a tiny wreath, about five centimetres in diameter, complete with flashing Christmas lights. The wreath, which fit easily into the palm of my hand, was just the right size for the motorhome. Peter and Ann had been tremendous volunteers, each walking with me in six provinces, and we'd miss them when they left the next morning to fly home for Christmas.

The merchants of Revelstoke presented us with a huge Christmas basket of goodies at a reception to welcome us to the town first known as "The Capital of Canada's Alps." After listening to our story, the mayor wrote a cheque for a generous donation, joining representatives of the Lions Club, the Rotary Club and firefighters, who also made presentations to Jesse's Journey.

On the morning of December 22, it was -16 C. as we hugged and said goodbye to the volunteers heading home for Christmas. The core members of the road crew were staying and one new recruit arrived to spend Christmas in the Rockies with us. More than one life was about to be changed.

Dianne Steward, who was born in the south of England, was a former medical secretary. With strawberry-blonde hair and sparkling blue eyes, she also had a lovely English accent. She hadn't been looking forward to Christmas on her own in London, so she called our office one day to say, "I don't have anyone, so if somebody on the road team wants to go home for Christmas, I could go to British Columbia." After a snow-delayed flight to Kelowna and a late-night drive through the mountains with an RCMP officer, Dianne arrived in Revelstoke at 2:30 a.m. Five hours later she was ready to go to work.

My friend Ted Eadinger, who was with us in Quebec and Saskatchewan, was back for another tour of duty and it didn't take him long to notice the new volunteer with the delightful accent. It was going to be a nice Christmas.

Bevin was still with us and Ed's wife Kay arrived from Newfoundland to round out the skeleton crew who would celebrate Christmas in the little town of Sicamous. Jesse's Journey would soon be moving south and down into the Okanagan Valley.

The road to Sicamous winds through some of the most majestic scenery in Canada. Just west of Revelstoke, surrounded by mountains, is Craigellachie, one of the most famous landmarks in Canadian history. It was at Craigellachie on November 7, 1885, that the last spike was driven, completing the Canadian Pacific Railway. At lunchtime, two days before Christmas, I took a picture of Ted and Dianne at the stone cairn that marks the exact spot where the last spike was hammered home. I had a feeling this might be a picture they'd keep for a lifetime together. Maybe it was the effect of Christmas or maybe I was just being a romantic, but it seemed to me even at that early stage that two people who needed someone had found each other in a place far from home. Day 259 left me feeling good and the reason for it was borne out when Ted and Dianne eventually married, a love found because two people had volunteered to help others with a commitment to Jesse's Journey.

Sicamous is called "The Houseboat Capital of Canada" due to the hundreds of houseboats rented each year to vacationers from the marinas on Shuswap Lake. A light snow with big picture-perfect snowflakes was falling when we reached the Monashee Motel, where we would spend Christmas Eve and Christmas Day. Jesse's older brother, Tyler, was due to arrive by bus from Vancouver and if the snow in the mountains wasn't too heavy, he should be in Sicamous in time for Christmas.

As so many service clubs had done many times before, the Lions and Rotarians of Sicamous worked together to surprise us by decorating our motel rooms. As the motorhome and vans rolled across fresh snow on the parking lot, we could see snow-covered Christmas lights on our balcony railings. It wasn't home, but it would our home for the holidays.

The Lions and Rotarians of Sicamous were a great bunch of people and went out of their way to make sure we had a merry Christmas. To make things easier, we learned names in relation to where people worked. Soon we were talking with our new friends, "hardware store John" and "grocery store Bob." On our first night in Sicamous, we were taken for a drive to look at the Christmas lights. I never imagined a town as small as this would have as many lights and with the snow falling and in the company of new-found friends, Sicamous did feel like home.

That seasonal delight was followed by a tour more pertinent to another season.

Houseboats manufactured in Sicamous are shipped all over the world. There were two levels on the houseboat we boarded, with a hot tub in the master bedroom on the second level and a gas fireplace to give the main-level family room a toasty glow. The kitchen had a huge island workstation and with a fridge and freezer, convection oven and microwave, there didn't seem to be anything missing. I was told this houseboat could be rented for about $4,000 a week. The purchase price was $286,000.

Our next stop was Moose Mulligan's Pub, where we were formally welcomed to Sicamous. With a glass of ginger ale I made a toast and thanked the group for all they had done to make our little troupe of Easterners feel at home. We had one more day on the road before taking a break for Christmas Day.

A CHRISTMAS TO REMEMBER

The morning of Christmas Eve was quiet in Sicamous. The snow that had been falling all night had yet to be ploughed and was about 6 inches deep. While the fresh white blanket was pretty to look at, it made walking difficult. The day that started peacefully would soon prove to be tiring, dangerous and beautiful, all at the same time.

It was still snowing when we reached our starting point east of town and got to work. The firefighters of Sicamous joined us to help collect donations and the sound of the siren echoing off the mountains attracted a lot of attention on a day most people were sitting by a fire or busy with last-minute wrapping.

The snow continued to pile up as we headed back to the mother ship for lunch. Almost completely covered with snow, the motorhome looked like a huge white lump. Ed, who always had lunch ready and waiting, said he thought Tyler would probably be late in arriving. He'd heard on the radio that buses from Vancouver to the interior were running late because of the snow. He didn't tell me there had been a crash involving a Greyhound bus and a tractor-trailer. Fortunately, no one was killed and we found out later that Tyler was on the bus in front of the one in the accident.

In the early afternoon it was snowing very heavily and we had to make a decision whether it was safe to continue. After the snowplough cleared what looked like a useable track, I decided to give it a try. Ed took the motorhome back into Sicamous, where it would remain until Boxing Day, and I stayed out on the road with the police to finish the distance for the day.

A young boy of 11 or 12 fought his way through the snow in the median to cross the road and make a donation. We saw him safely on his way, but the snow kept getting deeper and, though beautiful, it was starting to get dangerous. I had completed 26 kilometres of tough slogging. Visibility was poor and transport trucks were using their flashing lights as they crept past. In the fading light we headed back into Sicamous and our home away from home, at least for the next 48 hours.

Sicamous was silent on Christmas morning as we walked across the Trans-Canada to the Husky truck stop for a breakfast of orange juice, bacon, eggs and pancakes. Tyler had arrived safely the night before. There wasn't a car in sight and we joked about getting some sticks for a game of road hockey. Only in Canada could you play road hockey on the country's national highway on Christmas Day.

The unit Tyler and I were using had a small kitchenette with a stove. The Lions and Rotarians had decorated our rooms with strings of colourful Christmas lights and even gave us a turkey. By mid-afternoon, the smell of turkey roasting in the oven convinced us it was Christmas.

From our rooms we got a couple of mismatched Arborite tables with chrome legs that weren't exactly the same length. We pushed these together and added a collection of assorted chairs. With a tablecloth decorated with holly and berries, a handful of paper serviettes, a couple of tall white candles and whatever silverware and glasses we could find, seven of us – Ed and Kay Coxworthy, Ted Eadinger, Dianne Steward, Bevin Palmateer, Tyler and me – sat down to a Christmas dinner none of us would ever forget.

A motorhome is not an ideal place to hide Christmas presents and the days leading up to Christmas had been a bit of a comedy with everybody looking for secret spots. When you thought you'd come up with the perfect one, you'd discover something already hidden there. But when it was time to exchange gifts after dinner, it was amazing how many presents were produced from secret places in the motorhome and vans.

There were a lot of laughs as we opened gifts and every now and then over in the corner, "Bruce the Spruce," a foot-tall, sound-activated singing Christmas tree, would spring into action with another chorus of Jingle Bells. At the start of the day it was funny to see Bruce's mechanical jaw start to flap, but as the day wore on, tongue-in-cheek plots were being hatched to bring about Bruce's demise. Throughout the day, the phone lines hummed as everyone called family back in Ontario and Newfoundland.

On Boxing Day, we said goodbye to Sicamous. On the road we left the Trans-Canada for Highway 97A, which would take us south to Vernon and down through the Okanagan Valley. The road was narrower than the Trans-Canada, and at break time, as Ed tried to pull the motorhome as far to the side of the road as possible, he got it stuck in the snow. I walked on to the little town of Enderby while a farmer with a tractor helped Ed free the motorhome.

In Enderby, members of the Lions Club again demonstrated the immeasurable dedication and value of service clubs in Canada as they left their families to meet us and make a donation. One of the Lions who came to walk with me told me about his daughter, who was paraplegic as the result of a skiing accident 15 years before. She now spent her time giving lectures on having a positive attitude. I didn't get to meet her, but from the description, her outlook reminded me of Jesse and so many other boys like him.

Farther down into the Okanagan, it was noticeably warmer. The sun was shining and the temperature started to climb. We stayed on the road as long as possible, finishing in the dark before we drove to Vernon. I had only 25 little boxes left to move before the finish line in Victoria, but there was one ongoing problem that just wouldn't go away. There were few people, other than those on the road team, who knew the real condition of my legs and back. Despite soaking my feet in sea salt and water three times a day to keep them tough, they were in bad shape. As far back as Calgary, some nasty cracks had started to develop in my feet. My toes were an ugly colour and the question was, "Could I keep everything together for the remaining distance?"

RECALCULATING... MAYBE FOR THE LAST TIME

It was time to recalculate my expectations about the weather. I had anticipated a slightly easier workload once we were through Rogers Pass and into the Okanagan. But now we were here and the snow just wouldn't stop falling. It was discouraging. I thought it was unlikely to snow on Vancouver Island on the last four days of the journey, so the worst-case scenario was 21 more days of snow and tough going. If I anticipated the worst, anything better than that would be a bonus.

In Armstrong, we had breakfast with the Lions, who donated $500 to our project. On the road we were dealing with a mixture of rain and snow, which was sometimes good and sometimes bad. It was tiring to slog through the watery slush on the side of the road and it really made me sweat.

The air was sometimes warm enough that I could switch from a winter coat to my spring jacket, which was vivid red on Day 1 at Quidi Vidi but was now more of a washed-out pink. The rain and sun had faded it the same way a dream can sometimes fade. The colour on my coat would never return, but in the months on the road, I had learned that even if dreams fade, they never go away. While I was having tea and oranges at my second break, I leafed through a grocery store tabloid someone had left in the motorhome. My horoscope said my travelling would end soon. I hoped it was right.

South from Vernon to Kelowna, the temperature dropped and again it was snowing heavily. People were still stopping to make donations but by early afternoon, with the snow accumulating, the Ministry of Transportation had no choice but to ask us to leave the road because of poor visibility. We were happy to oblige and back at our motel, a difficult day on the road ended on a brighter note when the Rotary Club of Vernon made a $500 donation.

Forgetting about the weather for a few minutes, I called home early in the evening to talk to Sherene. We were both in a pretty good mood, perhaps because we knew we would soon be together again. But my absence had led to a bit of a silver lining for Sherene in the form of a newly acquired stage presence. I could hear the confidence in her voice as she told me about her most recent appearance to speak on behalf of Jesse's Journey. It was evident she had become comfortable speaking in front of an audience. I kidded her that when I got home, we could trade places. She could take on the full-time leadership of Jesse's Journey and I'd stay home, at least for a while. At the end of the day I had moved little box No. 263 and was one day closer to going home.

The last days of the year were spent winding through the heart of the Okanagan Valley's wine industry. From the highway I could see rows and rows and rows of leafless grapevines waiting for spring. British Columbia's wine industry began in 1860 when a missionary named Father Pandosy planted the first grapevines in the Okanagan. The wine was primarily for religious purposes and it wasn't until 1932 that the first commercial winery opened in the valley.

For the first time in days, the sun was shining and for the second time in the same year, there was a hint of spring. At long last, just as it did in Newfoundland, the snow was showing early signs of melting as we proceeded south in the Okanagan. Along the road, the spray from trucks left us covered in a wet patina of mud. But that didn't seem so bad when we heard about the problems behind us, where snow had closed the Trans-Canada from Revelstoke to Sicamous. Again, it seemed as if we'd been travelling in some kind of protective bubble when we also heard they were experiencing avalanches back in the Rogers Pass. I remembered how relieved I'd felt when we finally cleared the avalanche zone in the Rockies.

The day before New Year's Eve, I completed my 33 kilometres in what seemed like record time, finishing at 4:20 in the afternoon. I was glad to finish early because time had become an important commodity in the Pacific Time Zone. The three-hour difference between British Columbia and Ontario was difficult to deal with and one factor we might have overlooked in our original plan. The need to get up at 4 a.m. to do radio interviews that aired live to people in Ontario at 7 a.m. really made me start to feel like I was running on adrenaline. I called on the reserve tank again, reminding myself of the night I stepped into British Columbia and vowed, "I didn't come to the 10th province to quit."

These extra-early starts each day (you never do get back to sleep) were complicated by the fact that there seemed to be an event of some kind every night and another speech to make to another group wanting to know about Jesse's Journey. I kept telling myself to hang on for a few more days.

As I passed through Kelowna, the first man I met on the road one morning shook my hand and donated $100. Donations continued as I crossed the bridge that takes you from the east to the west side of Lake Okanagan. Traffic was backed up a long way, but people didn't seem to mind as they smiled, waved, honked their horns and reached for their wallets.

Donations came from all ages, from the young and the not-so-young. Two little boys climbed out of a car up ahead and ran back to meet me. They each gave us $20 and seemed pretty excited as their mom and dad took a picture of us. Back at the motorhome, Ed received a $50 donation from a widow who stopped to chat for awhile. She told Ed and Kay that every year on her late husband's birthday, she buys herself something new to wear. Then she looked up toward the heavens, smiled and said, "Honey, your taste is getting better every year."

The weather in the Okanagan can change in a big hurry and that afternoon, fog set in so thick that even with the powerful strobe lights on the Mickey van, it was difficult for others to see us. It was too dangerous to stay on the road and we were forced to go back into Kelowna. On the morning of New Year's Eve, I was thankful the forecast of continued heavy fog had proven false. In the morning air, as I was stretching my legs beside the motorhome, I joked with everybody that tomorrow we would be able to say, "This is the year we're going to finish the walk!"

The sun was shining and the mountain scenery was very pretty as we headed south from Kelowna through Peachland and Summerland toward Penticton. The orchards, fruit fields and vineyards in this part of the Okanagan Valley are blessed with 2,000 hours of sunshine each year, earning the area the nickname "the fruit basket of British Columbia."

A young RCMP officer was among those who stopped as soon as I was on the road. Although his eyes were shielded by sunglasses, I could tell he was moved by the story of Jesse's Journey. There was another young man who left his car running as he stopped to make a donation, only to find he had locked himself out of the vehicle. We lent him a cellphone to call his roommate, who had an extra key for the car. He was embarrassed. We were just grateful he pulled over.

Its got a bit scary along the road as people stopped right on the highway in the driving lane. They just wanted to shake hands and make donations. One woman said she didn't have any money but wanted to give us a bottle of champagne so we could ring in the New Year at midnight. It was certainly a different kind of donation.

DAY'S END AND YEAR'S END

On the last day of the year at the end of our day on the road in British
Columbia, it was just three hours until midnight in Ontario. Sherene sounded
tired when I called home to wish everyone a Happy New Year. The sound
of her voice reminded me I wasn't the only one paying a price to make this
project work. The daily road routine was taking its toll on me, but for all the
months I'd been away, Sherene had been keeping the home fires burning, far
from the spotlight and the attention we were getting. A team of volunteers
surrounded me every day, but Sherene was on her own looking after the
boys and quietly taking care of everything that needs to be done to keep a
household running and to make a house a home. I may have underestimated
the workload she would have to bear while I was away, but not her ability
to cope with it. As we said goodbye to each other and the old year, we had
managed to move 266 little boxes and there were just 20 days left on the road.

We spent New Year's Eve in Penticton, which is Salish for "a place to live
forever." Coast Salish refers to a cultural subgroup of First Nations in British
Columbia and extending down through Washington and Oregon in the
United States.

At dinner, Bevin borrowed wristwatches from everyone and after resetting
them, he lined them all up on his left arm so he could tell us when it was
midnight in each time zone in Canada, starting in Newfoundland. In the
heart of the Okanagan Valley, Western Canada's premiere wine-making
district, I toasted the New Year with a non-alcoholic wine and went to
bed. Tomorrow would be another day and another year.

As we left Penticton with our RCMP escort, people along the road applauded
us and donated generously. I climbed the long slow grade heading south to
Olalla and Keremeos. Our vantage point looking over Lake Okanagan put
us at the same height as small planes on their descent to Penticton airport.

The road to Keremeos was narrow and at some points the cliffs rose straight
up from the edge of the road. There were several hairpin turns and very little
shoulder, making the road difficult to walk. At Keremeos, the town that
calls itself "The Fruitstand Capital of Canada," I was joined on the road by
an RCMP officer in his scarlet dress uniform, as well as by members of the

Keremeos Lions Club. More than three dozen wooden fruit stands sat empty on the side of the road, waiting for the time of year when they would be filled with the valley's harvest of apricots, peaches and plums. Like so many Lions Clubs had done across Canada, the Lions of Keremeos presented us with a donation and pins for the road team. The Keremeos pin showed a tall mountain with snow-filled creases in the shape of a K. As I·looked up from the main street, I saw the mountain and the snow, just the way it was depicted on the pin.

Morning came early for the Jesse's Journey team making its way through the Okanagan. The evening before we had driven back to Olalla, where I spoke to the Lions Club. The next day started at 4 a.m. with a telephone interview with Breakfast Television in Halifax. After what had seemed like a very short night, the weatherman wasn't being all that kind. The road was covered with freezing rain, making it very slippery, especially on the banked curves. Ed tried to warm us at noon with a steaming-hot bowl of chili, but the rain and low-hanging clouds continued to obscure the tops of the mountains and made it a dreary day. On the road, a man and his two young daughters stopped to make a donation. He said I was a great inspiration but in truth, he was my inspiration on a day when almost no one else stopped.

It was still raining at the end of the day and in the dark we came to an accident scene lit up by the flashing yellow lights of a tow truck. A van had skidded off the icy road and plunged down the side of the mountain. It was lying on its roof in jagged rocks next to the river at the bottom of the cliff and cables had been attached to haul it up to the road. I asked the tow truck operator if anybody was killed. He said no, but the driver of the van had been taken to hospital. When he took a second look at me he said, "Hey, aren't you the guy who's walking across Canada for his son?" When I said yes, he told me to "Keep 'er going, pal. You're doing a good job." He had no idea how close those words mirrored by own thoughts. I was just hoping I could "keep 'er going" for another 15 days.

Through the Similkameen Valley, the road to Princeton passed through Hedley. The Nickel Plate Mine, which operated here for more than 50 years, generated more than $47 million in gold, silver and copper before shutting down in 1955. The story of the mine seemed to reflect the boom-and-bust history and the promise of riches attached to this part of the country in Canada's early years.

But to realize the promise of my dream, it seemed clear that slow, steady growth and sticking with the plan was probably a much safer course.

In the foothills of the Cascade Mountains, I struggled with ice along the twists and turns of the narrow road leading to Princeton. There were few donations and at the end of the day, after speaking to the Rotary Club at noon hour and the Lions Club at night, all I wanted to do was have my legs worked on and go to sleep.

We were in Manning Provincial Park, south of Princeton, and along the side of the road, the four to five-metre snowdrifts showed no sign of melting. I was so tired I couldn't remember where we started the day. All I knew was that it had been an uphill climb most of the day. The only good news was that we were climbing up and out of the fog. We had not been prepared for this dangerous road. It was much narrower than we had anticipated and was full of blind turns that once again forced us to use the two-way radios to play the cat-and-mouse game.

UNAVOIDABLE RISKS

Cat-and-mouse was a tiresome and dangerous piece of work that involved walking the road without the escort van behind me as protection. We hadn't had to resort to this since Northern Ontario, where the Trans-Canada twisted and turned through an almost endless series of rock cuts. Here in British Columbia on the blind curves, the van held its position with strobe lights flashing while I disappeared around the next curve in the road and hurried ahead to find another safe spot for the van to stop, this on a road with almost no shoulder. We then used the two-way radio to tell the people in the van it was safe to move to the next spot, where they would again tuck in at the side of the road. Then we'd start over.

The van, in turn, would let us know when a logging truck had passed and that we could expect it to reach us soon as it slowly climbed the hill. I kept my eyes forward while the volunteer on the road with me watched for the truck coming up behind. When the truck arrived, we stepped off the road to let it pass. The system worked well and gave us a margin of safety, except when there was a tractor-trailer or logging truck coming down the mountain in the opposite direction and we met three abreast. That made for a tight squeeze.

Fortunately, most of the truck drivers in the area knew all about Jesse's Journey and had a pretty good idea of approximately where we were on the highway. Throughout the day, I kept thinking this section of road was much more dangerous than Rogers Pass, the area we spent so much time worrying about. Sometimes the things we fear will hinder the path to a dream turn out not to be a problem. Fear is a word that describes a game played in our mind. The letters in the word can be designated as False-Evidence-Appearing-Real.

It was late in the day on January 5 when two men in a pickup truck stopped to make a donation. They asked if I was the man walking across Canada for his son. When I told the older of the two men, "Yes, that's me," he wanted to shake my hand. When I extended my arm to shake hands with the younger man as well, he apologized that his hands were so grimy. "There's no need to apologize," I said. "That's honest dirt."

Manning Park Lodge was buried under a thick blanket of snow when we returned that night. There were no telephones in the rooms so I couldn't call home. As soon as we were settled, I asked Ed if he could work on my legs. He had incredibly strong hands and as he worked his magic, I wondered where I would be without this Newfoundlander, who hadn't initially intended to have anything to do with Jesse's Journey. Ed Coxworthy, the man we nicknamed "the king of Newfoundland," was giving me almost a year of his life at no charge. That happens when you have a dream. Your belief encourages others to believe.

The lodge had a very interesting feature. Along lit pathways through a courtyard leading to the restaurant portion of the complex, some trees had been cut down to a level of about eight feet from the ground. From those stumps, wood carvers had created, in great detail, bears standing on their hind legs. The effect was dramatic.

From Manning Park to Hope there were very steep grades with signs warning truck drivers to check their brakes before beginning their descents. On some of these steep downhill slopes heading west were runaway lanes on the right hand side of the road. These were emergency escape ramps to help bring a runaway truck to a safe stop. The lanes, which turned upward like a ski jump, were made from tonnes of sand. The idea was that a truck that had lost its brakes could exit on one of these uphill ramps and come to a halt without damage or injury.

The jagged peaks, thick forests and plunging gorges in and around Hope served as the backdrop for the Sylvester Stallone movie First Blood. But Hope was not about "Rambo"-type characters. It was a quiet community amid giant fir trees where hope for a better future was reflected in its Friendship Gardens. The gardens commemorate a dark period in Canada's history, the internment of 2,000 Japanese-Canadians at Tashme Camp near Hope, during the Second World War.

FIVE THINGS ON MY MIND

Years before I ever saw the windswept rocky coast of Newfoundland, I came up with a set of precepts to help me turn my dream into a reality. The first thing I did was to set my goal and, as part of that, to confirm in my mind that the dream was personally meaningful, was challenging and that I was committed to seeing it through to completion.

The second step was to start planning how to reach that goal.

The third and perhaps most important element was to design the plan so we could win. This meant being realistic about my abilities and most of all, finding the right people for the right job to support me and help me realize the big picture.

The fourth factor was squarely on my shoulders alone. I had to stay focused and be willing to persevere and to commit to working harder than anyone else on the team. I knew I would have to take some risks and push myself to the limit. I also knew I would have to expect the unexpected.

In the appropriately named Hope, it was time to start thinking about the fifth of those precepts, something that hadn't yet come into play very much, and that was celebrating our success.

I hadn't kept a running count of our total mileage in my journal so I didn't know exactly when we would reach the 8,000-kilometre mark. It happened in Hope and as a surprise, some of the road crew went searching for a cake to mark the occasion. When they walked into a bakeshop in Hope, the magic that seemed to follow Jesse's Journey showed up again.

For a moment it looked like there wasn't going to be a celebration. The cakes had all been sold and the store was ready to close for the day. But the owner of the shop, who had noticed our vans around town and had seen me on television, realized the 8,000-kilometre mark was a pretty big deal for our team, so she picked up the phone and called her baker, who had already finished his shift and gone home. She asked if he would come back and bake just one more cake. "You know that guy who's walking across Canada," she said. "Well, he's here in Hope. He's walked 8,000 kilometres and they need a cake, so can you come in and make it?"

There was a pause and then the shop owner held the phone away from her ear and said to our road manager, "What colour do you want?" No one cared about colour; they were just happy to have a cake. The next question was, "What do you want it to say?" That remained a surprise for a couple of hours.

That night when we returned to our motel after a dinner meeting with Lions, Rotarians and members of the Hope Chamber of Commerce, I was called to a gathering on the motorhome. What I thought was going to be another routine briefing about departure times, road schedules for volunteers and police escort confirmation turned out to be a surprise party. The smiles on the faces of the road team told me they had pulled one over on me! There in the middle of the dinner table was a huge white cake trimmed with blue, green and yellow icing spelling out the words, "8,001 And Beyond Hope!"

The morning after I shifted little box No. 275, Hope's mayor and his mother joined us on the road for a short distance. By the end of the day we were in Chilliwack and the number of days left was down to single digits. The schedule showed we had seven more moves to make and we were just nine road days away from finishing. It was a good feeling.

FINDING A NEW DIRECTION

Earlier in British Columbia, when I knew we had less than a month to go, I had adjusted my thinking in terms of the weather and what we could expect. At that time I told myself to be mentally prepared for snow every day until we reached Vancouver Island. Now that we were just about out of the mountains, I changed the "forecast" and told myself it was likely more realistic to expect rain for the rest of the journey.

The day we reached Mission was the wettest day of the entire journey and that was saying something. It didn't just rain, it poured steadily all day and by mid-afternoon, radio reports indicated more than 40 millimetres or almost two inches had fallen.

And that day, No. 277, was the day Bevin picked to walk a full 33 kilometres with me for the first time since leaving St. John's. The demands on his schedule, including shooting video and doing advance work with the media, had never permitted him to spend an entire day on the road with me, although we had been together for shorter distances dozens of times. He kept saying he wanted to do it but his timing, in terms of the weather, wasn't great.

I can barely imagine his reaction if someone had told Bevin in April of 1997 that a year later, he would be at Kilometre 0 in St. John's, Newfoundland and taking those first tentative steps with me in a walk of more than 8,300 kilometres across Canada. He might have laughed with his buddies and probably would have forgotten about it immediately.

Back then Bevin was a young man rushing through a fast-paced world. But his decision to join the Journey was probably more life-changing for him than for anyone else who took part. In the months we'd been together on the road, he had wrestled with a ton of emotions and the result was a great maturing. His priorities in life had changed. As we walked along in the rain, he told me about going into big cities where busy people in a big hurry seemed to have a "get out of my way" attitude. He said it was different in smaller towns, where people seemed happier and showed greater caring for each other. The Journey had made Bevin ask himself what really matters in life.

From our earliest days in Newfoundland, Bevin had watched people from all walks of life pitch in to do whatever had to be done – laundry, dishes, driving and collecting money. He had noticed there were no egos on the road. It didn't matter if you were the CEO of a Fortune 500 company or a clerk in a grocery store. Out here, everyone was equal, and through the good times and the bad, everyone had stayed focused on the reason we were here.

As we passed Ruby Creek on the way to Mission, we walked beside two sets of railway tracks leading to Vancouver. People who wanted to shake my hand had been stopping. Some said it was a remarkable thing I was doing, but that wasn't quite right. What was really remarkable was what Bevin was doing, along with everyone else who had taken part in Jesse's Journey.

It was still raining the proverbial cats and dogs at midday when a group of Lions with a donation joined us on the road. They gave us a lot of information about some things we could see and some we couldn't. We learned that underneath the road we were walking on were telephone lines and two natural gas lines servicing Vancouver. Along the Fraser River, they pointed out where the salmon run occurs and a boom that keeps debris from floating downstream and becoming a hazard for shipping. They said that when logs caught in the boom are hauled from the river, inmates from two area prisons chop them into firewood for use by campers.

In view of the day-long downpour, you'd think the last thing we wanted was more water. But when we reached the top of another steep hill, we came upon a natural spring and used a couple of plastic cups from the van to toast Bevin's day on the road. A man and woman in a pickup truck stopped to fill some containers with the pure spring water and left a donation of $100. It seemed funny to be enjoying the clear-tasting water when water had forced us to change our shoes repeatedly throughout the day. On the motorhome there were running shoes drying in front of every available vent and socks, shirts, pants and jackets hung from makeshift clothes lines.

It was still dark the next morning as we left Mission to go to our starting point. By the time we met up with our police escort and got underway, the weather was getting warmer. After what seemed like an eternity of grey wet days, the sun was finally shining.

People continued to stop and make donations as I moved along the road toward Port Coquitlam. In Maple Ridge, the Lions Club presented Jesse's Journey with a cheque for $1,000. Two women who stopped were choked with emotion. They had a friend whose son suffered from the same disease as Jesse. The little boy was just six years old and already in a wheelchair. These women understood why I'd spent almost 10 months on the road. Farther along there was a father waiting to meet me. He said his son's name was Jesse too.

Jesse's Journey received a tremendous welcome in Port Coquitlam, home of Marathon of Hope runner Terry Fox. The mayor welcomed us and presented me with a key to the city. An excellent high school orchestra, boys and girls in matching green sweaters, played as corporate sponsors, service clubs, individuals and students gathered for the formal presentation of donations. After I spoke to the crowd, I was introduced privately to Terry's brother, Fred Fox. At the end of the ceremony the orchestra played O Canada. It was a proud moment.

After the reception I met a special young girl in the crowd. She was 11 and had her long blonde hair done up neatly in pigtails. After the first snowfall of the year, she had rounded up her friends and they went out to shovel driveways to raise money. She was with her mom and was proud to donate the $42 in coins she and her friends had raised to help Jesse's Journey.

Port Moody was next as we edged closer to Vancouver. It was a little scary in the traffic, even with a police escort. There were elementary school kids with balloons and banners along the far side of the road. Some were very small and we were concerned they might run out into the road. The police held up traffic while I jogged over to meet them. They were yelling and cheering as only kids can. I shook hands and one girl who might have been in Grade 6 or 7 said, "I'm really proud of you." After lunch and a stop at city hall, we headed out again, but we were running a little late.

In Burnaby, there were a lot of people applauding, yelling encouragement and making donations as we inched our way toward the bridge crossing over the Second Narrows to North Vancouver. The chaos of getting through another big city was repeating itself with more radio microphones and television cameras. It was dark and pouring rain again when we reached our finishing point at Centennial Theatre, where the mayors of both North and West Vancouver welcomed us to the West Coast.

One of the hardest things to do in a big city is move the motorhome through heavy traffic, especially when you're not familiar with the roads. In the downpour we'd been experiencing since late afternoon, and with the windshield wipers sweeping back and forth, the motorhome slipped into the stream of traffic making its way across the Lions Gate Bridge toward downtown Vancouver. In the morning the whole procedure would have to be repeated in the opposite direction as we crossed the bridge heading away from downtown to get to our starting point in North Vancouver.

Back on the road on the morning of Day 281, things seemed like they were happening in slow motion as the distance to Horseshoe Bay and the British Columbia ferry terminal got shorter. Lights from the RCMP escort vehicle flashed; cameramen ran to get in front of me. In the sunshine along the Sea-to-Sky Highway, I stopped at a waterfall and splashed several scoops of water on my face. Then it was almost as if I was outside of myself watching it happen as I walked across the grass that leads to the dock and the water's edge at Horseshoe Bay. It was January 14 and I had just finished walking the breadth of mainland Canada. I supposed I should be celebrating our success, but it wasn't time yet. There was still more work to do to reach the finish line at the Pacific Ocean in Victoria.

After our ferry ride across the Strait of Georgia, there would be just the length of Vancouver Island left to complete and Jesse's Journey, which began on an island on Canada's Atlantic coast, would finish on an island on Canada's Pacific coast. It was hard for me to believe the road portion of a Journey that I knew would continue to unfold was close to coming to an end.

By late afternoon the day had turned cloudy and cool and through all the handshaking, smiling and posing for pictures, I was anxious to head back into Vancouver.

MUSIC TO MY EARS

After we crossed the Lions Gate Bridge again, the motorhome rolled to a stop in the parking lot of the Bayshore Inn on Vancouver's waterfront. For the mother ship, it was the last stop on the mainland. As I stepped down to the pavement, I heard the first of the voices I'd been waiting months to hear. It was Jesse calling "Hey, Dad!" from a balcony above me and in a few minutes we were all hugging in the parking lot. It was overwhelming to hold Sherene in my arms and to see Jesse and Tim. I was finally together with the family I hadn't seen since August.

We spent the evening catching up on family news and sharing stories of our adventures on the road and the next morning, Sherene joined us for breakfast on the motorhome. It was the last Saturday of the journey. She was staying behind when our convoy left for Horseshoe Bay to board the ferry. Sherene, Jesse and Tim, would meet us at the finish line in Victoria in a few days.

Members of the Lions Club were at the ferry terminal to see us off and in Nanaimo, more Lions were among the service clubs waiting to welcome us to the island. Service clubs had passed the torch from one to the next all across the country. They had handed us off to the next club along the road as they all became a part of Jesse's Journey. Our encounters with these caring groups were often brief, yet unforgettable.

If there was a way to assess the sheer dollar value of the work done by the members of service clubs in Canada, I'm sure it would be in the billions. And that wouldn't begin to measure the worth of their good deeds and the good feelings that pour from their hearts.

The sky and the water were slate grey and it was raining when we docked in Nanaimo to begin the final portion of the journey. We stepped off the ferry and the beginning of our final few days on the road was heralded by the sound of bagpipes and by firefighters with flashing lights and sirens.

There were lots of donations as we wound our way through Nanaimo. On the southern edge of the city whose name was made famous by the baked confections known as Nanaimo bars stands one of the most impressive welcome signs in all of Canada. There are huge metal poles with giant metal sheets that suggest sails in a full wind. The blue trim and flags atop the "masts" create the effect of a tall ship. It left little doubt Nanaimo is an ocean playground with a rich seafaring heritage.

In British Columbia, they like to refer to rain as liquid sunshine. I still saw it as rain. But although it was wet, the road to Victoria was mostly flat and as we set our sights on Victoria, I took comfort in knowing there was very little chance we'd see snow again.

One man who stopped just outside Nanaimo to make a donation gave me a walking stick he had carved with the words "Jesse's Journey – Coast to Coast." At Ladysmith, which used to be known as Oyster Bay, we were the guests of honour at a banquet hosted by the town's service clubs. There were about 200 people on hand and by the end of the night almost $4,000 had been raised to help fund research.

From Ladysmith to Duncan, the clock continued to tick toward the finish line at Beacon Hill Park in Victoria, where I would dip my shoes into the Pacific

Ocean, just as I had done in the Atlantic almost 10 months before.

Through Lake Cowichan, the rain continued to fall. But the plan we had stuck to, with few alterations, for more than 280 days required us to finish just 20 kilometres of highway that day. The schedule had been fine-tuned for the last days of the journey so that I would have just 11 kilometres to walk on the final day. There was little doubt the end of the journey was getting close and each time I opened the door to the motorhome, I saw more familiar faces as people from home were starting to gather for the completion of the walk.

With just three little boxes left to be moved, the remainder of the journey across Canada could be counted in hours. I didn't know if it was due to building excitement along the road or the anticipation of completing the journey, but I hadn't been sleeping well. Phone calls were now pouring in from radio stations from Vancouver to Newfoundland. Interviews started at 5 a.m. and it seemed like every few minutes someone was sticking a cellphone into my hand for another chat with the media.

On the road, people said all kinds of things. I know they meant well but sometimes it was a little embarrassing. One woman threw her arms around me and said, "I love a man with guts." Another woman, who obviously knew about Jesse, shook my hand and quietly asked "How's he doing?" That was 10 times harder to deal with and left me choked with emotion and just wanting to move on as quickly as possible.

Despite the chaos and all the additional people clambering aboard the motorhome, Ed did his best to stick to our daily routine. On the third-last day I saw "the king of Newfoundland" wink as he served up scalloped potatoes and ham for lunch. I knew that when lunch was over, Ed would be the firewall between me and the waves of people who all wanted "just a minute" of my time. I closed the door to the bedroom thankful for a chance to rest for a few minutes. I knew how busy things would be for the next 48 hours. But after a somewhat broken sleep, there was a wonderful surprise waiting. I stepped off the motorhome into a group of 30 people who had flown all the way from London to be on hand for the final steps of Jesse's Journey.

At the end of Day 284 we returned to Duncan, "The City of Totems." As we had passed through a few hours earlier, I had admired the dozens of totem poles in the downtown. And I knew for sure we were in Duncan because I had it written on my hand. In the last few days I had resorted to writing the names of the places where I was speaking on my hand because I sometimes couldn't remember where I was. There had been a lot of shuffling back and forth between communities on the island to attend events and deliver our message. This "to-ing and fro-ing" and the heavy demand of early-morning phone calls with Eastern Canada had definitely left me feeling like I was running on fumes. In terms of our blueprint for success, staying focused was now the toughest part.

In Duncan, a native artist presented me with a print of a very intriguing painting. It was a close-up of the eye of a bear cub and in the reflection from the eye I could see a mother bear catching a fish in a stream as she showed her cub how to fish. The artist gave me an excellent explanation of the picture – that it reflects the responsibility of one generation to help the next, not just by telling them what we have learned but by demonstrating the "how-to" techniques we have acquired.

On the morning of my second-last day on the road, wisps of cloud hung in the tops of the fir trees as I walked through Mill Bay, chipping away at the few kilometres left before Victoria and the Pacific Ocean. As we waited for the Brentwood ferry to take us across Saanich Inlet to Brentwood Bay, a group of kids from a private school peppered me with questions about Jesse's Journey and the things I'd seen as I walked across Canada. They were very polite but seemed a little surprised that someone "as old" as I was could walk all the way across the country.

As we crossed Saanich Inlet, the ferry captain let me take the wheel for a minute. It was another nice moment to record in my journal, especially since the ferry didn't hit anything or sink while under my command!

When I stepped off the ferry, Sherene was waiting with her blonde hair blowing in the wind and the smile I had been missing for too many months. She was with family and friends, part of a growing group of supporters who would be with us as we moved closer and closer to Beacon Hill Park.

We finished up the bit of roadwork we had left and then the motorhome and the two mini-vans, Mickey and the other van, were moved ahead to Victoria. It was the last time the road crew had to unload their red duffel bags. After 10 months on the road in a play with a cast of thousands, the stage was set for the final day. There were 11 kilometres left to complete the walk from the Atlantic Ocean on the east coast of Newfoundland to the Pacific Ocean on the tip of Vancouver Island and I was very excited.

THE LAST LITTLE BOX

It was the morning of Day 286 and there was just one more little box to be moved. It was also my birthday and I was immensely grateful to the people of Canada for their wonderful gift. By the end of the day, we would have raised $2 million to launch the Jesse Davidson Endowment, which will eventually provide a million research dollars a year to find a cure for a disease that robs parents of their most precious gift – their children.

As I prepared for the last day, there was a touch of sadness similar to that final morning in 1995 when Jesse and I reached Ottawa at the end of our journey across Ontario. I was aware that when the day was over, those who had played such a big role in the Journey would be shifting their focus away from the routines they had followed for almost 10 months. The road crew would disband as its members caught flights home to the families they hadn't seen and lives that had been put on hold for nearly a year. In time, the road portion of Jesse's Journey would be just a memory for those who were there. But before that happened, there was one more day to complete.

As I climbed onto the motorhome for one of the last times, everything seemed like a series of "last ofs." I sat down to what would be my last bowl of Ed's Newfoundland porridge with brown sugar and milk. There was butter melting on the hot toast Ed set beside the strawberry jam and sliced oranges. With the steam rising from my last mug of breakfast tea, I laughed as I thought back to one of our great volunteers from Nova Scotia who gave Ed some motherly advice when she told him to be sure to slice the fruit. "Men will eat fruit if you slice it up for them," she said. "If you don't, forget it."

My eyes scanned the inside of the motorhome, which was full of familiar sights. There were the maps of British Columbia and Vancouver Island tucked behind the sun visor above the driver's seat. They would soon be put in a lower drawer already full of maps from all across the country. There was the little solid green light on the battery charger in one of the overhead compartments indicating the two-way radios were ready for their final day of use on the road.

There were dozens of mugs with colourful emblems from schools and radio and television stations in every province. There were jars full of lapel pins from cities, towns and villages all across Canada.

In front of me, hanging over the back of the driver's seat, was the red jacket I had worn that first morning in Newfoundland and many days since. It was bright red at the beginning, like a cardinal against a backdrop of white snow. Now, at best, it was a faded salmon colour. It had changed the way a lot of people involved with the Journey had changed. They'd had the adventure of a lifetime and for many it had been life-changing.

Now it was time to turn my mind to the final element of the five-part precept that had guided the whole of Jesse's Journey. It had been on my mind since Day 1 but I knew then there would be a lot of waiting before it came into play. With the end in sight, the day had come to share our success with others and encourage them to reach out for their dreams.

HELLO CANADA, WE'RE ON THE AIR!

Across the country, radio was the lifeline that let us stay in touch with people following the story of Jesse's Journey. The radio link began in earnest on Jesse's birthday back on April 10 when my friend Peter Garland broadcast his morning radio show from city hall in St. John's. That was the morning I dipped my running shoes in the Atlantic Ocean. Now, Peter and CFPL Radio in London were with us again, this time broadcasting live to an audience in Ontario from in front of the legislature in Victoria.

I was on the phone as soon as I woke up that last day and for the final time, Jesse's Journey checked in with stations as far away as Newfoundland. Through a satellite hookup to Halifax, I did an interview with CBC television. As I stood in front of the legislature in Victoria, I listened in my earpiece as an interviewer on the other side of the country told me she was going home to hug her kids.

The flashing lights of the RCMP escort vehicle let school kids along the side of the road know we were on our way. There were lots of horns being honked and motorists streaming by in both directions gave us a thumbs-up.

By lunchtime it was even more chaotic as people jostled into position for the last few steps of the Journey. The onslaught of interviews continued. Amid all the commotion, I sat down for my final sandwich-and-milk lunch on the motorhome. I hadn't been seated long when the door opened and I jumped up to hug a tiny lady with a big smile. This was a woman who called me every time I stepped into a new province. How she knew exactly when to call I never understood. But each time we were at our first break on our first day in a new province, the phone on the motorhome would ring and she would make a donation of $10,000. Her identity was known to only one or two others on the crew and she wanted to keep it that way. But on this final day of the Journey, she wanted to be there in person with the other well-wishers and to give a card of congratulations to "Jesse's dad."

As I lay face down on the bed in the back of the motorhome, my legs were being worked on for the last time. A lot of people had kept me in shape over the last 10 months and without them, I never could have made it. With just three kilometres left to go, this would probably be the most important afternoon of my life. I remembered the mental image I had in St. John's of 286 little boxes of work all stacked on one side of my mind. At the end of that first day, I mentally moved one of those little boxes to the other side, to the "completed" pile. Then there came a day in Ontario when there were more little boxes on the "completed" side than on the "still to go" side. By the end of this day, they would all be moved.

AND TOO SOON... IT ENDED

Victoria was covered by a thin layer of grey and white clouds and every now and then the sun poked through for a few minutes as we inched toward the Pacific Ocean. The last couple of kilometres had passed in a blur of smiles, handshakes, pats on the back, personal words of congratulations, cheers and applause. We were encased in the sound of a marching band with drums and bagpipes, accompanied by blaring sirens and honking horns. People I knew and people I didn't kept coming out of the crowd along the road and wrapping their arms around me.

Then almost before I knew it, and almost as if St. John's were just yesterday, my mom and dad were standing in front of me holding the banner that marked the finish – 8,272 kilometres from where I started at Quidi Vidi,

Newfoundland. I broke through the banner and as I held Sherene in my arms, I couldn't hold back a wave of emotion that swept over me like nothing I had ever experienced. We couldn't hide from the cameras clicking just inches away from our wet eyes. Sherene looked happy and I could tell she was immensely relieved we had all made it safely across the country.

Tyler had arrived to join the celebration and as I hugged our three sons, I knew the road portion of Jesse's Journey was over. I also knew I could finally admit, at least to myself, how much I ached. It occurred to me again that I might have fared better if I had done this at a much younger age, but in the same instant I again heard the question, "What wouldn't you do for your kids?" I now had the answer. There wasn't anything I wouldn't do. That's what I was thinking moments before being swallowed up in the crowd that had gathered around us.

I waited with my family for the cameras to move aside before I pushed forward to complete the last piece of business.

From the grass at the top of Beacon Hill Park, there was a long flight of wooden stairs down to the shore, where the Pacific Ocean lapped against the rocks and dozens of large logs that had broken away from booms and washed ashore. Tim came with me as I took the stairs down to the water and the waiting scrum of media people who had moved into position to capture the final moment. I was carrying a glass jug of saltwater that had been on the motorhome since I filled it on the morning of Day 1 in Newfoundland.

From the log-strewn shore I looked up to the crowd at the top of the hill. I could see Jesse and his trademark shy but proud smile as he watched from his wheelchair, with his mom and brother Tyler at his side. As soon as the television cameras and newspaper photographers were ready, I dipped my running shoes into the Pacific.

I then took the cap off the glass jug and poured out half of the water from the Atlantic. Then I submerged the jug and filled it to the top again. After resealing the top, I shook the jug to mix the waters of two oceans. The jug would go back to the motorhome to be taken home to London. And just like that, it was over.

At long last I heaved a sigh that perhaps suggested just how exhausted all of us on the road team were after almost 10 months on the road. I owed a huge debt of gratitude to an incredible team of people who could look back knowing we had raised awareness about a terrible disease and the need to invest in research. Across 10 provinces we had told the story of the devastation Duchenne muscular dystrophy wreaks on families. It was a story thousands of Canadians had never heard. It was a story about a disease that strikes boys almost exclusively and cuts their lives short.

On the road we had done what we set out to do. The Jesse Davidson Endowment was firmly established. But we knew there was a lot more still to do to realize the full potential of the dream.

After 286 days on the road, 286 little boxes of work moved and 8,272 kilometres walked, $2 million had been raised. In the morning we would head east, back to Ontario. With the satisfaction of knowing we had done our best, we were going home.

· EPILOGUE ·

Jesse Todd Davidson
April 10, 1980 – November 6, 2009

Jesse didn't live to see our dream completed. He was 29 years old when he died in November 2009 of the disease he had endured all his life. He will never know the thousands and thousands of Canadians whose hearts he touched by the way he lived his remarkable life and by the way he demonstrated what real courage is all about.

Jesse embraced everything he could in life. He was blessed with good friends, both male and female, and he cared deeply about them to the very end. Some of them he had known since his first days in school and they thought of Jesse as just a really great guy.

Awards and honours came Jesse's way but they never changed him. As a student, he was a high achiever and he was happiest singing in his high school choir and being president of his Junior Achievement group. He went on to graduate from college and when he went to work as an event planner, he showed people with disabilities of any kind that you can get out there and you can be part of everything that's happening.

Jesse didn't walk or run. He couldn't swim and he never used a skateboard. He never rode a bicycle. He couldn't lift his arms. And yet it was Jesse who was the sports fan in our family. He was there to see his London Knights win the Memorial Cup and he was loyal to the Montreal Canadiens.

Along life's road, Jesse received the King Clancy Award for service to the disabled. He was awarded the Order of Ontario, the Governor-General's Meritorious Service Medal and the Queen Elizabeth II Jubilee Medal. He was the inspiration for the charity that bears his name and he always had a smile and cheerful word for everyone he met. Jesse gave all of us a message about courage and hope for the future. Every day he showed us how far he would go for the people he loved.

His legacy is tangible. To date, more than $10 million has been raised for the Jesse Davidson Endowment and we are now able to give $500,000 a year to researchers seeking a cure for Duchenne Muscular Dystrophy. There is still much to do but thanks to Jesse's continued inspiration, we are on the right road.

Jesse was with his mom the night he took what would be his final ambulance ride to hospital. We knew he was in serious trouble and in the days that followed, clad in hospital masks and gowns, we never left his side.

He knew the gravity of the situation and he knew the routine. Unable to speak, we used the communication system we had worked out on other occasions when he was in intensive care. The letters of the alphabet were written out on five lines and as we took a pencil and pointed at the lines, Jesse would blink to let us know the letter he wanted was in that line. When we found that letter, we would repeat the process to find the next letter until we knew what Jesse wanted to say.

Our son knew all along we were in a race with time. He had known for a long time that despite how hard we were fighting on the research front, the cure we were working hard to find might not come in time for him. He accepted that and he wanted Jesse's Journey to be about all those other boys.

We seldom talked about what Jesse faced. We didn't have to. Jesse once told me, "Dad, when I'm not me any more, that's it." Jesse never cried and facing a terrible decision that no person as young as Jesse should ever have to make, his resolve never faltered. The last message he wanted us to understand came when he blinked his eyes in confirming that the letters he wanted from the sheet of paper were DNR – Do Not Resuscitate. On the morning of November 6, 2009, along with Jesse's brothers Tyler and Tim, we held hands in a circle at Jesse's bedside and as his mom and I held Jesse's hands in ours, he closed his beautiful eyes and slipped away.

It had been raining the whole week Jesse was in hospital. On the morning Jesse left us, when Sherene and I stepped outside the hospital, hand in hand, the clouds had disappeared. The sky was blue and the sun was shining.

The Jesse we knew was gone, but everything he loved and everything he stood for was still very much alive and he will live on in our hearts forever. At that very moment, somewhere, someone else was launching a dream. I wondered how far they would go to make it come true.

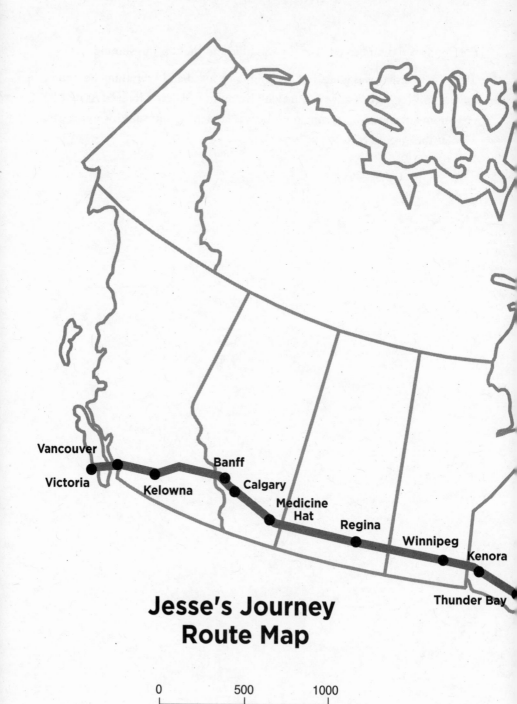

Jesse's Journey
Route Map

0   500   1000

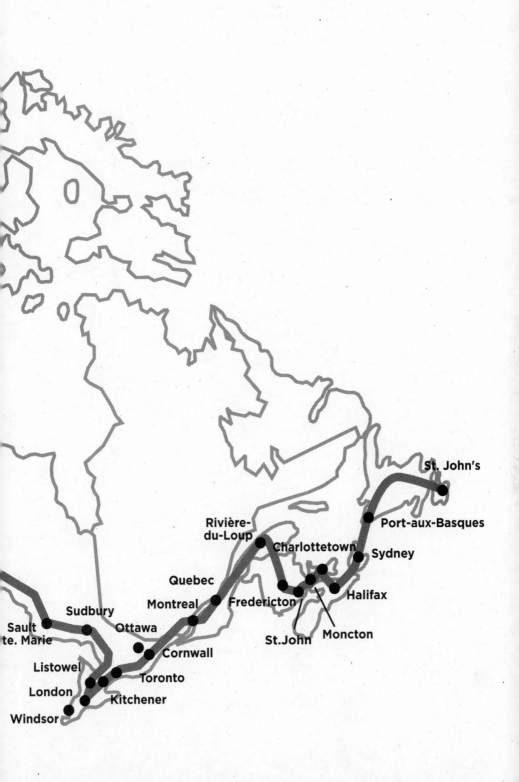

· WHEN THEY WENT HOME ·

In November of the year 2000, Jesse and John Davidson were presented with the Governor General's Meritorious Service Medal in a ceremony at the Citadel in Quebec City. While Jesse was unable to attend, his mother Sherene accepted the honour on his behalf.

In June of 2000 The Guinness Book of World Records recognized John Davidson's 286-day journey as a world record for the fastest crossing of Canada on foot.

Ed Coxworthy returned home to Bell Island, Newfoundland. He quit smoking in March of 2000.

Bevin Palmateer and Renata Van Loon married in September of 1999. They have two sons and live in Erieau, Ontario.

Trish Federkow the road manager, returned to school before taking up work in the human resources field in Toronto.

Michael Woodward, a founding member of Jesse's Journey, died in January of 2008. Jesse Davidson was instrumental in seeing that a scholarship was created in Mike's name.

Mario Chioini who escorted Sherene and Jesse Davidson to Paris, France, went on to teach school in Mexico. He is now a teacher at the American school just outside of Paris.

Ted Eadinger and Dianne Steward married in October of 2000. They live in London were Ted remains a member of the Jesse's Journey Board of Directors.

Maureen Golovchenko who managed the 'home' team and road volunteer Phil Spencer married in August of 2000. They live in London.

John Davidson returned home to his wife and family in London. He continues to work on the dream he and Jesse had of building an endowment fund that will generate at least a million dollars a year to fund research.

John is a sought after speaker encouraging people to follow their dream.

Jesse's Journey has raised more than $10,000,000 on the road to a cure for Duchenne muscular dystrophy.

The "Journey" continues...

· WHAT IT TAKES TO WALK ACROSS THE COUNTRY ·

635 loaves of bread
11 kilograms of brown sugar
572 litres of 2 percent milk
41 jars of jam
24 jars of peanut butter
3 bottles of cinnamon (popular on porridge)
Seven 2.25-kilogram bags of Quaker Oats
5,535 grams of raisins
227 kilograms of bananas
1,200 apples
1,800 oranges
11 kilograms of grapes
1,500 tea bags
75 cans of chili
110 cans of Campbell's soup
48 cans of fruit cocktail
40 bags of nachos

6 pairs of running shoes

· FINDING THE RIGHT ROAD ·

John Davidson is an award-winning speaker who has seen Canada from east to west and whose inspirational, illustrated presentation serves as a "how-to" for anyone pursuing a dream.

He describes himself as an "ordinary dad," but he also is a storyteller with 30 years of radio and television experience who uses his personal story to prove that all dreams are attainable with the right plan.

For information about having John Davidson speak at your next event, please visit: www.therightroad.ca or e-mail info@therightroad.ca or phone 519-645-8855.